THE EGO IDEAL

By the same author

Female Sexuality: New Psychological Views (with others), Payot, 1964;
   Michigan, 1970; Virago, 1981
Pour une Psychanalyse de l'Art et de la Créativité, Payot, 1971
Freud ou Reich? Psychanalyse et Illusion (with B. Grunberger), Tchou, 1975
Éthique et Esthétique de la Perversion, Champ Vallon, 1984
Creativity and Perversion, Norton, 1984; Free Association Books, 1985

JANINE CHASSEGUET-SMIRGEL

THE EGO IDEAL

A psychoanalytic essay on the
Malady of the Ideal

Translated by Paul Barrows

Introduction by Christopher Lasch

W. W. Norton & Company
New York ● London

L'Idéal du Moi. Essai sur la Maladie d'Idéalité, Paris, Tchou, 1975.
© Janine Chasseguet-Smirgel
This translation © Paul Barrows 1984

First British Edition 1985
Free Association Books
26 Freegrove Road
London N7 9RQ

First American Edition 1985
W.W. Norton & Company, Inc.
500 Fifth Avenue
New York, NY 10110
ISBN 0-393-01971-3

Published simultaneously in Canada by
Penguin Books Canada, Ltd.
2801 John Street, Markham, Ontario, L3R 1B4

British Library Cataloguing in Publication Data
Chasseguet-Smirgel, Janine
    The Ego Ideal: A Psychoanalytic Essay.
    1. Narcissism
    I. Title   II. L'Idéal du Moi. (*English*)
    155.2'32   BF 575.N35

    ISBN 0-946960-12-7
    ISBN 0-946960-13-5 (Pbk)

Typeset in Bembo by Folio Photosetting, Bristol
Printed and Bound in Great Britain by SRP Ltd, Exeter

Designed by Carlos Sapochnik

Contents

TRANSLATOR'S NOTE

Whilst I have retained the conventional Standard Edition version of certain terms (eg. the use of ego ideal, superego) this causes problems in some instances. As Bettleheim has clearly demonstrated (see *Freud and Man's Soul*, Knopf, 1982; Hogarth, 1983) the translators of the Standard Edition have at times departed from Freud's careful attempt always to write in clear everyday language and instead have developed their own pseudo-scientific jargon, even when Freud himself warned against such a procedure. The result is to distance the reader from the text. French translations of Freud, on the contrary, retain the everyday equivalents (cf. especially ich = moi = ego). Where necessary I have drawn attention to this discrepancy within the text and translated terms accordingly.

I wish to thank here the staff of the Tavistock Library for their invaluable and cheerful help with the Bibliography and hunting out references, Chris for the use of his word-processor and especially my wife, Kate, for her tolerance and support whilst I have been immersed in this task.

AUTHOR'S NOTE

The present work is a modified version of a paper given to the 34th Congress of Psychoanalysts of Romance Languages (Paris, April 1973). The few brief additions that I have made merely summarize replies made to those colleagues who were good enough to comment on my work.

There is currently a great deal of interest, in psychoanalytic circles, in the concept of narcissism, of which the ego ideal is an avatar. In France, Béla Grunberger has been studying this concept of Freud's since 1956. His work has opened up to psychoanalysis a new dimension of the psyche at the same time as making possible a better understanding of the often mysterious effects of the psychoanalytic process itself. His writings, now in one volume (B. Grunberger, *Narcissism, Psychoanalytic Essays*, New York, International Universities Press, 1979), constitute a breakthrough into a domain the importance of which is highlighted by certain contemporary socio-cultural phenomena. Whilst my hypotheses concerning the 'ego ideal' may at times be at variance with those he has put forward, without the latter they would doubtless never have seen the light of day. This book is, in consequence, dedicated to him.

I hope that my readers will be tolerant of a hazard that can befall an untranslated author. When I held the Freud Professorship at University College, London, I had no reason to expect that my lectures and seminars would be published, much less that this earlier work would be translated into English after *Creativity and Perversion*. Now that both have appeared I ask indulgence for repetitions of examples which, in some cases, I might have avoided if I could have foretold the future. The arguments of the books also overlap, but in ways which are part of what I wish to propose.

I wish to express thanks to my translator, Paul Barrows, and to my publisher and editor, Robert Young, along with his lively and efficient colleagues. I wish to add my gratitude to all those, whether in my field or not, whether in my family or not, whether living or dead, who have played a role in the formation of my own ego ideal.

Introduction

Christopher Lasch

The work of Béla Grunberger and Janine Chasseguet-Smirgel marks a new stage in the psychoanalytic study of narcissism. Grunberger's essays on narcissism have already been translated into English, but the relation between narcissism and the ego ideal becomes fully apparent only in the work of his wife and sometime collaborator. Some of her own work, to be sure, has also appeared in English, but a few scattered essays do not reveal its full range and theoretical significance. The present study shows for the first time the central importance of an understanding of the ego ideal. It is the work of a theorist of great originality and power.

Once the ego ideal is clearly distinguished from the superego, it becomes possible to make sense of much that formerly remained obscure in psychoanalytic theory. A proper understanding of the ego ideal restores to the psychoanalytic concept of narcissism something of its popular meaning of self-esteem. Narcissism is the state of archaic plenitude in which the ego serves as its own ideal, in Chasseguet-Smirgel's formulation. Following the suggestion thrown out by Freud in his pivotal essay, 'On Narcissism' — unfortunately abandoned in his later work, where 'ego ideal' and 'superego' appear as interchangeable terms — Chasseguet-Smirgel sees the ego ideal as the heir of primary narcissism: the heir, that is, of the infantile illusion of omnipotence and of the blissful feelings bound up with it. Separation from the mother shatters self-esteem because it forces the child to confront his own weakness and dependency — the gap between ego and ego ideal, which we spend the rest of our lives trying to close.

Chasseguet-Smirgel makes it clear, of course, that narcissistic wounds include much more than simply a blow to our self-esteem. The infant's growing understanding of its helpless, dependent position in the world shatters the illusion of perfect fusion with the mother and with the surrounding environment. It is this discovery of the boundary between the self and the not-self that opens the infant's eyes to its dependence on external sources of care and nourishment. The original experience of a contentment based at once on the illusion of absolute self-sufficiency and on the illusion of blissful union with the world gives way to a painful sense of inferiority. The memory of aboriginal contentment and grandiosity lives on, however, in the form of an ideal conception of selfhood, the ego ideal, on which the developing ego seeks to pattern itself. Often misunderstood simply as a role model based on internalized images of parents and other authorities, the ego ideal, as explained by Chasseguet-Smirgel, originates in the earliest experiences and embodies the 'fundamental human desire to return to the maternal womb'. Idealized parental introjects later serve as further reminders of lost perfection. 'Human evolution' as a whole, according to Chasseguet-Smirgel, grows out of 'nostalgia for a lost paradise'; all of us 'are always *à la récherche du temps perdu*'.

This unappeasable longing for an unattainable ideal of happiness — the 'malady of the ideal' — underlies both the most exalted human achievements and the most degrading forms of human folly. Its strength and persistence testify to the prematurity of the human infant, which Chasseguet-Smirgel, following Freud, regards as the dominant fact underlying all mental life. The human infant comes into the world too soon, endowed with ambitions that outrun its bodily powers. 'Human prematurity, which is at the origin of the formation of an ego ideal, probably gives to our instinctual life certain specific characteristics.' It governs the translation of bodily needs into the register of desire.

It makes pleasure more than a simple release from tension. Instinctual gratification serves at the same time to reduce the distance between ego and ego ideal. Yet the unattainability of their perfect union leaves desire always unsatisfied.

Humans are alone among animals in the constancy of the sexual impulse, and the absence of sexual periodicity in humans hints at the transformation of instinctual life by an overlay of narcissistic longing. In human beings, the sex drive is no longer instinctual in the strict sense; nor does any other biological drive remain uninfluenced by the narcissistic longing for primal union. Indeed this longing — rooted in the need to overcome the fact of separation and the consciousness of helplessness — becomes so intense that it can overwhelm even the self-preservative instinct itself. This is not because the ego ideal obeys a 'death instinct', but because the narcissism on which it is based, dating from a stage of mental life that antedates any sense of the distinction between the self and the outside world, has no understanding of death and therefore remains indifferent to the possibility of its own extinction. Among the many psychoanalytic concepts newly illuminated by the new understanding of narcissism and the ego ideal, the death instinct has always been the most problematic and inaccessible. We are now in a better position both to understand why it has to be rejected and to appreciate the insight behind it, which arises out of the train of speculations first broached by Freud in his essay on narcissism but was later obscured by his attempt to provide an instinctual basis for the disturbing possibility raised by the theory of primary narcissism — the possibility that something in the self longs to regress to a condition anterior to all tension and striving and cares nothing for the welfare of the bodily ego. The Nirvana principle, as Freud came to call it, seeks absolute release from tension and thus experiences even the promptings of the pleasure principle as a disturbing intrusion on the womb-like contentment it wishes to restore. But the Nirvana principle, we can now see, originates not in the 'death instinct' but in primary narcissism, with its illusion of everlasting life and its indifference to bodily demands.

Freud's intuition led him in the direction of something 'beyond the pleasure principle', something deeper and more obscure than the striving for libidinal gratification; but he assumed, in accordance with his theory of the primacy of instinct, that this something must itself be instinctual. Hence the ill-conceived hypothesis of a death instinct. Grunberger and Chasseguet-Smirgel have disentangled the Nirvana principle from the concept of a death instinct and posited instead a 'continual dialectic between the instinctual ego and the narcissistic self', in Grunberger's words. Their theory helps to explain, among other things, why the 'narcissistic person', as Grunberger writes, 'is one who loves himself well, but also one who loves himself poorly or not at all'.

Another Freudian insight, that frustration provides the motive force behind psychological development, becomes more fully intelligible in the light of Chasseguet-Smirgel's theory of the ego ideal. In its longing to recapture the experience of primal oneness and omnipotence, the ego ideal can follow either the short, direct, and regressive road marked out by the Nirvana principle or the long and difficult road of maturation and development. The second road is full of obstructions. It confronts the child with the full evidence of his inferiority and helplessness. But frustration also serves as an incentive to the child to master his environment, to struggle against adversity, to live up to the example set by parents and other authorities, to become an adult, and thus to recapture the sense of oneness not by denying the fact of separation but by overcoming it in the pursuit of an ideal — erotic, aesthetic, or religious — of devotion and self-sacrifice.

Idealized erotic passion, art and religion, according to Chasseguet-Smirgel, all serve to replace the original illusion of perfect fusion with experiences that recapture something of its euphoria but acknowledge the otherness of objects as well as their imperfections. An acceptance of the partner's limitations — the indulgence characteristic of tenderness — distinguishes a ripe and sensual passion from the idealization of love so characteristic of adolescence. In art, a representation of flawed beauty moves us more deeply than the idealized images held up by advertising and mass culture. In the same way, an insistence on the obstacles to salvation distinguishes religion, strictly speaking, from mysticism or from contemporary Jesus cults, which 'dissolve the face of the father and thus leap over the line separating religion from mysticism. The absolute reign of the son implies, as its latent content, union with the mother' — a union, that is, that acknowledges no impediments, in the form of paternal prohibitions or even in the form of a paternal presence, to its consummation.

It is the denial of these obstacles that defines the shortcut to Nirvana, the way of illusions. Chasseguet-Smirgel begins her study of the ego ideal with a study of sexual perversion, because it is here that the psychic mechanism of denial reveals itself most strikingly and most clearly betrays its narcissistic origin. Perversion, as Chasseguet-Smirgel explains it, is a strategy for the maintenance of narcissistic illusions. It denies both gender differences and generational differences; and the close connection between these two kinds of denial is clearly explained, perhaps for the first time, by Chasseguet-Smirgel's theory. Perversion embodies the illusion that the little boy is already a perfect partner for his mother, whom he endows with a phallus, moreover, in order to deny that she needs that of her husband. In women, the same kind of illusion takes the form of a fantasy in which the little girl bears a child without any paternal intervention.

Raised to an ideology in recent movements for sexual separatism, this fantasy springs from a need not to recognize the mutual dependence of men and women. Chasseguet-Smirgel quotes Valerie Solanas's *S.C.U.M. Manifesto*: 'Reproduction of the species is technologically possible without the help of the male. Henceforth women can reproduce only from women.' The denial of the male role in reproduction serves also to deny the difference between generations. If the mother has no need for a husband, she needs only her little girl or boy. By eradicating generational differences and differences of gender, perversion erases the more fundamental distinction between the self and the not-self, the source of every other distinction. It overcomes the anxiety and pain of separation by annulling any knowledge of the obstacles to the reunion of mother and child. Instead of overcoming these obstacles, it simply denies their existence.

Chasseguet-Smirgel's analysis of the ego ideal provides no support for recent programmes of sexual liberation and cultural revolution, which celebrate polymorphous perversity, gay rights, and a society without fathers; but neither does it uphold a normative schedule of psychological development, in the manner of ego psychology, or idealize the radically separate, autonomous ego as the end-product of that development. An emphasis on the ego ideal, as opposed to the ego itself, allows us to see that development lies not in a linear progression through clearly delineated oral, anal and phallic stages, culminating in the attainment of genital sexuality, but in a loving union with the world that nevertheless acknowledges the fact of its otherness.

By insisting on the links between sexual perversion and art, between narcissism and erotic passion, or between idealization and sublimation, Chasseguet-Smirgel makes us see that the most exalted activities have their basis in the most regressive longings and fantasies, which seek to restore a state of affairs in which the self merged imperceptibly with its surroundings. The eradication of this memory is no more the goal of a proper psychic development than is annulment of the knowledge of separation and dependence. Chasseguet-Smirgel invokes the distinction between being and becoming in order to clarify the difference between regressive and developmental solutions to the underlying problem of separation; but she does not mean to imply that development, which seeks to become and not to be an admired and envied parent, achieves its proper goal in the disavowal of connections with the outside world, in contempt for women, or in a repudiation of the feminine side of experience.

Chasseguet-Smirgel's insistence on the importance of matura-tion and development is best understood, then, not as a condemnation of homosexuality or as an effort to set up a rigorous norm of sexual behavior but as a critique of the *ideology* of perversion and of ideology in general, which originates in the need to preserve the infantile illusion of omnipotence. Some of the most illuminating pages in this work deal with group psychology — another aspect of Freudian theory that becomes fully intelligible only in the context of a proper understanding of the ego ideal. Whereas Freud saw the group as a revival of the primal horde, with the leader as a father-figure and the group as a band of brothers, Chasseguet-Smirgel argues that many forms of group psychology originate in the same illusion that underlies the ideology of sexual perversion.

Especially in the modern world, groups seem to find their dominant fantasy not in submission to the father but in collective reunion with the mother. 'The group is auto-engendered. It is itself an all-powerful mother. Group life organizes itself not around a central admonitory figure but around the group itself.' The group thus represents the 'hope of a fusion between the ego and the ego ideal by the most regressive means'. Nazism, for example, worshipped the mother goddess ('blood and earth') more than the father. It promoted a 'veritable eradication of the father and the paternal universe, as well as everything that derives from the Oedipus complex'. In Nazi ideology, according to Chasseguet-Smirgel, the 'return to nature, to early Germanic mythology, reveals an aspiration to merge with the all-powerful mother'. Group psychology in our time rests more often on the need for illusion than on the need for leadership, and modern ideology serves to promote the mass illusion of omnipotence. Groups tend to choose as their leaders not the man of action, the domineering father figure, but the master illusionist skilled in propaganda and the histrionic arts, who gives each member of the group the 'opportunity to think that he neither needs to grow up like, nor identify with, his father'.

Chasseguet-Smirgel brings her study to a close with some remarks, all too brief, on religion and science. Here again, she argues that mysticism and drug cults, unlike religion, follow the short cut to Nirvana. This analysis, incidentally, helps to explain why the death of God has not made men more independent and self-reliant. The collapse of religious illusions has only prepared the way for more insidious illusions, and science itself, instead of serving as an agency of general enlightenment, helps to reactivate infantile appetites and the infantile need for illusions by impressing itself on people's lives as a never-ending series of technological miracles, wonder-working drugs and cures, and electronic conveniences that obviate the need for human effort. 'At the level of primary processes, science is experienced as magic, thanks to its products.' It encourages an insatiable restlessness and impatience, 'as if men no longer knew how to accommodate themselves to the natural rhythms of life but had begun to function on the model of the machines they themselves have created. Thus science paradoxically acts as a powerful activator of illusion in its own right.'

It will be seen from these suggestions, linking illusions to ideology, that the concept of the ego ideal, as explored by Chasseguet-Smirgel, illuminates not only the psychology of narcissism in individuals but many of the connections between psychic life and society. It is a 'pivotal concept between the individual and the collective'. It addresses itself to the experiences that first lead the individual to an awareness of his separate existence. At the same time, it concerns itself with the whole range of psychic mechanisms, regressive and developmental, by means of which men and women seek to reestablish a satisfying connection with their surroundings. But this is not all. The concept of the ego ideal also helps to clarify the relations between man and nature. It reminds us that man belongs to the natural world but has the capacity to transcend it. It helps us to see, moreover, that the capacity for critical self-reflection, adherence to the most demanding standards of conduct, and moral heroism are themselves rooted in the biological side of man's nature: in the fear of death, the sense of helplessness and inferiority, and the longing to reestablish a sense of primal unity with the natural order of things.

Author's Introduction

How poor are they that have not patience!
What wound did ever heal but by degrees?
Thou know'st we work by wit and not by witchcraft
And wit depends on dilatory time.

Othello (Act II, Scene 3)

The expression 'the ego ideal' is sufficiently evocative (see Translator's Note, p. vii) to have an emotional impact even for the uninitiated reader who happens to chance upon it in a book or in the course of conversation. He or she will not, however, be able to grasp its precise significance. Psychoanalysts themselves, in this instance, are often not in a much better position than the non-specialist. Indeed one cannot but be struck by the fact that all analysts, more or less, talk about the ego ideal but that they do not always specify the significance they attach to the concept, as if there were some kind of tacit consensus in this regard. In fact, as we shall see (see Appendix), a study of Freud's writings shows that from 1923 the concept of the ego ideal was, literally, absorbed by that of the superego. Freud thereafter only very rarely mentions the concept, introduced (formally) in 1914. Between 'On Narcissism: an Introduction' and *The Ego and the Id* he uses it in various ways. It seems to me, however, that the same thing applies to the vocabulary of psychoanalysis as to language in general; that is, a word is introduced and continues to be used as long as it relates sufficiently to an object and is only rendered obsolete by the disappearance of the object. It is wrong of purists to wish to sweep away those words which put up such a resistance, retaining their hold on the language with the force given them by the existence of the idea or the thing which they designate. It is relatively easy to define the particular sense given in different instances to the concept of superego, even though this is not without its problems, depending upon whether one agrees with the Kleinians that it exists from the very first introjects, or with Freud that it is heir to the Oedipus complex, which moreover he puts relatively late. As far as the ego ideal is concerned, however, things are much more complicated. Consequently, in surveying the texts in which Freud writes about the ego ideal, I will cite some articles from before 1914 in which, whilst he does not specifically refer to it, he nonetheless seems to me to be considering a problematic which prefigures, and in some sense conditions, the introduction of this concept. The choice of these texts is itself not an easy one, as it is necessarily influenced by personal factors, namely — at least in a certain number of instances — by my own conceptions about the ego ideal. However, this subjective factor will, I hope, be tempered in part by the fact that a certain number of the ideas, which Freud took up again in subsequent works, do converge. There is a striking asymmetry between such a survey and a collation of those Freudian texts which contain references to precursors of the superego. All analysts would agree that, in the latter case, one would select those texts in which appear 'the censorship', 'the incest barrier', 'the critically observing agency' and 'the ego ideal' (in some of its functions). With respect to the ego ideal, such key words as 'overestimation' or 'overvaluation', as also 'narcissism', are of some use to us, but in my view (and here we are again involved in personal choices) we would also need to take into account such less precise allusions as 'ambitious phantasies' or 'family romance'.

There is another difficulty to be noted: anyone claiming to write about the ego ideal must take up some position concerning its links with the superego and how it stands in relation to this agency. Now, the ego ideal of 1914 and the superego of 1923 belong to different topographies. Consequently, in so far as one regards the ego ideal and the superego as not identical, at the same time as adopting the second topography, the ego ideal finds itself in the (uncomfortable) position of being astride two different conceptions of the psychic apparatus. If, furthermore, one recalls that the ego ideal of 1914 and the superego of 1923 are set in the context of two equally contrasted theories of the instincts, one cannot but be struck by the complexity of the problem. (The superego was introduced in 1923 in connection with the dualism of the life and death instincts of 1920.) One must hope, however, that a more clinically based approach can bring some clarity to this confusion.

Because of the form my presentation will take, but equally because of following the clinical material, I shall, virtually throughout this work, be writing about the ego ideal without reference to the superego, as if it were an autonomous entity. However, what might appear to be an artificial device is in fact in conformity both with the history of psychoanalytic theory (the ego ideal having appeared in Freud's work well before the superego) and with genetical development (the ego ideal being heir to primary narcissism and the superego heir to the Oedipus complex).

Granted that Igitur's 'malady of the ideal' (see Mallarmé) may apply to depression and even to Cotard's syndrome ('Igitur, threatened by the punishment of eternal life, that he vaguely senses') it is not with a study of this nosological entity that I am concerned. Some very good works have been devoted, both in France and abroad, to the role of the ego ideal in neurotic and melancholic depression. I am thinking particularly of Francis Pasche's 'De la dépression' in which he studies 'the depression of inferiority' in relation to the megalomanic ego ideal (Pasche, 1961) and of Béla Grunberger's 'A Study of Depression' and 'Suicide of Melancholics' (Grunberger, 1965, 1966) in which narcissism and its heir are seen as antagonists of the ego and the instincts. Abroad, the works of Edith Jacobson (Jacobson, 1953, 1946) also stress the role of the ego ideal in depressive structures.

To take up this question again would require a work to itself. My choice of subject has also been dictated by certain clinical reflections which have pushed me in a different direction, one in which, I hope, the reader will be good enough to follow me. Indeed, here again — along with other colleagues, I imagine — I have often been struck by the fact that some patients who have a very florid symptomatology, of a neurotic but also at times pre-psychotic character, sometimes alarming in physical appearance, prove on analysis to have a remarkable degree of insight (though this can apply equally to people met with outside the consulting room). They may have an intuitive sense of what they might be were it not for their inner conflicts. When they do undertake an analysis, they are supported through it, often against major resistances, by a sort of profound grasp of the stages they must go through in order to become themselves. By contrast, some patients who do not appear to be very ill and are perhaps socially very successful and clearly well-endowed intellectually show (over and above the classical resistances) a lack of understanding, that is quite as profound as is the intuition of the other patients, of what the analytic process is about and even, as I hope to show, about any kind of process whatsoever. The analyst then lacks the cooperation which, in the case of the former kind of patient, comes from the presence of a certain factor that I shall try to define. Perhaps it can be likened to the 'therapeutic alliance', so dear to American authors, which may in this way be defined more precisely and seen from a rather more classical analytic point of view. The delineation of the respective qualities of the ego ideal in these two types of structure should throw some light on problems such as, for example, the state of being in love, group phenomena, the different types of creative artist, the role of peers in the evaluation of our own ego . . .

Freud wrote that 'whoever understands the human mind knows that hardly anything is harder for a man than to give up a pleasure which he has once experienced. Actually, we can never give anything up; we only exchange one thing for another' ('Creative Writers', Freud, 1908). The Freudian concept of the ego ideal (1914) follows on directly from this observation. According to this, the ego ideal is a substitute for primary narcissistic perfection, but a substitute from which the ego is separated by a gulf, a split that man is constantly seeking to abolish. We will attempt to study some of the means used to this end whilst bearing in mind certain other Freudian propositions which, taken together, constitute a description of the human condition: 'However strange it may sound, we must reckon with the possibility that something in the nature of the sexual instinct itself is unfavourable to the realization of complete satisfaction' ('On the Universal Tendency . . .', Freud, 1912). And also:

> The ultimate ground of all intellectual inhibitions and all inhibitions of work seems to be the inhibition of masturbation in childhood. But perhaps it goes deeper; perhaps it is not its inhibition by external influences but its unsatisfying nature in itself. There is always something lacking for complete discharge and satisfaction — en attendant toujours quelque chose qui ne venait point ('Always waiting for something which never came'). (Note of 3 August, 1938, S.E. XXIII, p. 300. In French in the original)

And again: 'It is only later that the instinct loses that object (the breast), just at the time, perhaps, when the child is able to form a total idea of the person to whom the organ that is giving him satisfaction belongs' (*Three Essays*, Freud, 1905). And finally: 'What we call happiness in the strictest sense comes from the (preferably sudden) satisfaction of needs which have been dammed up to a high degree, and it is from its nature only possible as an episodic phenomenon' (*Civilization and its Discontents*, Freud, 1929). When the infant took himself as his own ideal there was no unsatisfaction, no desire, no loss, and this time remains with us as an example of perfect, unending contentment. Freud thus gives us to understand — until the last moment — that whilst man may chase endlessly after this lost perfection, he can never actually achieve it. It is this quest, it seems, that lies at the base of the most sublime achievements, but also the most baleful errors, of the human spirit. I hope that my work will contribute to an understanding of this apparent contradiction. Once again, references to the psychoanalytic literature on the superego as such will be limited. The subject has in fact been extremely well documented by Marcel Roch (Roch, 1966), and I would refer the reader to this, at the same time as expressing my gratitude to him for putting at our disposal such an invaluable tool.

'The malady of the ideal' is universal: all may not die of it, but all are afflicted. Hence a study of the ego ideal must lead to a consideration of man in general.

The reader might therefore be surprised to find that this work begins with an examination of the relationship between the ego ideal and perversion. In fact, it seemed to me that this point of departure would offer a better understanding of the role of the ego ideal in personality development which has *not* been hindered by certain factors tending to redirect its course, and from that point of view I think that my essay can be seen as a reflection on 'normality'. I think, furthermore, that the examination of the relationship between the ego ideal and perversion makes for a better understanding both of perversion itself and of certain mental states that display, along with it, a common nucleus that I have attempted to outline. This nucleus is present in structures with which we find ourselves dealing more and more. This work endeavours, then, to make some contribution to a study of the evolution of that pathology that so many works today focus upon.

The perspective of the work as a whole takes as its focal point man's biological immaturity and the Freudian concept of *Hilflösigkeit* (the infant's early helplessness, his inability to do things for himself). The violent end to which the primary state of fusion is brought by this helplessness obliges the infant to recognize the 'not-me'. This seems to be the crucial moment when the narcissistic omnipotence that he is forced to give up is projected on to the object, the infant's first ego ideal, a narcissistic omnipotence from which he is henceforth divided by a gulf that he will spend the rest of his life trying to bridge. This projection provides an impetus that then becomes the *primum movens* of his education and of his activities in other spheres. Thus the ego ideal is seen as a specific anthropological phenomenon (in the broadest sense of the term) which takes man beyond the simple quest for instinctual satisfaction.

To study the ego ideal is to study that which is most human in man, that which sets him farthest apart from the animal world, even more no doubt than the superego. In his *Outline of Psychoanalysis* (1938) Freud wrote that the superior mammals undoubtedly had a superego: he was referring in that case to dogs, as a letter of his to Marie Bonaparte indicates. It is this sense of nostalgia for a lost state of perfection that is so unique to man's condition. Man is an ailing animal, seeking after a time that has passed, a time when 'he was his own ideal' (Freud, 1914). He is involved in a constant quest for that part of his narcissism that was wrested from him at the time of the primary loss of fusion.

All too often psychoanalysts reduce the ego ideal to a *model* that the person is attempting to emulate. It seems to me that it cannot be understood in this way if, along with Freud, one considers it as 'the substitute for the lost narcissism of his childhood'. The choice of props for this narcissism in the form of models is only a consequence — of prime importance, certainly, as regards development, but secondary in relation to the person's deeper motivation — of the desire to bridge the gap between the ego as it is and as it would like to be (which in the last analysis always refers to the time when 'it was its own ideal'). The projection of this ideal on to a model is, for this reason, always somewhat derisory, and achieving the aim (i.e. resemblance with the admired model and hence its abandonment) can never be truly and finally satisfying, which can be a factor in progress. In fact, these models are only ephemeral, partial substitutes for a project that is much more grandiose and unattainable, save perhaps in orgasm, the most profound regression (psychosis) and death.

The narcissism that has been wrested from the primitive ego could be compared to the Platonic ideal seeking embodiment in some form, with the major difference that in fact it represents a quantity of energy. But it is the existence of the Ideal which predominates over the forms, which are only modest, successive versions of it. It is education (allied to the child's desire to free himself from his object, that is to say from his primary dependence) and the Oedipus complex that push the child to become autonomous through his identifications, giving to his ego ideal different forms. In other words, it is directed into different *ideals*, thus giving form (and hence limits) to his lost narcissism. One might, therefore, hypothesize the existence of a transcendent ego ideal over and above other temporary, and constantly revised, ideals.

Making money (or despising it, owning a luxurious house (or vaunting a bohemian life style), dressing in an amusing or original way, raising handsome children, practising a religion, taking to drink, adopting a particular ideology, loving and being loved, writing an intelligent book, creating a work of art, etc. — each of these may represent different ways of attempting to reduce the gap between the ego and its ideal. Yet it is no less true that, over and above the search for these satisfactions in themselves, man is inspired by something more profound, something more absolute, something permanent which goes beyond the changing *content*, the varied and ephemeral forms that he gives to his fundamental desire to find a lost perfection once again. These attempts, which are but staging posts on a road leading only to death, nonetheless inspire man in life. To my mind this view does not diminish the role of desire and pleasure nor, especially, that of the Oedipus complex. On the contrary, I would accord the incest fantasy and oedipal desire a fundamental significance by linking them to the ego ideal. Oedipal desire is sustained by more than the simple wish to reduce sexual tension, and in that it is profoundly human, because it too is linked to characteristics that are specific to the human condition: the immaturity of the little boy, his distress, his dependancy. It seems to me very necessary to differentiate the incest phantasy from the sexual instinct in general.

Consider — though I will have occasion to refer to other texts in which Freud writes about *Hilflösigkeit* — this extract from *Inhibitions, Symptoms and Anxiety* (1926):

The biological factor is the long period of time during which the young of the human species is in a condition of helplessness and dependence. Its intra-uterine existence seems to be short in comparison with that of most animals, and it is sent into the world in a less finished state. As a result, the influence of the real external world upon it is intensified and an early differentiation between the ego and the id is promoted. Moreover, the dangers of the external world have a greater importance for it, so that the value of the object which can alone protect it against them and take the place of its former intra-uterine life is enormously enhanced. The biological factor, then, establishes the earliest situations of danger and creates the need to be loved which will accompany the child through the rest of its life.

It follows from this view of *Hilflösigkeit* and its consequences that the Oedipus complex — that is, incestuous desire and its derivatives — must be seen not only as the 'nucleus of the neuroses' but also as that of the human psyche in general.

CHAPTER ONE

The Ego Ideal and Perversion

She took her into her bedroom and said to her: "Go into the garden and fetch me a pumpkin." Cinderella went off straightaway and picked the most beautiful she could find, and took it to her godmother, unable to guess how this pumpkin could get her to the ball. Her godmother hollowed it out, leaving only the skin, and tapped it with her magic wand, and the pumpkin was changed in a flash into a beautiful golden carriage. Then she went and looked in her mouse trap where she found six live mice; she told Cinderella to lift the trap door of the mouse trap very gently and as each mouse came out she gave it a tap with her wand and the mouse was immediately transformed into a beautiful horse, giving her a magnificent team of six beautiful, dappled, mouse-grey horses. As she was worrying about how she could make a coachman, Cinderella said, "I will go and see if there isn't some rat in the rat trap; we will make a coachman with that." "You are right," said her godmother, "Off you go and see." Cinderella brought her the rat trap, which had three large rats in it. The fairy chose one of the three, because of its wonderful beard, and with a tap changed it into a portly coachman with one of the most beautiful moustaches you have ever seen. Then she said to her, "Go into the garden and you will find six lizards behind the watering can; bring them to me." No sooner had she brought them than her godmother changed them into six footmen who straightaway climbed up behind the carriage in their fine livery and stood there as if they had never done anything else all their lives. The fairy then said to Cinderella, "Well then, now you have all you need for going to the ball. Doesn't that please you?"

In 1914, when Freud introduced the concept of the ego ideal into psychoanalytic theory, together with that of narcissism, he made the ego ideal heir to primary narcissism ('On Narcissism: an Introduction', Freud, 1914). Unable to give up a satisfaction he has once experienced, man 'is not willing to forgo the narcissistic perfection of his childhood' and 'seeks to recover in the new form of an ego ideal that early perfection that he can no longer retain. What he projects before him as his ideal is the substitute for the lost narcissism of his childhood in which he was his own ideal.'

According to this text, man was forced to give up the narcissistic perfection of his childhood by both the 'admonitions of others' and 'the awakening of his own critical judgement'. In fact, as Freud states in a note to 'Instincts and their Vicissitudes' (1915), the disruption of this primitive narcissistic state is linked to the person's experience of helplessness which forces him to recognize the existence of the 'not-me', of an object which he will, at a later point, invest with his lost omnipotence. The idea that the recognition of the object has its origin in the infant's early helplessness and hence in his *dependency* (a constant theme in Freud's work) figured already in the *Project* (Freud, 1895, Part I, General Scheme):

> At first, the human organism is incapable of bringing about the specific action (i.e. an action capable of lowering internal tension through an *experience of satisfaction*). It takes place by *extraneous help*, when the attention of an experienced person is drawn to the child's state by discharge along the path of internal change — e.g. by the child's screaming. In this way the path of discharge acquires a secondary function of the highest importance, that of *communication*.

As we know, it is precisely this narcissism — 'projected before him' — which forms the ego ideal and which is also subsequently invested in other objects, in the case of the boy centering on the father figure at the time of the Oedipus complex. Without as yet elaborating this in detail, it should be noted straightaway that there is a long process of evolution from the moment when a person takes himself as his own ideal to that when he makes over his narcissism to his homosexual object, the father, who then becomes his model or, as one might otherwise put it, till he forms the project of trying to identify with him. Now, in my view, a study of the obstacles to the evolution of the ego ideal can afford us a clearer idea of the relationship between the ego ideal and the development of the individual in general. The example of the pervert seems particularly significant in this respect. Numerous authors have devoted themselves to the study of the superego of the pervert, a topic which does indeed pose many questions. However, the problems raised in relation to the ego ideal are no less interesting and can both enlighten us about certain basic perverse mechanisms and throw some light on the general functioning of the ego ideal.

A feature of the aetiology of the perversions that has often been noted is the very frequent occurrence of an attitude of seduction and complicity on the part of the mother towards her child. My own clinical experience is entirely in accord with this finding. The pervert will readily say: 'I did not have to take my father's place, I always had it', or will recount how his mother took him into her bed whilst father slept in the dining room, or else will recall scenes in which his mother undressed in front of him, kissed him on the mouth, or lavished constant adoration on him in the form of caresses, tender words and a certain spiritual intimacy coupled with an unwonted physical promiscuity. These intense exchanges between mother and son seem to take place within a closed system, a system from which the father is excluded. Freud (1931), writing on 'Female Sexuality', said, 'Where seduction intervenes it invariably disturbs the natural course of the developmental processes, and it often leaves behind extensive and lasting consequences.' To my mind the important thing in the present context is that it is as if the mother had encouraged a self-deception on the part of her son by making him believe that he, with his infantile sexuality, was a perfect partner for her, and consequently had no reason to envy his father, thus bringing to a halt his development. His ego ideal, instead of moving on to invest the genital father and his penis, remains thereafter attached to a pregenital model.

It goes without saying that the crucial factor is that the deception be maintained. This illusion (that the pervert is a suitable partner for the mother and will one day possess her) is relived in the transference. One pervert patient believed (this was no longer a fantasy) that the analysis would end in a sexual relationship between myself and him. Ruth Lebovici (1956) mentions the same belief in a patient of hers. The illusion is sustained in a whole range of circumstances, even when the mother's attitude does not in fact correspond to the schema just described. For example, one perverse patient seems, on the contrary, to have been rejected by his mother. Nonetheless, various factors combined to lend to the account, given to him by his mother, of the circumstances of his conception, a central position around which his perversion became organized. As a young virgin, she supposedly danced naked with the father of the child, and it was on this occasion that she was made pregnant, without penetration having taken place. It was the delivery that supposedly deflowered her. This case (communicated to me by a colleague) illustrates well how in such a representation of the primal scene the father does nothing which the child, with his pregenital sexiality, is not equally capable of doing, e.g. dancing naked. In addition, in this account of a Christ-like birth, the mother gives to the son an even more 'genital' role than the father, since it is he who deflowered her in the act of being born.

The family constellation of another (fetishistic) patient seemed to be even further removed from the prototype I have described. His father had for many years shown obvious signs of paranoia. His mother was described as being the soft and submissive victim of this tyrant of the household, who also wrote anonymous letters and made holes in the bedroom walls of various members of the family with a gimlet, in order to be able to spy on them, etc. It seemed as if everything conspired towards blocking any path that might lead the patient to an identification with the genital father, since the behaviour of this father — identified with an anal sadistic, phallic maternal imago — lent itself particularly to the phantasy of a father without a genital penis, but with a fetishistic gimlet in its place. Here again the little boy can comfort himself with the illusion that he has no reason to envy his father on a genital plane. The child, with his infantile anal sadistic eroticism, could claim to be his equal.

One can understand, in this light, why a girl who is loved too tenderly by her father, who ostensibly prefers her to his wife — a situation often met with — does not become perverse, but neurotic; and also perhaps why perversion is less common in women than in men. Freud noted that amongst the children of a single family, the boys often became perverted and the girls neurotic (*Three Essays*, 1905 and 'Civilized Sexual Morality', 1908). It seems to me that the girl can never be completely certain that she is a satisfactory object for the object, because her father is an object who has made her wait, and because she has previously experienced a relationship with the mother that was inevitably frustrating. This is not true only by virtue of those early conflicts that neither sex can avoid, but also because of the intrinsic restriction for a girl of being born to someone of the same sex who is not her 'true' sexual object (as B. Grunberger has emphasised in 'Outline for a Study of Narcissism in Female Sexuality', 1964). In addition, the daughter did not receive the same kind of cathexis from the mother as would be accorded to a boy, except in the case of mothers who are themselves perverse (as in the case described by Robert Bak, 1971).

Francis Pasche (1956) explains the process of fetishism (to my mind the same explanation applies to all the perversions) as being due to the presence of an obstacle to the idealization of the father. No doubt this lack of projection of the ego ideal on to the father by the future pervert can also be seen as a function of the two axes of male sexuality described by Denise Braunschweig and Michel Fain in their thought-provoking work *Eros et Antéros* (1971) — the maternal instinct and the oedipal structure — the father having failed to come between the mother and her baby by reclaiming her as his wife.

However, we should not forget, in describing this schema, the contribution of the young male himself: his desire to be his mother's partner and to blot out with all the means at his disposal the reality that goes against this desire. The parents' attitude tends either to confirm him in this, at the expense of sexual truth, or to thwart him in various more or less inappropriate ways (leading to neurotic or even psychotic solutions when there is a lack of maternal erotic and narcissistic cathexis), or to lead to a satisfactory development of the ego through a gradual weakening of the maternal bond. But in no case is the parental attitude responsible for the existence of the child's desire. It only serves to direct the choice of possible solutions. In fact, the distortion of the ego ideal when not projected on to the father is accompanied by a corresponding distortion of reality and hence of the ego.

Joyce McDougall, whose remarkable work has greatly extended our understanding of the perverse structure, emphasises the role of the integration, into our apprehension of reality in general, of the difference between the sexes, and the denial to which this is subject in the case of the pervert. The thesis is not new, but what the author stresses — and this entirely accords with my own conclusions — is that the sight of the female genital organs lacking a penis is not only terrifying in as much as it confirms the possibility of castration, but also because the mother's lack of a penis causes the child to recognize the role of the father's penis and no longer to deny the primal scene (McDougall, 1971).

Indeed, I consider that the bed-rock of reality is not only the difference between the sexes, but that which corresponds absolutely to this, like the two faces of a coin: namely, the difference between the generations. The reality is not that the mother has been castrated; the reality is that she has a vagina that the little boy's penis cannot satisfy. The reality is that the father has a penis and prerogatives that are still only potentialities in the little boy. The denial of the mother's lack of a penis masks the denial of the presence of her vagina. If the sight of the female genital organs is so 'traumatic', it is because it confronts the young male with his inadequacy, because it forces him to recognize his oedipal defeat — a defeat that Catherine Parat has so vividly described in her paper on 'The Oedipal Organization of the Genital Phase' (Parat, 1966).

Freud asked himself in 'Fetishism' (1927) why it should be that, since no man escapes the sight of the female genital organs and the fear of castration that follows from this, some are affected to such an extent that they become homosexuals or fetishists, whereas the great majority develop along the path of normal heterosexuality. Perhaps one might suggest that those who become perverts are those who, often with their mothers' encouragement, have not been able to reconcile themselves to giving up the illusion of being able to be a satisfying partner to her, whereas the factors that favour the projection of the ego ideal on to the father help the little boy to overcome his fear of the female organ lacking a penis. If it is true that by attributing a phallus to his mother the fetishist is defending himself from fears of castration, he is at the same time defending himself from a recognition of the genital relationship between his parents. If his mother has a penis, she has no need of that of the father — the adult male — and he, the little boy, can satisfy his mother with his pregenital sexuality. The boy has, as Freud said in the 'Dissolution of the Oedipus Complex' (1924), only very vague 'notions' as to what constitutes a satisfying erotic intercourse, but knows that certainly the penis must play a part in it.

In *An Outline of Psychoanalysis* (1938) he again writes about the oedipal phase when the little boy 'begins to manipulate his penis and simultaneously has phantasies of carrying out some sort of activity with it in relation to his mother'. Curiously, Freud had gone much further in recognizing the masculine desire to penetrate a corresponding organ when in 1908 ('On the Sexual Theories of Children') he described the 'obscure urges to do something violent, to press in, to knock to pieces, to tear open a hole somewhere'. 'But', he added,

when the child thus seems to be well on the way to

postulating the existence of the vagina and to concluding that an incursion of this kind by his father's penis into his mother is the act by means of which the baby is created in his mother's body — at this juncture his enquiry is broken off in helpless perplexity. For standing in its way is his theory that his mother possesses a penis just as a man does, and the existence of the cavity which receives the penis remains undiscovered by him.

Could it have been made any clearer that this theory bars any access to an awareness of the role of the father? And might it not be thought that it exists solely in order to maintain this misapprehension?

One might, at this point, wonder to what extent the whole conception of the male oedipal position, as described by Freud, needs to be revised (and many have been the attempts) in the following light: to assert that at the time of the Oedipus complex the male child has no desire to penetrate the mother (having no awareness, even unconsciously, of the existence of the vagina) seems to me to be confirming male defences generally and that of the pervert in particular.

This view would reduce to some extent the dramatic role of the Oedipus complex and also the decisive part it is given in the development of the ego and the related sense of reality. It may be noted that Catherine Parat, in the paper cited earlier, and also Béla Grunberger in his papers on 'The Analytic Situation' (1956) and 'The Oedipus Complex and Narcissism' (1967), by emphasizing the child's biological immaturity at the time of the Oedipus complex and the resultant narcissistic wound, have a view of the Oedipus complex based on an awareness, at least at an unconscious level, of the difference between the sexes. Moreover, for Catherine Parat, 'the differences between the sexes — their complementarity — are a typically oedipal discovery'. Further, it seems to me that the necessity to maintain the illusion of the lack of difference between the sexes, which corresponds to a denial of the difference between the generations, the one governing the other, which is common to all perversions, would explain why fetishism can be found in all the perversions, as Rosolato has shown (1967). This is also the view of R. Bak for whom 'fetishism is the basic perversion' (Bak, 1969). Moreover, as early as 1905 Freud considered that the search for the woman's penis played 'a large role in the multiple perversions'.

When the child is obliged to acknowledge the difference between the sexes and their complementary genitality, he finds himself obliged at the same time to acknowledge the difference between the generations which, for the pervert, is equivalent to being consigned to the void. Everything possible must therefore be done to avoid this awful awareness. Pregenital sexuality, its erogenous zones and part objects, must itself be subject to a process of idealization. This had already been noted by Freud in the *Three Essays*: 'It is perhaps in connection precisely with the most repulsive perversions that the mental factor must be regarded as playing its largest part in the transformation of the sexual instinct. It is impossible to deny that in their case a piece of mental work has been performed which, in spite of its horrifying result, is the equivalent of an idealization of the instinct'. When Freud introduced the ego ideal into psychoanalytic theory in 1914, he stressed the fact that idealization relates to the *object* and sublimation to the *instinct*. We will have occasion to come back to this very important distinction. However, we may note here that in his 1905 text he does actually refer to an *idealization of the instinct*, which is distinct from sublimation since it concerns precisely a component instinct discharged directly in the perverse act.

It seems indeed quite possible to envisage the *idealization* of an instinct in the (very frequent) case in which the perverse act, and not only its object, is overvalued. One has only to read Sade to find the most repulsive coprophilic acts being treated as a pleasure of the gods and those who do not practice them being treated with contempt for being neither 'connoisseurs' nor free spirits. Was not Olympus, after all, peopled by Gods and demi-Gods: Aphrodite,

Eros, nymphs and satyrs personifying human sexual desires in an idealized (deified) form?

Some degree of narcissistic cathexis of the instincts is an inherent requirement for their integration, that is to say, for their acceptance by the ego, their 'egotization' — as Grunberger has many times emphasized. Otherwise the instinct remains alien to the ego, suffers various vicissitudes, for example, repression or projection, and, in extreme cases, gives rise to the 'influencing machine'. This narcissistic cathexis is to be distinguished from sublimation since the (sexual) *aim* of the instinct remains unchanged. With the idealization of an instinct something is added to this egotization. To idealize an instinct (or an object) is to give it a dimension, a value, a significance, a brilliance that it does not intrinsically possess (which may not relieve it of any of its crudity; the crudity itself may be elevated to the skies). It is to exalt it by making it pass for something that it is not. Seen in this perspective, the pregenital instinct is idealized in order to give oneself and others the illusion that it is equal and even superior to the genital instinct. If, in the course of 'normal' development, the ego ideal is projected on to the genital father and genitality, the latter, once attained, cannot be the object of idealization. Since it represents an end-point it cannot be evaluated against anything but itself. This is also why genitality, combining as it does all the component instincts, cannot be symbolized. The symbol being a substitute, genitality could only be a substitute for itself. The concept of the global and unifying nature of genitality is a constant of Freud's work from the *Three Essays* right through to the *Outline*, in which he again writes of sexuality that 'the complete organization is only achieved in the genital phase'.

The idealization of love, and the projection of the ego ideal on to the object when in love, are of a particular order that I will come back to. The idealization of pregenitality always corresponds to the overriding need to repress and to counter-cathect the fact, glimpsed at some level, that this is not 'the real thing'. The standard, in other words, nonetheless remains that of genitality (and the genital father), as we shall have occasion to see.

As regards the idealization of the pregenital part object by the pervert, Freud has written of the *reverence* of the fetishist for the fetish ('Fetishism', Freud, 1926). The idealization of the fetish has been particularly emphasised in France by Pasche and Renard in their article on perversion (1956). In his work on 'Régression, perversion, névrose', Francis Pasche emphasizes the pervert's idealization of the object (1956, pp. 106, 107, 108).

Glover (1933) has also studied the phenomenon of the pervert's idealization of pregenital part objects. According to him, the pervert never idealizes adult objects but always 'part objects: food, faeces, urine, sexual zones', the objects of the anal-sadistic phase holding a particularly privileged place: 'In a typical case the anal ring was phantasied as a kind of halo suspended in the sky. It was then contemplated, adored and idealized. The qualities attributed to it were mystical and the whole attitude of the patient was religious in type.' This curious glorification should not, however, surprise us. A religious attitude towards the part object (originally the fetish was a god), and in the sexual act itself, is common amongst perverts. A patient, for example, having masturbated with perverse erotic fantasies, announced to his analyst, 'I have said Mass again' (Jean Guillaumin — personal communication). One child, whose father was a doctor, spent his Sundays saying Mass in his father's consulting room. It goes without saying that this represented a substitute for playing at doctors, which itself was equivalent in this case to imitating the mysterious activities in which his father engaged with his clients in the secrecy of his consulting room, and thus related to the primal scene. Later the patient developed the habit of wanting to be beaten with a crucifix in a very ritualized way. (I have heard of someone else who played the same game of saying Mass in similar circumstances as a child, but who later became a priest.)

The ceremony surrounding religion is easily superimposed on the ceremonial of the pervert, not only because in both cases an element of ritual is involved (a point on which I cannot dwell here) but also because both involve idealization. In *Die Frömmingkeit des Grafen von Zinzendorf*, O. Pfister emphasized the connection between religious reverie and perverse eroticism, as quoted by Freud in 'On the History of the Psychoanalytic Movement' (1914). It will be recalled that for Freud: 'Idealization [the projection of primary narcissism on to the object *who then becomes the carrier of the ego ideal*] is possible in the sphere of ego libido as well as in that of object libido. For example, the sexual overvaluation of an object is an idealization of it' ('On Narcissism: an Introduction', Freud, 1914). How are we to understand such a marked propensity on the part of the pervert to idealize his part objects and the perverse act itself? (This is the companion to the tendency, in someone who has cathected his ego ideal in the father, to then project it into his total love object in the state of being-in-love). We should, I think, always bear in mind the need he has to maintain the deception of being an adequate partner for his mother, notwithstanding the infantile pregenital nature of his sexuality. As Joyce McDougall has stressed, genital love is despised by the pervert in so far as it is the prerogative of the castrated father. It might be said that 'daddy-type love' is devalued to the advantage of the pregenital sexual games of the child. (As is well known, there is today a strong collective current tending to denigrate procreative genitality, as a 'repressive' form of sexuality, in favour of a 'liberated' sexuality.)

For McDougall, the pervert has the impression of being in on a secret of the Gods, of having discovered a special 'recipe'. He is at the same time amazed to note the interest shown by those of his kind in women as genital objects. Hence, for him the idealization of the perverse act and of part objects is an absolute necessity. It must help him rid himself of, and counter-cathect, a perception that would otherwise evoke in him a feeling of real inadequacy, namely that the genital father has powers that he lacks. For somewhere in the mind of the pervert there exists, nonetheless, an ego ideal that is more reality-based and that, in analysis, appears under the guise of, for example, the father returning from the wars as an injured hero, or having become alcoholic or, again, as the brilliant captain of industry who is the victim of the economic crisis. The image of the father's earlier splendour had been kept carefully repressed in order to protect the illusion of the pervert being the mother's sole object (and also because of the guilt feelings that it arouses). Its appearance in the analysis is often accompanied by intense depressive affect: the house-of-cards of the illusion collapses at the same time as nostalgic feelings in relation to the father are coming to the fore. One way to avoid the tragic feeling of having been attracted by a mirage at the expense of authentic object relations is to glorify the whip and the boot, flagellation and coprophagia, asserting the superior pleasures and beauties of these to genital coitus with a woman.

Glover comments amusingly about the pervert's idealization: 'However devoid of idealization of adult relations he may be his geese are usually regarded by him as swans.' For ultimately it is the pervert's very being that is in question. His geese (his objects, his instincts) are at the same time his own pregenital phallus that he endeavours to pass off as equal to the father's genital penis. As in the story of the Emperor of China's Nightingale (Chasseguet-Smirgel, 1968) it is a matter of the less valuable phallic symbols (the clockwork nightingale, the goose) attempting to pass themselves off as equal or superior to the others (the real nightingale, the swan). In my essay, which took Andersen's fairy-tale as its starting point, I suggested that there was a parallel between the person who fabricates something 'fake' and the pervert. I showed that the 'fake' phallus was a fetish — a word that shares the same root as 'factitious' — standing for the pervert's pregenital (fecal) phallus that he endeavours to impose as a genital penis. In the course of this I referred to some artistic, literary and intellectual productions whose originators, because of their conflicts, were unable to identify with the oedipal father, introjecting his genital penis. The narcissistic fulfilment obtained through the creation of a 'fake' phallus may have the power to deceive. However, numerous examples show that the creator of a 'fake' lives under the threat that the imposture will be discovered, that the fecal penis — the fetish — will show through the brilliant veneer covering it, just as the pervert fears (more or less, according to his ego organization) the exposure of his 'secret',

namely that his miraculous sexual 'recipe' and his idealized objects
are nothing but petty infantile games played with fetishes, or even
more obviously fecal objects, and that he himself has only, in place
of a conquering phallus, the pathetic penis of a pre-pubertal little
boy. (An exhibitionist patient only showed his penis when it was
semi-erect. On analysis it appeared that he wished to stir up
women — as mother substitutes — *despite* the pathetic — infantile
— appearance of his genitals.) His swans are decidedly only geese
(strip off the prince's clothes and you are left with only a
pauper).

Through the idealization of his instincts and his part objects,
the pervert achieves a sort of narcissistic fulfilment since this leads
to an idealization of his own ego. He can thus merge himself with
his idealized pregenital objects, and the revered fetish reflects
back the transfigured image of his own infantile attributes. In this
way he manages to approximate more nearly the time when he
was his own ideal. He admires himself in his glorified instincts, in
his exalted objects, as he used to admire himself in his mother's
eyes, where he sought confirmation of his adorable perfection.
However, the ever-present possibility that the disguise masking
the infantile and truncated nature of his ego will be seen through,
makes him particularly exigent as to the quality of all that
surrounds him, particularly in the aesthetic sphere. He will seek
out the most exquisite curios, the most accomplished works of art,
the most well-turned poems, the most refined decor. Glover
(1931) has remarked that 'the perverse activity is more freely
exercised when certain aesthetic conditions are fulfilled'. The
pervert is a man of taste, a knowledgeable amateur, an aesthete
rather than a genuine artist, his creative powers being impaired by
the impossibility of an identification with the father such as is
necessary for the process of sublimation. Like Oscar Wilde, his
genius goes into his life, his talent into his work.

This explains, to my mind, how it is that in some perverts the
most exquisite refinement can exist side by side with the most
repulsive practices, for the idealization that gives such a delicate
and aesthetic touch to his surroundings, far from preventing him

from doing so, actually permits him, under other circumstances, to poke needles into rats and to enjoy it (Proust).

In the inspired film of the Czech director J. Herz, *L'Incinérateur de Cadavres*, the hero, played by the magnificent actor R. Hrusinsky, is a perverse, criminal, psychotic character who disguises the anal sadistic nature of his necrophilia by idealizing his trade (he works in a crematorium). He explains to an apprentice that cremation allows the soul to be liberated from the body (clearly identified as something dirty that he helps it to be free of), how death is something both beautiful and useful as it puts an end to suffering, etc. (He himself becomes the murderer of his wife and children who are of 'impure' blood.) He loves 'beautiful music', buys 'beautiful' pictures (though the anality that he tries imperfectly to disguise is discernable in their *kitsch* taste), takes walks in 'pretty' cemeteries where he admires the statues. His wife is an 'angel', and his marriage to her has brought him an 'angelic life'. He caresses the faces of dead young girls, combs their hair and then combs his own. (The comb here is similar to a fetish.) He is at the same time mystical, fascinated by Buddhism. He has a vision of an immense collective crematorium in which, in the end, souls will be set free quickly, quicker than in an ordinary crematorium. He starts to work for the Nazis and finally identifies himself with the Dalai Lama. It is clear that in this instance mysticism serves to glorify anal sadistic activities and to diminish their 'fecal' nature, as also to transform excrement into gold and the digestive process — which, like cremation, is a form of combustion — into a kind of miraculous alchemy, freeing the soul from the piece of scrap that is the body. B. Grunberger (1959) describes the digestive process as consisting of a 'breaking down of the ingested food and its successive reduction to increasingly undifferentiated units, gradually losing any original particularity, and finally forming a homogeneous mass, the fecal bolus', and points to the connection between this and, amongst other things, the Auschwitz *gauleiter*'s description of his camp as 'the world's anus'. Similarly, the hero of the film comments that the ashes that are the end-product of the process of cremation are completely homogeneous: 'Absolutely identical with each other'. It is scarcely convincing to maintain that it is sufficient for this psychotic pervert to claim to have done these things 'in the name of the superego' to render them legitimate. It is, above all, his own ego that is in question, and the possibility of maintaining a narcissistic cathexis of it through an idealization of his pregenitality and of his objects generally.

Thus, the pervert's affinity for art and what is beautiful seems to me to be explicable in terms of his *compulsion to idealize*, which is no less strong than his sexual compulsion. Nevertheless, the counter-cathexis of genitality and genital objects, as well as the absence of projection of narcissism on to the father, are rigorously maintained. (This state of affairs may culminate in a 'fecalization' of the father and his world.) Failing such an idealization of pregenitality at the expense of genitality, he would become profoundly depressed. It is to my mind primarily to such a failure of this 'transference' of the ego ideal, of genitality and of the father on to the instincts and part objects that we owe the fact that we sometimes find ourselves with a pervert on our couch. Moreover, the prospects for the treatment of the pervert seem to me to depend on the mobility of the ego ideal, that is to say on the possibility of a narcissistic recathexis of the father's image, which at a certain level is very bound up with the relative weakness of anti-depressive mechanisms and the inadequacy of substitutive mechanisms (for example addiction).

2 The Development of the Ego Ideal

The child therefore receives its individual education much later than the animal; but it is, in consequence, much more susceptible to the influence of the species. The many ministrations, the continuous care that its early state of helplessness requires, maintains and increases the attachment of fathers and mothers and, in caring for the body, they cultivate the mind. The time required by the former to gain in strength turns to the profit of the latter.

Buffon, *Natural History*

Where the inclination of the male child to avoid having to confront rivals, castration and painful oedipal defeat (present to some extent in everyone) has not been supported and encouraged, his ego is led to look for, to discover, and to admire that which makes the father his mother's chosen object. Hence he forms the wish to be like him at some time in the future. In Freud's terms he 'projects (this) before him': the father will become the boy's ego ideal. Man's *biological immaturity* is the foundation-stone of the concept with which we are concerned here. It owes its origin to the child's early helplessness (*Hilflösigkeit*) and to the way in which this brings the state of primary fusion to a violent end. It is impossible to recover this fusion with the mother immediately through incest (and he who has not been castrated — who, in other words, has not lost his omnipotence — is incestuous) because of physiological immaturity (genital deficiency). This prompts the development of the ego ideal, the 'project' of identification with the genital father containing, within the implied incest phantasy, the hope of a return to this state of primary fusion. I would remind the reader here of Ferenczi's theory of genitality as described in his admirable *Thalassa* (1924) in which he establishes that the wish to return to the mother's womb is the most fundamental human desire. Genital coitus allows this desire to be satisfied in three ways: 'The whole organism attains this goal by purely hallucinatory means, somewhat as in sleep; the penis, with which the organism as a whole has identified itself, attains it partially or symbolically; while only the sexual secretion possesses the prerogative, as representative of the ego and its narcissistic double, the genital, of attaining *in reality* to the womb of the mother.' (I would specify that for me — and in this I follow Freud's conception — the primary narcissistic state extends over a period of time which includes some time prior to the birth itself.) The pinnacle of human development thus contains within itself the promise of a return to the mother's womb or, in other words, to the most primitive phase of development. We are urged forwards by a sense of longing for a wonderous past (for a time when we were our own ideal). Between these two points in time, however, there lies the whole of man's psycho-sexual development. Incestuous fixation is the lack of mobility in the libido of the little boy, who cannot give up his aim of sexual possession of the mother. It is implicitly linked by Freud himself to the intra-uterine state and the difficulty of giving this up, when he writes in relation to the problem of negotiating the oedipal phase: 'The comparison with the way in which the skull of a newly born child is shaped springs to mind at this point: after a protracted labour it always takes the form of a cast of the narrow part of the mother's pelvis' ('Contribution to the Psychology of Love', Freud, 1912). In 1924, in a note added to the *Three Essays* he writes: 'Rank has traced attachment to the mother back to the pre-historic intra-uterine period and has thus indicated the biological foundation of the oedipus complex.'

If sexual union with the mother represents a possible means of recapturing the primary state of narcissism, then the distinction that Freud drew in his 1914 text between narcissistic and anaclitic (or 'leaning-on type') object choice is attenuated since, at the outset, both aim at recapturing the state of narcissistic at-oneness that preceded the loss of fusion with the primary object.

In Freudian theory, in the form it took from the time of the *Three Essays* and the introduction of the dualism of sexual instincts and ego instincts, sexuality is closely linked to the bodily functions. Sexual satisfaction is seen at first as merely offering a bonus of pleasure, and only later as something to be sought in its own right. An additional and complementary view would see sexuality linked to the desire to rediscover the cosmic ego (Federn) of primary narcissism. The mother, who would be both the anaclitic object and the object the child wishes to unite with to regain the primitive sense of fusion, would then be the chosen sexual object, by a kind of dual 'leaning-on'. 'The development of the ego consists in a departure from primary narcissism and gives rise to a vigorous attempt to recover that state. This departure is brought about by means of the displacement of libido on to an ego ideal,' noted Freud in his 1914 text. If one accepts Freud's view then it seems to me to serve as a justification for all those attempts to understand human evolution in terms of a longing for a paradise lost, even though the idea will be elaborated in differing ways (Ferenczi, Grunberger).

It can be seen that failure to achieve this ideal, and the obstacles that are run up against in attempting to reach it (in particular the 'incest barrier' in the oedipal phase), may cause a regression towards a more archaic form of 'narcissistic reinstatement', or even towards psychotic megalomania in which the original lack of differentiation between internal and external perceptions recurs. The originality of the ego ideal is, in fact, that it represents a link-concept between absolute narcissism and object relatedness, between the pleasure principle and the reality principle, because it is itself a product of the severance of the ego from the object. (The ego ideal is, in Freud's words, 'a level of development of the ego'.)

It was in *Totem and Taboo* (1912) that Freud demonstrated the particular status that he accorded the ego ideal, shortly before giving it its name, thus drawing on the magic technique of the primitive animist, which rests upon the omnipotence of thoughts. As is well known, he distinguishes three phases in the evolution of man's view of the universe — animistic, religious and scientific — and he traces the fate of the omnipotence of thoughts through these:

> At the animistic stage men ascribe omnipotence to *themselves*. At the religious stage they transfer it to the gods but do not seriously abandon it themselves, for they reserve the power of influencing the gods in a variety of ways according to their wishes. The scientific view of the universe no longer affords any room for human omnipotence; men have acknowledged their smallness and submitted resignedly to death.

Freud compares the animistic phase to narcissism, the religious phase to the point at which, having developed object relations, narcissism is projected on to the parents, and the scientific phase to the stage of maturity in which the individual accepts the exigencies of reality (although he is sceptical as to whether this phase is ever completely attained, detecting traces of animism in 'modern life'). It is the religious phase, says Freud, that 'would correspond to the stage of object choice of which the characteristic is a child's attachment to his parents'. The projection of infantile narcissism on to the parents, who constitute the ego ideal, can thus be seen as a step towards the achievement of a sense of reality and of object relatedness, since primary megalomania is given up in favour of the object. At the same time the formation of the ego ideal corresponds to the reality principle in that it does not choose the shortest path of discharge to achieve satisfaction (as it would following the pleasure principle).

I have stressed several times that the ego ideal implies the idea of a *project*. Fain and Marty (1959) talk, even more concretely, of a *hope*. Project and hope imply postponement, delay, a temporal perspective — all of which are characteristic of a mental state governed by the reality principle. Together they suggest the idea of *development*, of *evolution*. In fact it falls principally to the mother — at least in the early stages of life — to encourage her child to project his ego ideal on to successively more evolved models. Carefully dosed frustrations and gratifications serve to encourage the child to give up certain satisfactions, linked to the acquisition of certain functions and to a certain 'way of being', in order to acquire new ones. Each stage of his development must afford him sufficient gratification for him not to be tempted to regress, and yet sufficient frustration for him not to be tempted to remain at that stage (to become fixated), in short, for the the *hope* that will allow the child to continue to climb the steps of his development to be sustained. The child is thus guided by his mother, who helps him to project his ego ideal 'before him', fostering its motivating role or, in other words, ensuring that it continues to keep an aspect of 'promise'. Fain and Marty (1959) have written of the need for 'a certain pressure exercised by the object as ego-ideal, which tends to direct the subject in a progressive sense, whilst satisfying his passive and receptive desires'. Certain phenomena of 'cathectic loyalty' can be understood in this light ('Analysis Terminable and Interminable', 1937), as noted by Freud in the case of the Wolf Man (1918) who, he said, 'obstinately defended any position of the libido which he had once taken up from fear of what he would lose by giving it up and from distrust of the probability of a complete substitute being afforded by the new position that was in view. This is an important and fundamental psychological peculiarity, which I described in my *Three Essays on the Theory of Sexuality* as a susceptibility to "fixation".' Perhaps one can understand this difficulty in giving up one phase of development for a new one, this libidinal inertia, at least in part, as being linked to early deficiencies which prevented the child (the future Wolf Man) from cathecting his *development* as such, in which the projection 'before him' of his ego ideal plays an important role. Each new acquisition is always effectively accompanied by the (at least partial) loss of the object and 'way of being' of the preceding phase, and hence implies some mourning. (Weaning, for example, implies mourning the breast and an oral-narcissistic mode of functioning.) How is one to proceed if the new acquisition fails to compensate for that which has had to be given up (if, for example, being able to feed oneself is not invested with some value)? What is to be done if the giving up of passive anal satisfactions is not followed by the establishment of active anality with the mastery and pride which this involves, at a time when the rigours of bowel training are being introduced? Here we touch upon problems linked to the 'pleasure of the functioning' studied by J. and E. Kestemberg (1965). The narcissistic confirmation that Grunberger refers to must, therefore, be appropriately available if the child is to make advances; if it is insufficient, the ego cannot acquire any cohesion. (The mother's narcissistic cathexis of her child as a 'whole' is linked to the physical care and caresses she lavishes on him, bringing together in this way his body ego and psychic ego and conferring value on his different functions. Amongst certain mammals, if one of a litter is not licked by the mother, it will die. If she forgets to lick his genital organs, he will not urinate.) If the narcissistic confirmation is excessive, it may result in perverting development by preventing the ego ideal from being cathected in the genital father, as we have seen in the case of the pervert. In fact in this instance narcissistic confirmation is coupled with sexual seduction. The child is then, *par excellence*, the 'erotic plaything' Freud referred to ('Contributions to the Psychology of Love', Freud, 1912), the sexual seduction itself constituting the narcissistic confirmation the child is so avid for: that he is a suitable partner for his mother and hence corresponds to his own ego ideal. It is not that Eros and Anti-Eros are opposed; rather it is precisely their excessively total and precocious coming together that brings about the perverse fixation. The mother's role is indeed very delicate, and risks oscillating between too much and too little. When narcissistic and instinctual satisfactions are ego syntonic they increase self-esteem (as Freud showed in

'On Narcissism') and diminish the gap between the ego and its ideal. They take from the ideal some of its megalomania, and may ultimately lead to its premature extinction, or at any rate that of its 'motivating' force. By contrast, excessive frustration lends it a primitive character and a propensity to regression. The absence, at the outset of life, of narcissistic gratification can lead to a premature genitalization of the instincts (c.f. Melanie Klein's views on the flight into genitality). The child's narcissism then remains split off from its instinctual life and cathects an exaggerated ego ideal.

Man's biological immaturity, which is responsible for the development of an ego ideal, most probably endows our instinctual life with certain peculiar characteristics. Thus it does not seek simple, automatic discharge, nor does pleasure derive purely and simply from the lowering of tension. Since any satisfaction that is achieved is accompanied by a reduction of the gap between the ego and the ego ideal, any ego syntonic instinctual pleasure is inseparable from a narcissistic satisfaction due to the recathexis of the ego by a quantum of liberated narcissistic libido. Naturally conflicts will appreciably modify this schema. As Grunberger has shown, in particular in 'Observations on the Distinction between Narcissism and Instinctual Maturation' (1960), there is a degree of antagonism between narcissism and the instincts (in particular anality), which it is an essential goal of analysis to reduce. His views are, in the long run, less pessimistic than those put forward recently by D. Braunschweig and M. Fain who, it seems to me, regard this antagonism as irreducible.

If, for the little boy, the projection of the ego ideal on to the father holds out the promise of being able to abolish the gap separating ego ideal and ego through the realization of an incest phantasy, the same cannot be said for the little girl since for her this realization does not have, *a priori*, the same sense of a return to a primitive state of fusion which is only possible through union with the primary object. (This factor can perhaps be added to those I described in the chapter on 'The Ego Ideal and Perversion' in accounting for the fact that perversion is less frequent in women than in men.) Seen in this light, it is only mother-daughter incest that can have the true value of incest for the daughter. This is, implicitly, the view of Ferenczi, who finds himself obliged to write of an identification by the woman with the man's penis in coitus in order to ensure a symmetrical satisfaction for both sexes of the desire to return to the mother's womb. The fact that it is only incest with the mother that represents a return to the original state of fusion is, amongst other factors, picked out by various authors (C.-J. Parat, B. Grunberger, D. Braunschweig and M. Fain). This allows one to appreciate why it is that father-daughter incest rarely leads to psychosis, whereas mother-son incest is responsible for the boy's 'psychic death' (S. Lebovici). This psychic death is the result of the destruction of the ego's development which had been initiated by the impossibility of union with the mother. The coincidence of ego ideal and ego that thus occurs sweeps away the acquisitions of the process of developing manhood, now rendered useless and inconvenient for the realization of this fusion, and culminates in serious distortions of the ego.

Indeed, if the complete, total satisfaction that the child knew in the state of primitive fusion had persisted, not only would he never have detached himself from it, as Freud noted in 'Contributions to the Psychology of Love'; but neither would he ever have acquired either the differentiation of the psychic agencies, or the ego functions. It is the experience of frustration that prompts the development of the ego and the perceptual-conscious system. It is the giving up of a certain number of satisfactions and successive objects that prompts the need to find substitutes for them and to effect displacements (i.e. the acquisition of symbolic activity and sublimation). It is from having to delay satisfaction that phantasy life, the elaboration of a desire, language, etc. is born. All the developmental phases affect these acquisitions through the specific contributions they each make. It is the anal phase that allows the child to emerge from the primary undifferentiated state, gives him an inside and an outside, situates him in time and space. It is the oedipal situation and the incest prohibition that consolidate the acquisition of the *third dimension*.

(This is sensed intuitively by Michel Thevoz in his book on the Swiss painter, Soutter.) Immediate gratification leaves us in immediate proximity to the object, immersed in it. Successive frustrations (which may after all, *post facto*, acquire an oedipal significance) and the triangular situation allow us to maintain a distance from the object, affording us a certain perspective. One has only to listen to Marguerite Sechehaye's patient (*Autobiography of a Schizophrenic Girl*) — describing the terror in which she lived, at the time of the outbreak of her illness, of seeing objects thrusting themselves upon her, through the loss of this sense of perspective — to understand that this is no mere figure of speech. In other words, access to reality and the existence of the ego and of secondary process are only possible in the absence of a total satisfaction of our desires, a satisfaction that union with the mother would bring. In the same vein, Michel Gressot (1966) has stressed the role of the incest prohibition as a 'key-constellation' preventing regression, 'a foundation for the other prohibitions', 'a guarantee of weaning through prohibition of incest'. All these acquisitions, which are what make us human beings, would fall away like a house of cards, if that which was responsible for their original creation was removed.

On the other hand, the primal scene signifies the loss of hope of genital fusion with the mother. One can understand in this light that it represents an essential precipitating factor in depersonalization, namely, as I had occasion to demonstrate in a contribution to the 20th Congress of Psychoanalysts of Romance Languages (Chasseguet-Smirgel, 1958), regression to a phase in which object relations are dissolved to make way for primitive fusion. If he is to avoid harmful consequences to himself, it is only through a substitute object that man can rediscover the lost sense of at-oneness in, as we shall see, the state of being in love. In other words the full attainment of this sense of at-oneness is forbidden him. Freud postulates that 'something in the nature of the sexual instinct itself is unfavourable to the realization of complete satisfaction', and he attributes this to two factors: the first is that, because of the incest barrier, 'the final object of the sexual instinct is never any longer the original object but only a surrogate for it' ('On the Universal Tendency . . .', 1912). We shall have occasion to return to the second factor in question.

If the only incest is incest with the mother, then the girl should experience an insatiable homosexuality. This is a conclusion reached, incidentally, by the authors of *Eros et Antéros*, following quite a different path. However, the differences between the sexes impels the girl towards her father. Even if her eroticism runs counter to her wish to eliminate the gap between ego ideal and ego through a primary narcissistic fusion, it is nonetheless the case that for the girl motherhood is a solution that allows her to reconcile, in a sense, her erotic wishes which are directed towards her father with her wish to recapture the primitive state of fusion with her mother. The mother can reexperience with her child, admittedly on a much more evolved level, the sense of fusion which as a child she experienced with her own mother. It can be seen that, for obvious reasons, the girl is led to situate her wish in the future. And hence she is led to constitute for herself an ego-ideal that will include the project of becoming a mother — as mother, but also as the father's wife, who has been given a child by him. Along with Ruth Mack Brunswick (1940), in the article she wrote jointly with Freud, I consider that the wish for a baby is something that appears very early, prior to penis envy. (I am not concerned here with the little boy's wish to have a baby.) But whereas she considers its sole origin to be the desire to take over the principal possession of the omnipotent mother, I believe this desire also includes that of reconstituting the primary mother-infant unity. The companion to the boy's perverse deception regarding the difference between the sexes and between the generations, which installs him as mother's partner, would be, in the girl's case, the denial that the child needs to have a father. In other words she would deny all that period of development from the loss of the primary narcissistic state to the onset of the oedipal phase, since — short of being delirious — the little girl can hardly believe herself capable of making a baby immediately, except in symbolic form or in phantasy. Symbolism and phantasy are, of course, linked to the need to give up immediate or hallucinatory gratificaton. Indeed, the bearing of children without the male playing any role is written into the S.C.U.M. (Society for Cutting up Men) Manifesto: 'Reproduction of the species is technically possible without any need for a man. Women could henceforth reproduce only women' (Valerie Solanas, *S.C.U.M. Manifesto*).

The toy known as a Russian doll no doubt represents the expression of the little girl's phantasy of being able to give birth immediately to another little girl, already pregnant, etc., by-passing all that development that culminates in the oedipal phase. It is perhaps no coincidence that the doll is of popular Russian origin, the exclusion of the paternal role, together with the phantasy of the mother's omnipotence, reflecting, in all likelihood, the Russian people's relationship to the maternal figure so pertinently described by Alain Besançon in *Le Tsarévitch immolé* (1967).

However, one should not lose sight of the fact that if the little boy — cases of actual incest excepted — never does actually reestablish a state of primary fusion with the mother, neither does the little girl's identification with the mother, when she herself becomes a mother, represent the equivalent of a genuine return to the original state. What has once been acquired is never totally lost (even in the most deeply regressed psychotic one can still find slight traces of this, often hard to recognize but pathetically present), because even if pregnancy and motherhood cause the woman to regress this regression still contains very important oedipal elements. More evolved wishes can also find expression in motherhood (otherwise mothers would not want to have sons, for example). In addition, the incest barrier also plays its role in the mother's oedipal response: she is forbidden to reincorporate the child she has borne.

I do not find it possible to agree entirely with Ferenczi when he says that anality, like orality, represents — through the combined use of ego-instincts and sexual instincts — an attempt to realize the wish to get back inside the mother's body. He says that this occurs initially through the use of the teeth to penetrate her body, then through identification with the (containing) mother, the child's own intestinal contents being identified with the child. Orality does represent one way of attempting to recreate the primitive state of fusion, by the inclusion within the ego of the external world (the breast), through introjection rather than through biting. Even so, from the moment of the appearance of the teeth (and weaning), along with toilet training, the picture changes. On the one hand, the child acquires new modes of incorporation (which then become selective), and on the other, he employs a new form of narcissistic and instinctual gratification, namely the exercise of control. His new acquisitions foster the development of an active and autonomous ego ideal. Differentiation from, and dominance of, others becomes the chosen narcissistic goal, apparently opposed to the preceding goal of passive fusion, although, of course, anality has its own possibilities of specific forms of passive gratification.

These pregenital ego ideals are short-term ideals which substitute provisionally and partially for the genital, oedipal ego ideal which represents the promise of narcissistic fulfilment. The genital oedipal ego ideal embodies all the pregenital ego ideals in the same way, so to speak, as Hegel writes of 'going beyond yet preserving' (*aufheben*). As I see it, it is as if the genital ego ideal had as its mission to promote the development of an ego formed through the successful integration of all its constituent parts, via the identifications made at different stages of its development (which is what the 'genital ego' is). The ego ideal has its exigencies as to the manner in which the ego is constituted and does not tolerate faults in this edifice.

I first formulated this hypothesis in a very brief 'Clinical Note on Examination Dreams' (Chasseguet-Smirgel, 1967). In fact, it was as much a theoretical as a clinical note. I will summarize it very briefly:

It should be recalled that the interpretation of examination dreams — one kind of typical dream — proposed by

Freud rests on the assertion, attributed by him to an
"experienced colleague", that it is only exams that have
actually been passed successfully that form the basis of such
dreams. For Freud, such an "anxious examination dream"
appears when the dreamer has some responsible activity
ahead of him the next day: "What is regarded as an indignant
protest against the dream: 'But I'm a doctor, etc., already!'
would in reality be the consolation put forward by the dream,
and would accordingly run: 'Don't be afraid of tomorrow!
Just think how anxious you were before your Matriculation,
and yet nothing happened to you. You're a doctor, etc.,
already.' And the anxiety which is attributed to the dream
would really have arisen from the day's residues."

Granted, but would it not be simpler and more in accord with the
wish of the dreamer to dream that he succeeded in his project?
Why this complicated detour?

Various examples from clinical work have led me to the
following hypothesis: exams sanction the different stages of our
scholastic and university career. They correspond to the
different stages of our development and maturation (in many
languages the final school exam is called the *matura*). In most
cases, the exam which one has passed in reality, and which one
dreams about, is felt to have been passed by luck, by fraud or by
mistake. Whatever the case, the success is experienced as
undeserved. The symbolical maturity gained in this way is felt to
be a sham and not founded on real integrations. In my view it is
the ego ideal that is dissatisfied with these defects in the ego,
that are improperly camouflaged by an apparent success. It is the
narcissistic desire, operating under the aegis of the ego ideal, to
make good these faults in maturation by a reworking of the
defective process that is expressed through these examination
dreams. This desire, which mobilizes one or more instincts,
comes up against obstacles that have not yet been removed and
this generates anxiety.

The exam which Freud confides to us he dreams about most

often, in a chapter of *The Interpretation of Dreams* devoted to examination dreams, is an exam that he passed with the help of a little cheating (hence masking a deficiency):

> In my dreams of school examinations, I am invariably examined in History, in which I did brilliantly — though only, it is true, because [in the oral examination] my kindly master (the one-eyed benefactor of another dream) did not fail to notice that on the paper of questions which I handed him back I had run my finger-nail through the middle one of the three questions included, to warn him not to insist upon that particular one.

In Section H of Chapter VI of *The Interpretation of Dreams*, Freud studied what he called 'hypocritical dreams' which 'offer a hard test to the theory of wish fulfilment'. Having recounted Rosegger's famous recurring dream, taken from *Fremd Gemacht* ('Along with my modest career as a student and man of letters, I have for many years dragged around with me, like a ghost from which I could not set myself free, the shadow of a tailor's life . . .'), Freud offers the account of one of his own dreams that he considers related to that of Rosegger:

> As a young doctor I worked for a long time at the Chemical Institute without ever becoming proficient in the skills which that science demands; and for that reason in my waking life I have never liked thinking of this barren and indeed *humiliating* [my italics] episode in my apprenticeship. On the other hand I have a regularly recurring dream of working in the laboratory, of carrying out analyses and of having various experiences there. *These dreams are disagreeable in the same way as examination dreams* [my italics] and they are never very distinct. While I was interpreting one of them, my attention was eventually attracted by the word '*analysis*', which gave me a key to their understanding. Since those days I have

become an 'analyst', and I now carry out analyses which are very highly spoken of, though it is true they are 'psycho-analyses'. It was now clear to me: if I have grown proud of carrying out analyses of that kind in my daytime life and feel inclined to boast to myself of how successful I have become, my dreams remind me during the night of those other unsuccessful analyses of which I have no reason to feel proud.

Freud gives many interpretations of his dreams: they may represent punishment dreams, masochistic impulses in the mind or equally the 'deeply rooted wish for youth'. Here I think one is again essentially concerned with the wish not to disguise a narcissistic defeat (a factor in *humiliation*), such as that symbolized by the failure of the chemical analyses, set against the success of the new 'analyses'. I would therefore suggest the hypothesis that a failure to negotiate adequately *all* the stages of development, whatever the ego's apparent success and manifest adult character, will create tension between the ego and the ego ideal. Just as no desire can be hidden from the superego, no disguise can deceive the ego ideal.

An examination dream recently told me by a patient has provided me with the opportunity to bring together some new elements in support of my hypothesis.

Every time I am in a state of crisis [says Alix] I have the same dream. I fail my baccalauréat and I tell myself "Still you have gone on to more advanced studies so it doesn't matter." At the same time I have an idea that these studies are invalid because I do not have my baccalauréat, because this is missing.

In reality, I did indeed fail my baccalauréat even though I was a very good pupil. The good Sisters never failed to point out to me the sacrifices my parents had made for my studies. I could not go on to further studies until ten years later, when a regulation was passed allowing entry through a special exam.

It would take too long and, I think, is unnecessary to report the patient's associations concerning the 'crisis' that she gives as the origin of her dream. A few brief comments will suffice.

In this instance we find, contrary to the dreams Freud described, a dream about an exam that the dreamer had indeed failed; the patient seems to have come to grief because of unresolved oedipal problems (her elder sisters had not gone in for studies). She had, subsequently, the opportunity to take a 'special exam' which she passed and which apparently (objectively) made up for her previous failure but which did not however succeed in covering up the real *deficiency* (her own term) which the failed baccalauréat symbolized, namely that within her own ego, in this instance the lack of integration of her rivalry with her elder sisters. The wish of the dreamer seems to me to be not to accept a simple cosmetic operation that would disguise the deficiency but to deal with it in a real way by confronting her oedipal difficulties. If she repeats the same dream at each moment of 'crisis' in her life, it is because each time she is faced with the same dilemma: whether to tackle the root of the problem or whether to skirt round it, to have it vanish by means of a 'special exam'. The ego ideal prefers absolute solutions. Of course in the analytic situation this dream is addressed to the analyst; and the analytic process (unlike certain forms of psychotherapy and all forms of psychiatric treatment depending on drugs) is, by definition, a method which is not content with papering over the cracks, 'making good' faults, but puts in question the whole of the personality, the entirety of its development (Balint's 'New Beginning'). Seen in this light, examination dreams are, *par excellence*, 'programme dreams' and translate the intuition that one can have of the nature of the analytic process before having the slightest conscious awareness of it.

It seems possible to envisage the existence of an innate programme of psycho-sexual development (as of the ego and the instincts) just as there is an absolute biological necessity for the embryo to develop according to the specific signals that come from the organizers, as the tendency for wounds to heal over follows a natural course, the different mechanisms coming into play according to a pre-established sequence. Freud was no stranger to this idea. Thus in Lecture XXII of the *Introductory Lectures on Psychoanalysis* (1917) he writes:

> It is not our belief that a person's libidinal interests are from the first in opposition to his self-preservative interests; on the contrary, the ego endeavours at every stage to remain in harmony with its sexual organization as it is at the time and to fit itself into it. The succession of the different phases of libidinal development probably follows a prescribed programme. But the possibility cannot be rejected that this course of events can be influenced by the ego, and we may expect equally to find a certain parallelism, a certain correspondence, between the developmental phases of the ego and the libido; indeed a disturbance of that correspondence might provide a pathogenic factor.

Equally we have seen earlier that he wrote about 'the natural course of the developmental processes' (1931).

Kurt Eissler suggests that the course of development is in some sense controlled by a 'meta-plan of the ego', whilst Anna Freud (1966) considers that there is an *innate tendency to complete development* (her italics). Again Freud, studying 'The Dissolution of the Oedipus Complex', manages to reconcile a *phylogenetic* view of the Oedipus complex with an ontogenetic one:

> Another view is that the Oedipus complex must collapse because the time has come for its disintegration, just as the milk teeth fall out when the permanent ones begin to grow. Although the majority of human beings go through the Oedipus complex as an individual experience, it is nevertheless a phenomenon which is determined and laid

down by heredity and which is bound to pass away according to programme when the next pre-ordained phase of development sets in.

In the same text he also writes, 'It is also true that even at birth the whole individual is destined to die, and perhaps his organic disposition may already contain the indication of what he is to die from. Nevertheless, it remains of interest to follow out how this innate programme is carried out and in what way accidental noxae exploit his disposition'.

If, then, one accepts that genitality implies an integration of pregenital organizations with 'a correspondence between the developmental phases of the ego and the libido', it can be seen that where the ego ideal has been projected on to genitality it will demand this kind of integration, in other words, that development must involve every phase becoming integrated. If the inevitable renunciation of primary narcissism is accompanied by its being separated off in the form of an ego ideal, and if this ego ideal implies the promise of a return to that primitive state of fusion through an identification with the genital father sexually united with the mother, one can see that this ego ideal fosters the achievement of the full genitality that is necessary for the accomplishment of the original project. Between the initial project and the promise of its realization in genital coitus, the baggage with which the child came into the world has been gradually filled by his instincts. Any failure in this integration is experienced at the level of the genital ego ideal as a castration since it destroys the ordering of the component parts over which genitality establishes its primacy, a primacy which is thereby impaired. As is well known, disturbances in development and conflicts between the psychic agencies render the achievement of this integration problematic (and hence leave the ego ideal dissatisfied). Freud gave as the second reason for the difficulty the sexual instinct has in attaining complete satisfaction precisely this problem of the integration of the component instincts, particularly the coprophilic and the sadistic ('Contributions to the Psychology of Love', 1912). I would therefore suggest that the character of the ego ideal is such that it naturally promotes maturation. (Cosnier, 1970, makes a distinction between this 'maturative ego ideal', to which I have had occasion to refer elsewhere, and a megalomanic ego ideal which, in certain people, may exist in parallel, a view close to some of those developed in the present work.) This character is affected by severe disturbances in development, such as I have attempted to describe in the case of the pervert, to the extent that it is rendered virtually inoperative.

When I was completing my bibliography I came across a definition of certain of the ego ideal's functions very close to that which I have tried to develop here. It is that of Gerhart Piers (Piers and Singer, 1953):

> The ego ideal is in continuous dynamic interfunction with the unconscious and conscious *awareness of the ego's potentialities*. This part of the ego ideal must contain the *goals* of what has been variously termed "instinct of mastery" (Hendrick) "mastery principle" (Fenichel), etc. A better term for what I have in mind might be "maturation drive". It would signify a psychic representation of all the growth, maturation and individuation processes in the human being.

The author goes on to draw certain inferences from this concerning the relationship between the ego ideal and shame.

If one wants to relate this view of the ego ideal to the dualism Eros-Thanatos, then the ego ideal can be seen to be in the service of Eros: between its point of departure (primary narcissism) and its projection on to the genital organization, it inspires man to negotiate 'those detours taken by life in its rush towards death' (*Beyond the Pleasure Principle*, Freud, 1920). These detours are themselves, as we have noted, linked to the establishment of the reality principle, even if the organizing principle of the ego ideal is the discharge of tension through a return to the original state. The upheavals of development mean that the individual runs the risk of abandoning these detours in favour of the shortest route to achieving the ever-longed-for satisfaction, that is through regression, a mechanism that can be seen as being linked to the activity of the death instinct.

In *Beyond the Pleasure Principle* Freud writes about the tendency, which is never given up, to repeat a primary satisfaction: 'No substitutive or reactive formations and no sublimations will suffice to remove the repressed instinct's persisting tension; and it is the different in amount between the pleasure of satisfaction which is *demanded* and that which is actually *achieved* that provides the driving factor which will permit of no halting at any position attained, but, in the poet's words "Presses ever forward unsubdued" (Faust).' If the phantasy of union with the mother is a powerful organizing principle of our psycho-sexual life, if this is what 'presses (us) ever forward unsubdued' (and, in the worst cases, backwards), then what becomes of it after the dissolution of the Oedipus complex? Such is the question to which we must now turn.

3. The Ego Ideal, Being-in-Love, and Genitality

And, on a sudden, day seemed joined to day,
As though the hand that hath the power had sped
A second sun to make the skies more gay.

Beatrice stood, her eyes still riveted
    On the eternal wheels; and, constantly,
    Turning mine thence, I gazed on her instead;

'Twas even thus a change came over me,
As Glaucus, eating of the weed, changed race
And grew a god among the gods of sea.

Dante, 'Paradise', Canto I, *The Divine Comedy*

The early efflorescence of infantile sexual life is doomed to extinction because its wishes are incompatible with reality and with the inadequate stage of development which the child has reached. That efflorescence comes to an end in the most distressing circumstances and to the accompaniment of the most painful feelings. Loss of love and failure leave behind them a permanent injury to self-regard in the form of a narcissistic scar, which in my opinion, as well as Marcinowski's, contributes more than anything to the "sense of inferiority" which is so common in neurotics. The child's sexual researches, on which limits are imposed by his physical development, lead to no satisfactory conclusion; hence such later complaints as "I can't accomplish anything; I can't succeed in anything". The tie of affection which binds the child as a rule to the parent of the opposite sex, succumbs to disappointment, to a vain expectation of satisfaction or to jealousy over the birth of a new baby — unmistakeable proof of the infidelity of the object of the child's affections. His own attempt to make a baby himself, carried out with tragic seriousness, fails shamefully. The lessening amount of affection he receives, the increasing demands of education, hard words and an occasional punishment — these show him at last the full extent to which he has been scorned.

Such is the dramatic picture Freud sketches of the oedipal child in *Beyond the Pleasure Principle* (1920). The giving up of the oedipal object appears, in this context, to be linked to the painful recognition by the child of his size, of his inadequacy. For the child it is the tragedy of shattered illusions.

In 'The Dissolution of the Oedipus Complex', four years later, Freud goes back to this same picture: '. . . the absence of the satisfaction hoped for, the continued denial of the desired baby, must in the end lead the small lover to turn away from his hopeless longing. In this way the Oedipus complex would go to its destruction from its lack of success, from the effects of its internal impossibility.' It will however be recalled that in this very text, without giving up the idea of a spontaneous dissolution of the Oedipus complex prompted by its unrealizable nature (and hence involving a submission to reality), Freud stresses the role of the castration complex and the setting up of the superego. In an earlier chapter I recalled the thesis that the incest barrier represents a protection for the oedipal child against the wound to his narcissism of having to recognize his own impotence. The interdict safeguards the illusion. The difficulty is to know to what extent the giving up of the oedipal object — which, in my view, is confused, at some level, with the object of primary fusion — is complete and definitive, to what extent one thinks of the oedipus complex coming to a *violent end*, even in the 'ideal' case envisaged by Freud. It will be recalled that for Freud 'the process ... is more than a repression. It is equivalent, if it is ideally carried out, to a destruction and an abolition of the complex' ('The Dissolution of the Oedipus Complex', Freud, 1924).

C. Parat's paper on this topic expresses the matter with great subtlety:

> In the more fortunate cases, after the modifications of the latency period, after the enrichment of identifications and sublimated cathexes, after the upsurge of puberty, the culmination would be the possibility of establishing a love involving both an object-related and a narcissistic element. If it is impossible to speak about the oedipal situation without speaking about love, neither can one speak about love without evoking the oedipal situation. Oedipal love represents the first genital constellation, the first model of love.

Parat takes up Freud's celebrated formula in the *Three Essays*: 'The finding of an object is in fact a refinding of it, an allusion to the lost primary object.' (I would emphasize that I understand that the primary object has not yet been differentiated from the ego and that it is only experienced as an 'object' *a posteriori*.) She adds, 'This refinding, on the opposite shore of the unavoidable oedipal crossing, helps to give to the love relationship its dimension of pleasure regained, of an ancient kingdom previously glimpsed, lost and found again.' However, in the genital love relationship, the object is not an 'oedipal substitute'. Parat emphasizes, in parallel with this, the fragility of the genital oedipal structuring that she is describing: 'Any endogenous or apparently exogenous difficulty leads to a revival of the oedipal conflict.'

Following Christian David in this, she thinks that 'love is always built up in part, but only in part, on the old oedipal love'. At the same time love helps to efface 'the oedipal narcissistic trauma'. One can see therefore that for Parat the love that characterizes the genital oedipal organization is based at one and the same time on both the model of primary love and that of oedipal love — without, however, being an exact copy of either. She hypothesizes that following the dissolution of the oedipus complex a new dimension is acquired, which will be reflected in the type of love that characterizes the structure then dominant. However, her emphasis on the ever-present possibility of a reactivation of oedipal conflict shows that she does not give much credence to the idea of a complete disappearance of the Oedipus complex, at an unconscious level as well, such as Freud pictured — admittedly as an 'ideal'.

As for David, in his interesting book *L'Etat amoureux* (1971), he too demonstrates the dual origin of love:

> The reciprocal prompting of an outburst of passion, in addition to its oedipal sources, originates in the simultaneity of the revival of separation traumas. Now, one of the main aims of being-in-love is, without doubt, to eliminate their consequences, to enter into a world of at-oneness and communion. Solitude is to be definitively cast out; never again will one be left out, at least one other being will be near at hand who can be understood always and in everything. Understood by the slightest gesture, wordlessly, *as a mother understands her child* [my italics], as a dog understands its master.

At the same time, even more than Parat, he stresses that love cannot be reduced to its oedipal origins, that each and every love represents a new creation. I am not however in agreement with him when he attributes the division between oedipal love and so-called 'genital' love essentially to the lack of knowledge of the difference between the sexes prior to puberty. I have said earlier that this view of the oedipal situation that Freud has bequeathed us seems to me to serve to confirm us in our defences and itself represents an attempt to bind the narcissistic wound inherent in the oedipal situation. David, equally, speaks of 'the oedipal wound ever ready to reopen' and hence ever present in the unconscious. The two authors that I have just quoted acknowledge, therefore, the oedipal and narcissistic-fusional sources of the state of being in love, whilst also attributing to it some specificity in relation to dual origin.

D. Braunschweig, in her paper *Psychanalyse et réalité* (1971), writes as follows on oedipal structuring: 'Furthermore, clinical experience has shown us that, in cases where this structuring has been firmly established, the giving up of the oedipal object, which in the course of an analysis follows the ending of the repression of the representations of this object and of the desire attaching to it, also contains within it an elaboration of primary mourning.' This observation, which links the primary object and the oedipal object, is entirely in accord with the hypotheses I have attempted to formulate here. However, the notion of a total, real mourning of an oedipal object containing the 'primary object' seems to me to be hard to maintain. Or rather, more precisely, it is to the extent that the oedipal wish has been reinforced by — has 'leant on' — the wish to rediscover the primary object, that its complete disappearance from the unconscious seems to me to be problematic. Were it indeed to be so — were this dual mourning to be achieved completely — the ego ideal would be reabsorbed and the idea of rediscovering a lost paradise would be renounced. In fact, what we find is that during the latency period there is a relative de-idealization of the parent of the same sex (what Anna Freud has called 'disenchantment') linked, it would seem, to oedipal disappointment. The child gives up taking his father as a model, in order to take possession of the mother, but does so to the advantage of other models (his teachers, for example). This development coincides with his relative detachment from the parental objects and what is commonly called his socialization The oedipal conflict is, however, only dormant and will be reactivated by puberty as also by that other period of physiological upheaval in women: the menopause. (There would seem to be a parallel development in men when they lose their powers of procreation.) The perennial nature of oedipal desire (and of the desire to rediscover the primary object which underlies it) appears clearly in this phase of the woman's genital life.

Hélène Michel-Wolfrom (a well-known gynaecologist who died some years ago) reported that most of the women who came to consult her in their fifties about their menstrual periods having stopped, believed themselves to be pregnant. This denial of a reality that is experienced as a mutilation and the wish for a child that replaces it can be directly linked to the oedipal situation, if I may judge by one moving case that I had in treatment.

A woman doctor, the mother of a family, whom I had in analysis some fifteen years ago, came back eight years after the end of her treatment because of a recurrence, since the cessation of her periods some months previously, of hypochondriacal anxieties and fears due to the beginning of the menopause. She came four times and stopped the sessions herself once we had understood, with the help of some very rich dream material, how the menopause had rekindled her desire to have a child by her father. She dreamt, for example, of a man resembling her father using a pole to 'stir up' a large cabbage in a huge cooking pot. (In France boys are said to be born in cabbages.) The menopause represented the final loss of this hope, and was experienced as the result of a punishment inflicted by the mother for her guilty wishes. She had come to ask me — in the maternal transference — not to punish her by depriving her of her procreative powers. Needless to say this wish and these fears had been elaborated at length during her analysis. Her periods recommenced during the week of this brief treatment, and I have every reason to suppose that she accepted their subsequent disappearance better, since she had no further recourse to my help.

Similarly, as is well known, pregnancy and the birth of a child reactivate oedipal and, of course, preoedipal conflicts in women (and in men). What is, perhaps, not so well known, (I became aware of it through the case of one patient) is something which goes beyond the fact that the desire for a child classically involves the wish to relive the relationship with the mother, and, at an oedipal level, to have a child by the father. The birth of the actual child may, on the contrary, be experienced as a disappointment to the extent that the 'real' child is not the father's child. Thus one patient, who had passionately wanted to have a child and who had undergone long and trying treatment for her infertility, developed a depressive state after the eagerly-awaited birth. This depression could not simply be attributed to the causes which are generally invoked. During the sessions in which she was complaining of her depression, she spoke of a 'liaison' that she had had prior to her marriage which, despite having lasted for several years, had never led to a full sexual relationship. Whilst I was still perplexed by the appearance at this time of the image of her former partner, she brought a dream in which she did have sexual relations with the man in question who was married, in the dream, to a bank employee. In reality her father's mistress was a bank employee. The birth of the child had, then, awakened oedipal longings, the depressive affects being due to the fact that the 'real' child obliged her to work through her mourning for a child of her father's. (Denise Braunschweig, in her discussion of C. Parat's paper, stresses that 'whenever any project that corresponds to a phantasy the unconscious content of which is linked to the vicissitudes of instinctual development, has an outcome in reality . . . there is a revival of narcissistic suffering because the phantasy is not confirmed' and writes on this subject of the 'unbridgeable gap between the oedipal wishes of childhood and current satisfactions'.)

In general, my own observations are in accord with those of Parat when she notes that: 'It is as if each restructuring can only be accomplished by way of a re-experiencing of the oedipal conflict and with the help of this re-experience.' I would readily ascribe this resexualization of the more tender instincts having an inhibited sexual aim, post-oedipal vestiges having the superego's sanction, to a reactivation of — or to a loss of — the hope of attaining to the primitive sense of fusion. The fusion abolishes the divide between the ego and its ideal, each time a libidinal upheaval (physiological or not) again puts in question the economy of the person. In short, it is as if the acquisition of a sense of reality, which is only possible once the oedipal object and a return to the earliest state have been definitively renounced, were a state — when it is achieved — that is extremely unstable. This observation is in accord with that of Freud in *Totem and Taboo* (1912–1913) regarding man's problematic achievement of the scientific phase, 'which no longer affords any room for human omnipotence; men [having] acknowledged their smallness and submitted resignedly to death'. One might even wonder whether reality, looked full in the face, would not have the blinding radiance of death. For after all, where would man find the spur that 'presses [him] ever forward unsubdued' were he not bolstered by the hope of being able to repair some fundamental breach (Grunberger's 'narcissistic reestablishment')? To abandon the hope of finding the ultimate satisfaction at the end of all the detours imposed on the instincts' journey by the reality principle, would bring with it a death-dealing regression.

One might therefore say on the one hand that the renunciation of the oedipal object, with the dissolution of the oedipus complex, has only a relative value, and that, on the other hand, the bridging of the divide between ego and ego ideal is never absolutely renounced. The latter, through pregenital integrations, will have taken on lesser dimensions through the satisfactions that have been obtained, the acquisitions and identifications that have been made, which, by reinforcing self-esteem, liberate part of the narcissism retained by the ideal and permit a recathexis of the ego. However, as I have said earlier, the narcissistic wound inflicted by oedipal disappointment, if it leads to a real and absolute mourning of the object in both its senses, can result in a dissolution of the ego ideal or, on the contrary, if the wound remains open, in the Ideal becoming immeasurably enlarged through a renewed appropriation of narcissism from the ego to its own profit, widening the rift that separates it from the ego, and leaving a gaping wound. In fact, in most cases, we witness the setting up of an Ideal that is mid-way between these two extremes. This seems to me to be due to three essential factors:

(1) To the setting up of the superego, heir to the Oedipus

complex, which in the light of the works of Jones, Grunberger and
C. Parat may be seen as an agency protecting the narcissism of the
oedipal child by attributing to a prohibition that which is actually
the product of his intrinsic sexual poverty, the superego acting as a
balm to the narcissistic wound and preventing a haemorrhage of
libido from the ego to its ideal (another eventuality might be a
regression of a psychotic nature).

(2) To the initiation of sublimatory activities, which is of
particular importance in the post-oedipal period (we shall return
to the question of the relationship between the ego ideal and
sublimation later), this last point being linked, amongst others, to
the displacement of the projection of the ego ideal on to new
models.

(3) To the possibility of looking for the lost sense of fusion in
love, with an object who is no longer the oedipal object (although
it may to all intents and purposes be cathected as such).

In addition to this third element, with which we are concerned
at present, it will be recalled that Freud sees as the focal point of
being-in-love the projection of the ego ideal on to the object: 'We
see that the object is being treated in the same way as our own ego
so that when we are in love a considerable amount of narcissistic
libido overflows on to the object. It is even obvious, in many
forms of love-choice, that the object serves as a substitute for
some unattained ego ideal of our own . . . The whole situation can
be completely summarized in a formula: *The object has been put in
the place of the ego ideal.*' Freud emphasizes the impoverishment
suffered by the ego in this process: 'The ego becomes more and
more unassuming and modest, and the object more and more
sublime and precious, until at last it gets possession of the entire
self-love of the ego, whose self-sacrifice thus follows as a natural
consequence. The object has, so to speak, consumed the ego.
Traits of humility, of the limitation of narcissism, and of self-
injury occur in every case of being in love.'

Already in 'On Narcissism: an Introduction' (1914), of which
Group Psychology and the Analysis of the Ego (1921) seems in many
ways to be a continuation, Freud said, 'Libidinal object-cathexis

does not raise self-regard . . . a person in love is humble.' Now this 'limitation of narcissism' is only apparent. Were it real it should bring with it depressive affects; this is far from being the case. The exaltation accompanying love serves as a reminder to us. It has rightly been compared by David to the manic state. 'Exaltation', 'ecstasy' — these are terms closely associated with being in love, the etymology of which (elevation, being transported out of oneself and the world) is the exact opposite to that of 'depression', which signifies 'sinking in'. In one chapter of his book David very pertinently and subtly juxtaposes mourning and being in love. Writing about love — admittedly reciprocated love — the author exclaims, 'Here it is no longer the shadow of the object that falls upon the ego, it is the ego that is illuminated by the sudden radiance of the object rising towards it,' and also, 'The radiance of the object illuminates the marvelling ego, which is dazzled yet also exalted by this sudden brilliance.' Only a lack of reciprocity brings some correspondence between love and mourning, writes the author. I would perhaps go even further than David here. Indeed, I do not consider that the ego is exalted only in the case of reciprocal love. It seems to me that in love — from, indeed, the very first instants, from the moment of choice — subject and object represent the objectivization of the relationship between the ego (the subject) and the ego ideal (the object). In other words, the subject finds itself close to its incarnate ideal. Immediately, the long-awaited disappearance of the gap separating them is experienced as having taken place, at the level of an hallucinatory wish-fulfilment, through anticipation. Only a long series of disappointments, of repeated refusals, will lead the rejected lover to attempt to effect the necessary detachment and hence to accomplish the work of mourning (in the same way that failure to achieve satisfaction puts an end to hallucinatory wish fulfilment). But the first moments of love — independent of the object's response — are full of exalted joy, of an expansiveness of the ego. It is indeed the radiance of the object (of the ego ideal) that falls on the ego. I think that Freud's proposition that 'the object absorbs, devours as one might say the ego', might be understood as 'The ego ideal absorbs, devours the ego', that is, as the fusion of the two agencies in the feast, or as the rediscovery of the original tie preceding the differentiation of me (ego) and not-me. It may be noted how much the contrast between the shadow and the radiance of the object is stressed here. A whole range of phenomena that imply a more or less ephemeral plunge into the world of primary narcissism (with, it must not be forgotten, a concomitant abolition of the differentiation of the agencies of the psychic apparatus) are equally depicted as a blinding light. The inspiration of the artist or intellectual is described as 'illumination', visions of the virgin and the saints, or manifestations of the divinity are accompanied by dazzling light, by brilliant rays — Moses and the burning bush, for example. Theosophy, a mysticism that aims at union with God, is a form of 'illuminism' and visionaries in general are said to have received some special kind of 'illumination'. Psychotics present their delirious intuitions as a sudden access of 'lucidity', as an understanding that has come to them 'in a flash of lightning'. Insight is often experienced as a 'fulguration'. The poet Prévert says of children in love that they are 'bathed in the glow of their first love'. As for the lover's recognition at first sight of his object, it is often referred to as a thunderbolt All these are indications that a certain fusion has immediately taken place at some level, the agencies have ceased to be partitioned off, the boundaries of the ego have been erased.

Whilst being-in-love may constitute one of the most likely post-oedipal outcomes for the ego ideal in as much as it is characteristic of adolescence (albeit there may be infantile prepubertal loves), it does not necessarily represent a genital oedipal organisation in Parat's sense. Indeed one is well aware — and Freud underlines this ('Being in love and hypnosis', in *Group Psychology*, 1921) — that the poetic love of the adolescent may be devoid of conscious sexual desire or may, when the synthesis between the sensual current and the affectionate current is faulty, lead to impotence. In these instances one can understand the state of being in love as representing a manifestation of the desire to rediscover the state of primary narcissism through the projection of the ego ideal on to the object in a regressive fashion, without the psycho-sexual developmental gains, which are in fact inadequately integrated, being involved in this search. Pregenital sexuality — and in particular anality — as well as the full orgastic capability acquired with puberty, instead of being seen to afford new means of achieving the sense of at-oneness that is so desired through a sensual union, are felt to be incompatible with the process of idealization and to be an impediment to the achievement of a lost bliss. The split between instinctual maturity and the narcissism described by Grunberger is here particularly apparent. The 'radiance' of the object then joins battle with the shadows of the instincts, that of the anal component in particular (the themes of light and brightness that were touched on earlier being seemingly antithetical to anality). This love is 'ethereal', the weight of the flesh having been taken from it.

So it is with those loves from which physical consummation is excluded; at times a single encounter, a barely glimpsed face have sufficed to give birth to the dream of a celebration of the marriage of ego and ideal. Dante and Beatrice, Laura and Petrarch are thus ever heros for us, in the sense in which Rank uses this word, since they are incestuous in the *mystical union* of ego and ego ideal. The courtly love of the 12th century — the age of cathedrals, of crusades to the Holy Land, of the quest for the Holy Grail, and of the Cathar heresy at its height — falls entirely under the sign of the split between narcissism and the instincts. At its most extreme the object is but a pretext for the glorious assumption of the ego and being personified is an impediment to this.

Does not the troubadour vow fidelity to his lady — often a distant princess he has never seen — even beyond old age and death, that is to say beyond the vicissitudes of the flesh? In a most interesting article Jacques Sedat (1972) recalls the rites of courtly love and the fundamental state of lack of (physical) satisfaction which represents the prerequisite for the attainment of delight:

My heart takes no delight in any love
Save that I have ne'er enjoyed

exclaims Jaufré Rudel, poet of the distant lady. This delight is
neither pleasure (which is after all limited) nor mere joy, but
beatitude itself: 'The refusal of pleasure, the suppression of
appetite for satisfactions, is the renunciation required prior to
setting out in quest of delight' (Sedat).

Behind this manifestly oedipal love — the troubadour is
always a bachelor and chooses a lady who is wife to a noble
lord — it is easy to discern the latent homosexuality but also,
and especially, the search for a pure narcissistic exaltation, the
elation procured by the imaginary contemplation of the
object, 'through the eyes of the soul', to whom the
troubadour unites himself over and beyond the contingencies
of the flesh, of perishable matter, of space and time. This is
just as the mystic visionaries lose themselves in God in the
experience of ecstasy, just as the Platonist attains to the idea,
beyond the multiplicity of its embodiments, beyond
embodiment itself. In the *Symposium* the aim is to succeed in
seeing 'Beauty itself, in its integrity, in its unalloyed purity,
rather than a beauty impaired by human flesh, human colours,
a host of other mortal trifles'.

If one takes into account the development of the ego as
described by Tausk (1919), who postulates the existence of a
psychic ego prior to a body ego, the latter experienced at first
as something separate that it will be the task of the
psychic ego to integrate, it is understandable that on the road
back to primary narcissistic fusion the subject experiences his
body as a worthless garment to be cast off in order to go
beyond the bounds imposed by embodiment. It is the
description of this process that Grunberger emphasizes in his
work on melancholy (1966): 'There exists in each of us a
tendency to try and overcome our dependency in relation to
our mortal selves.' We are here faced with a gnostic way of
thinking, and as Pasche (1959) has shown with great

penetration, the avatars of this are timeless. For him Western thought (be it religious or atheistic) is definable in relation to gnosticism. (This seems indeed to be even more manifest today than at the time Pasche presented his remarkable paper.) For the gnostic, man must free himself from matter, from his earthly trappings. His body must become a body of air, then an ethereal body and finally a pure luminous and spiritual essence (see Leisegang, *La Gnose*). For it is at that point that he will attain the Spirit and the Radiance of God. There is consubstantiality between his spirit and the divinity. Ridding himself of his body therefore allows him to accede to union with the divine, to perfect knowledge.

This fusion with the divine clearly represents a return to the union of ego and ideal, to the primary undifferentiated state. It seems to me to constitute at the same time a transgression of the incest barrier. 'Knowledge' in the Bible is synonymous with coitus. To know a woman is to penetrate her, so would not perfect knowledge be that of the mother? Man must not eat of the fruit of the tree of knowledge. He must for ever be separated, cut off from the supreme knowledge. Incest is forbidden him. That courtly love has to do with gnosticism seems sufficiently clear if one looks at certain of the rites noted by Sedat, in particular, the contemplation of the naked woman and the *Asag*. This concerns an ascesis relating to the purification of the sight and of the feeling of love. The *Asag* is a trial involving chaste cohabitation with the lady, a cohabitation that excludes *the deed*. (The anal reference is evident here. In English this is more apparent in the related word 'doings'.)

Pure love is *Fin' Amors*, that is to say, a love that is perfect, complete. These rites can be likened to certain gnostic (and especially Cathar) practices, although the contempt for the body is not so conscious. (Pasche recalls the metaphors — clay, blight, mire — used in gnostic writings to refer to the body.) One can see that this split between narcissism and the instincts in certain forms of love, far from representing an attainment of the genital phase, expresses but a painful nostalgia for the state of primary fusion which is confused with the fusion of ego and ideal. Rather than bind his instincts together the person abandons them in order that he may soar up, an immaterial body, towards 'the Daughters of Fire', blending 'dream and life' and attempting in this way to escape 'the dark sun of melancholy' (allusions to Gérard de Nerval, a well known poet of the last century who was psychotic). These angelic loves that lead towards regression are often sketched upon a psychotic background, especially when they persist or arise after adolescence.

The revival of oedipal feelings in adolescence often makes the repression of the sensual current very marked. That the state of being in love, experienced in this way, should be primarily the prerogative of the adolescent should come as no surprise if we recall the enormous economic changes that he has to confront. The separation that he effects at that point between his ego ideal and the whole of his maturation represents in any case, most often, only a moment in his development, as if the instinctual upheaval he is undergoing required a certain amount of time to be integrated. Being in love may then be seen as an attempt at a compromise between the violent sexual instincts of the adolescent and his anti-instinctual 'thirst for the ideal and for purity', for it is indeed a woman (or a man in the case of the young girl) who is the object of them, although this object may, in early adolescence, be of a homosexual nature. The sexual instincts — even if repressed — are nonetheless directly involved, and the adolescent is usually well aware of this fact. He may, for example, be more conscious of the split that is operating within himself. In other words, in adolescence being in love contains within it the germ of a future reunification of narcissism (projected on to the object in the form of an Ideal) with the sexual instincts, which is not the case when the adolescent adopts an ideology, this adherence being essentially ascetic whatever the manifest content of the ideology in question. However, in certain cases — and one has only to glance at any newspaper to verify this — the love of adolescents, even when there is an accompanying physical relationship, does not brook being subject to life's contingencies. The least obstacle may push the couple to suicide, death then being experienced as the triumph of primary narcissism over reality. (The obstacle generally comes from the parents, who in that case occupy the role of both oedipal rival and of a reality that upsets a pre-established narcissistic fusion.)

It can happen that not only is the lover's exaltation not in the least diminished by the fact that the object fails to respond to the love that is borne it, but that the lover loves, and only wishes to love, in silence ('My soul has its secret, my life has its mystery, and she whom I loved never Knew ought of it . . .') as if the least attempt at realization threatened to break the spell. Think of those adolescent loves for distant idols, sometimes long dead — Rudolf Valentino, James Dean . . .

If love may be based upon a very regressive type of organization of the ego and the libido, can one still maintain the idea of a specific form of object relationship linked to the genital organization of the libido and — not to mince words — can one speak of 'a perfect form of love' (Freud) under the primacy of the genital organization, or should one abandon this notion as being purely moralizing and normative? Two apparently opposed lines of development seem to have somewhat obscured the problem. The first, that of Reich, consists of putting the accent on orgastic capacity and the function of the orgasm. Orgastic capacity defines health and the *norm*: 'The genital character is controlled by a *normal libidinal economy*. The title of 'genital character' is justified by virtue of the fact that only orgastic primacy and potency (determined by a well-defined character structure) can ensure a libidinal economy that conforms to the norm.'

In the chapter devoted to 'The Genital Character and the Neurotic Character' in his *Character Analysis*, W. Reich writes about the character armour:

> This character of the Ego consists of various elements of the outer world, of prohibitions, instinct inhibitions and identifications of different kinds. The contents of the

character armour, then, are of an external, social origin . . . The development from a primitive state to the civilization of today demanded a considerable restriction of libidinal and other gratification. Human development has been characterized by increasing sexual suppression; in particular, the development of patriarchal society went hand in hand with an increasing disruption and restriction of genitality . . . In order to avoid real anxiety (occasioned by actual external dangers) people had to inhibit their impulses; aggression has to be held down even if people, as a result of the economic crisis, are at the point of starvation, and the sexual instinct is shackled by social norms and prejudices. A transgression against the norms means actual danger, such as punishment for "theft" or infantile masturbation, jail for incest or homosexuality. To the extent to which real anxiety is avoided, the stasis of libido and with that the stasis anxiety increases. Stasis anxiety and real anxiety are in mutual interaction: the more real anxiety is avoided the more intense becomes stasis anxiety, and vice versa. The unafraid individual satisfies his strong libidinal needs even at the risk of social ostracism.

The character armour protects a person from the external world and spares him (real) anxiety at the same time as it stores up the anxiety coming from the stasis of libido (libido not discharged through genital orgasm).

In the genital character 'periodic orgastic discharges of libidinal tension reduce the instinctual demands of the id on the ego' . . . Certainly the ego of the genital character is equally armoured, but it chooses how to wear this armour and is not under its *rule* [my italics] . . . The genital character may be extremely joyous, but can also know intense anger. It reacts to the loss of the object with sadness, without being overwhelmed by it; it can experience passionate love and implacable hatred, etc. As to the psychic agencies, they coexist peacefully: 'The super-ego of the genital character is *sex-affirmative* [Reich's italics]; for this reason, there is a high degree of harmony between id and superego. Since the Oedipus complex has lost its cathexis, the counter-cathexis in the super-ego has become superfluous.' [In the same chapter the superego is defined as 'a foreign body from the external world, full of threats and prohibitions' . . .] On the practical level one might say that there are no sexual prohibitions at the level of the superego. The superego is unaware of sadism not only for the reasons indicated above, but also because the absence of any libidinal stasis precludes the activation of sadistic tendencies . . . *The ideal ego and the real ego resemble each other, and this translates into an absence of tension* [my italics]. As for the ego, 'the ego takes over, *without any guilt feeling*' [Reich's italics], the genital libido and certain pregenital tendencies of the id for gratification . . . The ego, as a result of sexual gratification, is under little pressure from either the id or the superego.

This golden age of Psyche, when the lion lays down with the lamb, is possible because of orgasm. The neurotic, for his part, is, on the other hand 'incapable of an orgastic liberation of his floating and un-sublimated libido'. As is well known, according to Reich the absence of orgastic liberation (linked to 'real' anxiety about the external world) causes the libido to be redirected into infantile objects which are resexualized — hence the actualization of the Oedipus complex in the neurotic — and into the pregenital phases of the libido.

It would seem that the essential criticism that one can make of Reich's conception of the genital character (and it seems pertinent to recall that it dates from the years 1928–1932, a time when he was still a member of the psycho-analytic movement) is that it is precisely so centred on the orgasm. Nathaniel Ross (1970) notes that clinical evidence indicates that there is no parallel between orgastic capacity and maturity of object relations. Similarly Charles N. Sarlin (1970) emphasizes the entirely auto-erotic significance that orgasm may assume. As for Heinz Lichtenstein (1970), he assigns to the orgasm as one of its essential functions, following Eissler in this, that of confirming the person in his sense of his own existence, a function entirely independent of object relatedness, capable even of being in complete contradiction with an evolved level of the latter.

Perhaps I may be permitted a hypothesis as to the privileged place of orgastic capacity in the Reichian system, a hypothesis that seems to me to be validated by the later deelopment of Reich's writings when he passed 'From Psychoanalysis to Orgone Biophysics' (*Character Analysis*). Taking the character armour as a starting point, he was led to describe a muscular armour the nature of which takes on more precision as one gradually proceeds through his work. Thus this armour is described as being segmental, comprising several rings. One schema demonstrates that 'the direction of orgonotic streaming is transverse to the armour rings'. The streaming is moved onwards by wave-like contractions. The schema and the commentary upon it unquestionably evoke the peristaltic movements of the intestines. An insufficient relaxation of the armour prompts the following remark (in capitals in the text): 'AS SOON AS THE EXPRESSION OF GIVING MEETS ARMOR BLOCKS, SO THAT IT CANNOT FREELY DEVELOP, IT CHANGES INTO DESTRUCTIVE RAGE.' The whole of this description is indicative of problems at the level of bowel training. I think that one might put forward the idea that the armour (be it character or muscular armour) which is, it should be recalled, of external origin, corresponds to a frequent persecution phantasy, namely that of being gripped and immobilized in the rectum of the persecutor who prevents one from acting. This phantasy is activated at the time of bowel training, since the parent implementing the training aims to block the child's (anal) discharge, making it dependent upon his or her good will, as if the child were enclosed in the sphincter of his 'trainer'. Orgasm is, then, nothing other than an equivalent of the anal discharge experienced as a triumph over the trainer-persecutor whose grip has been broken. The armour-rectum thus represents likewise the projection of a regressive, restrictive superego (Reich identifies the armour with *the rule*. Cf. above).

In fact *orgasm per se* does not seem to me to have any specific status. It consists indeed in a discharge of tensions and this is, intrinsically, nothing but an evacuation (Alexander refers to 'drainage') even if the tensions in question are of a more complex nature than those of an anal order. But as soon as the predominant phantasy, in orgasm, becomes that of making the enemy let go his hold (even if this phantasy may be operative in many on an oedipal or pregenital level), it is an abuse to accord this an orchestrating role in a theory of genitality implying the full achievement of psycho-sexual development in all its aspects. I would recall Freud ('Instincts and Vicissitudes', 1915): 'The word love . . . can only begin to be applied . . . after there has been a synthesis of all the component instincts of sexuality under the primacy of the genitals.' It will be understood also that by attributing the lack of coincidence of Ego and Ideal and the absence of complete enjoyment to external factors, Reich maintains the megalomanic phantasy that it might be possible to attain the Absolute.

Counter to this line of development is that of Bouvet and his description of 'the genital object relationship' (1956). Indeed, contrary to Reich, he does not give a central position to the manifestation of the instinct in his discussion but rather inverts the factors, describing a structure whose elements seem to correspond to the concept of genitality, as against the pregenital object relationship that he has previously described, and without there being any reference to the instinctual roots of his description. For example:

> Here the ego has acquired a stability that is not threatened by the loss of a significant object. It remains independent of its objects . . . Affects and emotions are graduated, from feelings of which there is but a trace to manifest passion . . . And above all, since the instincts which provide its driving

force have been genitalised they no longer have the character of an ungovernable, unlimited, unconditional need for possession, that would include a destructive aspect. They are truly tender, loving and if the person is, for all that, not especially giving . . . he is in this instance capable of understanding and of adaptation to the other person's situation.

This description has very often been criticized. This does not mean, however, that it may not contain some elements of truth. That which gives it the moralizing and normative character that is so often commented on is its apparent gratuity. It appears to be cut off from its instinctual base and to exist alongside it, but not in relation to it, or rather the links that unite them are not apparent.

We have here, therefore, two descriptions of genitality, of which the one emphasizes certain instinctual capacities entailing, *ipso facto*, the appearance of full human relationships, while the other involves a description of well-developed object relations that implies the attainment of genital primacy. In both cases we sense the presence of a valid intuition, but the mechanism whereby one order of phenomenon is converted to another, and its reciprocity (the manifestations of the instinct and the object relationship) remain mysterious. In both cases we can recognize an equal 'scientific' puritanism.

M. Balint's extremely amusing critique of the concept of genital love (1948), in the most misogynous article in the whole of psychoanalytic literature, seems to me paradoxically to furnish several arguments in favour of an attempt to define genital love, an attempt that takes us back to Freud. (The misogyny appears between the lines throughout the article, but it becomes manifest when the author comes to advance the point of view that love first appeared in a homosexual form between the brothers of the primal horde, then at the end of his essay when he protests against women's claims to equality.) Balint is led to revise the psychoanalytic concept of 'tenderness' as a component of genital love. He arrives at the conclusion (based on a number of etymologies) that 'tenderness' suggests disease, weakness, immaturity and asks, 'How has genital love, the mature form of love, got mixed up with this doubtful company? ' He remarks that 'we are expected to give and are expecting to receive, kindness, regard, consideration etc. even at times when there is no genital wish, no genital satisfaction to be felt. This is contrary to the habit of most animals, which show interest for the other sex only during heat. Man, however, is supposed to show unfailing interest in, and regard for, his partner for ever.'

A parallel phenomenon to this everlasting demand for regard is man's prolonged childhood. Whereas amongst animals filial ties are very quickly undone, man 'is expected to, and usually does, pay love, regard, respect, fear, gratitude to his parents for ever. Something similar is demanded in love.' And the author goes on to conclude that genital love is 'an artefact of civilization like art or religion' and that 'it is enforced upon us, irrespective of our biological nature and needs'. Balint maintains that we find 'full genital function coupled with infantile behaviour' (that is to say, tenderness). On this matter he also writes: 'What we call genital love has really very little to do with genitality, in fact it uses the genital sexuality only as a stock on which to graft something that is essentially different.' In short, according to the author, this something that is essentially different being archaic (tenderness) leads one to think that love represents a danger which, in similar fashion to psychosis and toxicomania, threatens the weak ego.

This text leads to a number of considerations centred on two points. In the course of his argument the author compares man to animals. Would it not be possible to delineate human genitality all the better precisely by focusing on the essential differences between human development and animal development; that is, in man, his immaturity and the existence of the incest barrier? A second argument advanced by the author consists in demonstrating that, in order to attain to genital love, genital sexuality must be coupled with an archaic, heterogeneous element (tenderness). In 'Contributions to the Psychology of Love' (1912), Freud says that the origin of tenderness corresponds to the primary infantile object choice. On this basis one can demonstrate the necessity for such a conjunction in order that a relatively advanced form of object relationship may be achieved. It combines archaic elements — which are experienced with the primary object — and developed sexuality. Genitality includes all the developments of maturation, and the genital object subsumes the primary object. In addition, doesn't the Oedipus complex imply a desire other than the mere discharge of sexual tension? The object at that point takes on at least as much importance as the instinct. It is, by definition, with the Oedipus complex that the object ceases to be that 'variable' in relation to the instinct that Freud speaks of in 'Instincts and their Vicissitudes' (1915).

Sexual satisfaction is no longer sought for its own sake; it is entirely subordinated to the object — the father or the mother. On the contrary, the search for a satisfaction that can be obtained with an interchangeable object — which is only a means of discharge — would take us back to the anal phase (all faeces being alike), to the part object, to auto-erotism (in the 1905 sense) or to organ pleasure. The fact that, in genital love, the object counts for at least as much as the instinctual discharge is a relic of the negotiation of the oedipal phase. In this man is in no way comparable to animals who, not being aware of an incest barrier, are not aware either of oedipal desire, that is to say, the predilection for one object above all others. It is also oedipal desire — and its non-fulfillment in both its phases — which explains the (relatively) perennial nature of filial attachment ('It is precisely those sexual impulses that are inhibited in their aims which achieve such lasting ties between people' ['Being in Love and Hypnosis', Freud, 1921]), an attachment that man's biological immaturity had already previously brought into being by making the child entirely dependent on those around him.

It is rather curious to note that certain authors who take an interest in the form of the genital organization of the libido and its links to object relations, omit to mention that the genital love to which they refer is post-oedipal and that it for ever bears the stamp of the oedipal phase.

Such was not the case however with Freud, whose emphasis on the necessity for that confluence of the *sensual* and the *affectionate* currents which 'alone ensures a completely normal attitude in love' ('On the Universal Tendency . . .', Freud, 1912) seems to me, on reflection, to constitute the basis for what might be said, even today, about genital love. (This confluence might, moreover, be likened to what Abraham had to say about the post-ambivalent character of the genital phase.)

Even if Freud does not mention 'genital love' there can be no doubt that the idea of a complete form of love — 'complete object love' ('On Narcissism, an Introduction', Freud, 1914), 'real, true love' ('Being in Love and Hypnosis', Freud, 1921) — is often present in his work (we have just seen that he also speaks of 'normal' love). When he studies the difficulties facing human love, which often translate precisely into a lack of confluence of the two currents, it is with constant reference to the oedipal situation. When the child reaching puberty (that is to say, for Freud, at the time of the establishment of genital primacy) comes up against the incest barrier,

> it will make efforts to pass on from these objects which are unsuitable in reality, and find a way as soon as possible to other, extraneous objects with which a real sexual life may be carried on. These new objects will still be chosen on the model (imago) of the infantile ones, but in the course of time they will attract to themselves the affection that was tied to the earlier ones. A man shall leave his father and his mother — according to the biblical command — and shall cleave unto his wife; affection and sensuality are then united ('On the Universal Tendency . . .', Freud, 1912).

One can see that for Freud genital love is conceived as result-ing from the conjunction of the wishes, the instincts, the affects of which the mother was the object — as primary object and as oedipal object — with the entirety of the sexual instincts that the child has been forced to repress or to metamorphose because of the incest barrier, and which, with the new object, may be given free rein. This is the case unless there is an oedipal fixation which, through the identification of the actual love object with the incestuous object, leads to impotence or to a splitting of the affectionate from the sensual current. The affection is then expressed in relation to overvalued (idealized) objects which are substitutes for the incestuous object, whereas the sensual current is directed towards denigrated objects. Today we would emphasize rather the split between oedipal mother (overvalued) and pre-oedipal mother (devalued), the aggressive instincts linked to the pregenital maternal conflict only being able to manifest themselves in relation to unworthy objects.

'As soon as the condition of debasement is fulfilled, sensuality can be freely expressed, and important sexual capacities and a high degree of pleasure can develop' ('On the Universal Tendency . . .', Freud, 1912). It will be appreciated that it is not a matter here of any link between orgastic sexual discharge and the establishment of a developed relationship. This discharge may be highly satisfying *because* it is experienced with a despised (anal) object, whilst an object relationship that is apparently well developed might hinder sexual capacity. Nor is it a question of morals. There is no punishment for not having succeeded in establishing a developed object relationship. It may even afford considerable pleasure. However, the oedipal injury will not be removed, to the extent that it can be by being in love, any more than the gap between ego and ideal will be filled. Sexual satisfaction with an object invested with the wishes that were directed towards the incestuous object (and towards the primary object) cannot be achieved. Thus 'one of the ideals of sexual life, the focusing of all desires upon a single object, will be unattainable' (1915 note to the *Three Essays*). The concept of a maturative ego ideal such as I have attempted to delineate earlier allows one to understand how the ego ideal may drive the ego to achieve each and every integration in order to make the realization of its project of fusion possible, in a way that encompasses all the capacities acquired during its development.

Following Ferenczi, this view sees genitality as a means of rediscovering the primary object (and a time when the ego was its own ideal) in another way than by regression. It might be likened to Abraham's essay (1924) in which, the oral-narcissistic stage being preambivalent, the genital stage is described as post-ambivalent. The one and the other are therefore characterized by an absence of ambivalence, the one rediscovering itself in the other after the long trajectory effected by the ego and the instincts. However, the complete absence of ambivalence is inconceivable, save in the presence of total satisfaction. Because of his immaturity and the incest prohibition, man will always experience a gap between his wishes and their satisfaction, such that genitality as definitive reconciliation of man with himself and his object is of the order of an Ideal, when presented to us as a stage that might really be achieved in a permanent way. Then, I fear, we are also into the realms of illusion. On the other hand, denial of the tendency in man to effect a synthesis both of the instincts themselves and of these unified instincts with affection is even more based upon illusion. For this would constitute an abolition of the gap between wish and satisfaction, between the Ego and the Ideal, by a denial of its very existence, through a suppression of the very notions of development and maturation and hence of difference.

The post-oedipal outcome of the wish to rediscover the primitive state of fusion may, in the best instances, be able to profit from the developments in the ego and the instincts whose flowering is the achievement of full orgastic capacity, or in other words of a fusion including the integration of genital and pregenital instincts. The object still remains an aid to the projection of the ego ideal as in the case of the adolescent described above but, it seems to me, to a lesser degree, because the instinctual satisfactions obtained in sexual relations when they are ego syntonic diminish the quantity of narcissism projected, part of which comes to recathect the ego, and in return makes it available for new object cathexes. A satisfactory development of ego and instincts in a context of genital primacy seemingly favours love rather than the state of being-in-love. If the exaltation of being-in-love is necessarily accompanied by immersion in the boundless universe of narcissism where love means forever, successful genital development is seemingly more suited to supplying love its daily bread. The ego ideal that has cathected development has shed some of its megalomania and can bear the relative, and hence the commonplace. The state of being-in-love is, by definition, a state; love implies the establishment of a relationship, and of a lasting relationship. As Freud emphasizes: 'It is the fate of sensual love to become extinguished when it is satisfied; for it to be able to last, it must from the beginning be mixed with purely affectionate components — with such, that is, as are inhibited in their aims — or it must itself undergo a transformation of this kind' ('Being in Love and Hypnosis', Freud, 1921). Now, I doubt in fact that being-in-love, as opposed to love, engages primarily the affectionate current. Projection of the ego ideal on to the object is not the equivalent of affection, and this latter is often entirely absent from passion. Affection, or tenderness, as its etymology indicates, is the opposite of hardness, that is to say, of aggressivity. It represents a voluntary suppression (and not a repression) of violence. Innocence and fragility arouse compassion. The projection of the ego ideal on to the object does not of itself make the latter an adequate representative of weakness (by which I mean that narcissistic cathexis is not the equivalent of affection). Affection seems to me to be inescapably linked to tolerance, to a possibility of putting up with the faults and imperfections of the partner, hence of having a less demanding, less absolute ego ideal. (This relates primarily to the early mother-infant relationship which, at a certain level, the couple recreate.)

The picture of the ego ideal as it emerges within the context of the love characteristic of the oedipal organization of the genital stage seems to me to be made up of complex elements that I shall attempt to summarise:

— The hope of rediscovering the lost primary sense of at-oneness is not given up, but the ways of achieving this will be different; it will no longer essentially be sought through an incestuous phantasy, although this may be reactivated in passing.

— Sublimatory activity and complete sexual satisfaction permit a narcissistic recathexis of the ego which diminishes the ego ideal by the same amount.

— The (internal and external) reality that can afford narcissistic and instinctual gratifications is positively cathected. To some extent the ego ideal will be projected on to the very means of access to reality. At an intellectual level truth will be preferred to illusion, science to superstition. In love, the partner will be loved with his or her limitations and vulnerabilities and not for an illusory perfection (it is in this, moreover, that the cathexis to which they are subject is essentially different from oedipal cathexis).

— What remains of the pursuit of the primitive sense of fusion and incestuous gratification through love will be manifest principally in attachment to the object (I am not, of course, concerned here with those cases of pathological fixation that have nothing to do with love).

Freud paid considerable attention to the exclusive nature of object choice in love. He wrote: 'The trait of overvaluing the loved one, and regarding her as unique and irreplaceable, can be seen to fall just as naturally into the context of the child's experience, for no one possesses more than one mother and the relation to her is based on an event that is not open to any doubt and cannot be repeated' ('A Special Type of Choice of Object', Freud, 1910). Indeed, if in the anal stage the object, modelled on the faeces, is interchangeable, the Oedipus complex — as I have said above — brings about a radical alteration to object choice (but infidelity is, for Freud, a possible sign of oedipal fixation, the substitutive objects leaving the subject permanently dissatisfied).

In 'Being in Love and Hypnosis' Freud attributes permanent attachment to the object to the 'certainty [of] the revival of the need which had just expired'. This somewhat utilitarian view, based upon the experiencing of satisfaction and the search for an identity of perception which is facilitated by the stability of the object relation, is completed in Chapter 12 of *Group Psychology and the Analysis of the Ego* by some considerations on monogamy:

> The last two remarks will have prepared us for finding that directly sexual impulsions are unfavourable to the formation of groups. In the history of the development of the family there have also, it is true, been group relations of sexual love (group marriages); but the more important sexual love became for the ego, and the more it developed the characteristics of being in love, the more urgently it required to be limited to two people — una cum uno — as is prescribed by the nature of the genital aim. Polygamous inclinations had to be content to find satisfaction in a succession of changing objects.
>
> Two people coming together for the purpose of sexual satisfaction, in so far as they seek for solitude, are making a demonstration against the herd instinct, the group feeling. The more they are in love, the more completely they suffice for each other . . . It is only when the affectionate, that is, personal, factor of a love relation gives place entirely to the sensual one, that it is possible for two people to have sexual intercourse in the presence of others or for there to be simultaneous sexual acts in a group, as occurs at an orgy. But at that point a regression has taken place to an early stage in sexual relations, at which being in love as yet played no part, and all sexual objects were judged to be of equal value, somewhat in the sense of Bernard Shaw's malicious aphorism to the effect that: "Being in love means greatly exaggerating the difference between one woman and another".

Indeed it seems to me that this exaggeration of the difference is to be ascribed not only to oedipal love — the loved parent being unique — but also to a reparation for the fact of not having been the unique object of the loved parent. In love the object is unique as one is oneself narcissistically unique, and as one wishes to be for the object (one of the reasons underlying compulsive infidelity seems to me to be a wish to reverse the previously experienced oedipal situation).

Love — as Freud will repeat — is a force that tends to fragment the collectivity. This is why it is attacked by all totalitarian regimes as 'egotistical', 'possessive', 'individualistic'. However, to all those other characteristics that have been ascribed to genitality, might one not add that the person attaining the so-called genital organization is an *individual* ? An examination of the relations between the ego ideal and the phenomena of the group will, I hope, enable me to justify this remark.

4. The Ego Ideal and the Group

Every morning vehicles take the workers to the countryside and bring them back again in the evening. They carry standards, have celebrations, feast on cakes. Every woman, if she wishes, has three men: husband, lover and a father to her child. For single people there is bayaderism.

'That suits me' said Bouvard. And he became lost in dreams of this world of harmony.

Through control of the climate the earth would become more beautiful; through the cross-breeding of races human life would be longer. Clouds would be controlled as lightning is now, it would rain on towns at night to clean them. Ships would traverse the polar seas, unfrozen by the aurora borealis.

Flaubert, *Bouvard and Pécuchet*

We'll all go to paradise. (Song, 1972)

Anticipating a later discussion, we may distinguish here and now that, at a certain level, there exists a fundamental difference between the ego ideal, heir to primary narcissism, and the superego, heir to the Oedipus complex. The first represents — at the outset at least — an attempt at recovering lost omnipotence. The second, in a Freudian perspective, is a product of the castration complex. The first tends to reinstate Illusion, the second to promote reality. The superego comes between the child and the mother, the ego ideal — as I have said — pushes him towards fusion. The setting up of the superego provides some relief from the limitless demands of the ego ideal by instituting the incest

barrier and by transforming the child's intrinsic impotence
into obedience to an interdict. This allows him not only to
save face but to obtain a narcissistic gratification from this
very obedience. It is also true, in a general sense, as F. Pasche
stresses in his article 'De la Dépression' (1961), that it is often
easier to obey a set of moral principles than to become a
personality in one's own right. It is nonetheless the case that
the wish to be one's own ideal, as at the beginning of life,
seems never to be given up entirely by most men. To
differing degrees, it persists unchanged despite the vicissitudes
it suffers at another level, in parallel with the development of
the ego. The latter seemingly undergoes in this a splitting
process analogous to that described by Freud in the case of
the fetishist.

The Freudian superego is the last of the agencies of the
psychic apparatus to appear. As is well known, when Freud
introduced the superego into his second topography he did
not distinguish it from the ego ideal. Thus he writes:

> The superego is, however, not simply a residue of the
> earliest object choices of the id; it also represents an
> energetic reaction formation against those choices. Its
> relation to the *ego* is not exhausted by the precept 'You
> ought to be like this' (like your father). It also comprises
> the prohibition: 'You may not be like this' (like your
> father) — that is, 'You may not do all that he does; some
> things are his prerogative' ('The Ego and the Superego',
> in *The Ego and the Id*, Freud, 1923).

Within our present perspective we might say, continuing to
make a distinction between ego ideal and superego, that the
positive injunction emanates from the heir to narcissism and
the negative from the heir to the Oedipus complex. It should
also be recalled that, according to Freud, many adults never
acquire a true 'moral conscience' resulting from internalized
prohibitions, nor experience real 'feelings of guilt', but only
'social anxiety'. They do not possess a superego and are only

prevented from doing wrong by the fear of being found out (*Civilization and Its Discontents*, Freud, 1929). This idea had already prompted similar remarks in 'On Narcissism: an Introduction' (1914) and in *Group Psychology and the Analysis of the Ego* (1921) (Chapter VII, 'Identification') whilst Freud had not yet introduced the second topography.

In 1932, studying 'The Dissection of the Psychical Personality' (*New Introductory Lectures*, Freud, 1932) he is even more radical: 'As regards conscience God has done an uneven and careless piece of work, for a large majority of men have brought along with them only a modest amount of it or scarcely enough to be worth mentioning.' It seems that little account has been taken of this proposition of Freud's in the psychoanalytic literature. On the contrary the accent has been put on the universal severity of the superego — omitting, it seems to me, to distinguish between several orders of factors which are all ascribed to the heir to the Oedipus complex. It seems, indeed, that in certain circumstances, this agency — of but recent creation, at times virtually non-existent according to Freud, and in any case seemingly fragile — may be swept away, as it were, by the sudden reactivation of the old wish for the union of ego and ideal. It was a patient of Alexander's who remarked that the superego is soluble in alcohol (Alexander, 1938). It is indeed therefore narcissistic elation, the meeting of ego and ideal, that dissolves the superego. Group phenomena seem particularly suited to provoking the disappearance of the superego. Freud had already noted this in *Group Psychology and the Analysis of the Ego*:

> For us it would be enough to say that in a group the individual is brought under conditions which allow him to throw off the repressions of his unconscious instinctual impulses. The apparently new characteristics which he then displays are in fact the manifestations of this unconscious, in which all that is evil in the human mind is contained as a predisposition. We can find no difficulty in understanding the disappearance of conscience or of a sense of responsibility

in these circumstances. It has long been our contention that "social anxiety" is the essence of what is called conscience.

and also:

> In obedience to the new authority (that of the group) he may put his former 'conscience' out of action, and so surrender to the attraction of the *increased pleasure* [my italics] that is certainly obtained from the removal of inhibitions. On the whole, therefore, it is not so remarkable that we should see an individual in a group doing or approving things which he would have avoided in the normal conditions of life.

Freud further said: 'We should have to admit that in any collection of people the tendency to form a psychological group may very easily come to the fore.' As is well known, Freud considered the group to be 'a revival of the primal horde' which consisted of 'an individual of superior strength among a troop of equal companions . . . The primal father is the group ideal, which governs the ego in the place of the ego ideal' whereas the members making up the group, having thus replaced their individual ego ideals by one and the same object, can identify with each other. The cohesion of the group depends essentially on its relationship to the leader who pushes the constituent members to abandon their individuality. Each member of the group is thus assimilated with the others:

> When an individual gives up his distinctiveness in a group and lets its other members influence him by suggestion, it gives one the impression that he does it because he feels the need of being in harmony with them rather than in opposition to them — so that perhaps after all he does it "for love of them . . ." So long as a group formation persists or so far as it extends, individuals in the group behave as though they were uniform.

And again:

> An individual's private emotional impulses and intellectual

acts are too weak to come to anything by themselves and are entirely dependent for this on being reinforced by being repeated in a similar way in the other members of the group. We are reminded of how many of these phenomena of dependence are part of the normal constitution of human society, of how little originality and personal courage are to be found in it, of how much every individual is ruled by those attitudes of the group mind which exhibit themselves in such forms as racial characteristics, class prejudices, public opinion, etc.

This blotting out of individual personalities — which is linked to the identification of the members of the group with each other, having established a common ego ideal by projecting it on to the same object — the leader — seems then to be all the more absolute according to the intrinsic weakness of the individuals. In the primitive horde,

> The will of the individual was too weak; he did not venture upon action. No impulses whatever came into existence except collective ones; there was only a common will, there were no single ones. An idea did not dare to turn itself into an act of will unless it felt itself reinforced by a perception of its general diffusion.

In addition there would be a wish to impose uniformity on the members of the group having, as its origin, fraternal rivalry:

> If one cannot be the favourite oneself, at all events nobody else shall be the favourite . . . No one must want to put himself forward, every one must be the same. Social justice means that we deny ourselves many things so that others may have to do without them as well, or, what is the same thing, may not be able to ask for them.

Discussing the herd instinct Freud affirmed that 'all the members must be equal to one another . . . Many equals, who can identify themselves with one another, and a single person superior to them all'. Rather than define man as a gregarious animal he calls him a *horde animal*, 'an individual creature in a horde led by a chief'. Taken together, Freud's propositions take us back to a situation that relates to the father complex, the chief being a substitute for the father, the individuals making up the group representing an analogue of the sibship.

As I see it, not all human gatherings, least of all the group correspond to this schema, which applies to a relatively evolved situation. A particularly illuminating article by Didier Anzieu (1971) supports the thesis that I shall be attempting to defend here. The author establishes an analogy between the group and the dream. Any group situation will be experienced as hallucinatory wish fulfilment. In addition 'in a thousand different ways in the course of the history of ideas, the group has been imagined as this fabulous place in which all wishes will be satisfied', whether it be 'the *Utopia* of Thomas More, Rabelais' Abbey of Theleme, Fourier's phalanstery, Jules Romains' companions . . .' (Anzieu, 1971). According to the author, in the group as in the dream, the psychic apparatus undergoes a triple regression. Temporally the group has a tendency to regress to primary narcissism; topographically, the ego and the superego can no longer exercise their control. The id takes possession of the psychic apparatus with the ideal ego which '*seeks to realize a fusion with the omnipotent mother and the introjective restoration of the lost primary love object* [my italics]. The group becomes, for the members, the substitute for this lost object.' (Regression of form is manifest through the recourse to modes of expression that are permeated by primary process, similar to the first exchanges of infant and mother.) Anzieu shows therefore that a group that operates by itself (without any controlling organism having the function of reality testing) '*would naturally function within the order of illusion*'.

Three successive observations of training groups, which the author has experience of as leader, will bring out certain themes that are constituents of the group illusion. There is the setting up of an egalitarian theory: 'That the heights and depths should be levelled, leaders brought down to size, everyone reduced to the common denominator.' This proposition is interpreted by the author as the negation of the difference between the sexes and, in a more general way, that of the primal phantasies. Egalitarian ideology defends against castration anxiety. Equally there also appears in the group a denial of the primal scene. The group is self generated. It is itself an omnipotent mother. It is not organized around a central person (the leader), but around the group itself. The group illusion is then a realization of the wish to 'heal one's narcissistic injuries' and to identify oneself with the good breast (or with the omnipotent mother).

It seems to me that Anzieu's work allows one to take better account of certain group phenomena. Indeed what he describes is very precisely the fulfilment of the wish for fusion between the ego and the ideal by the most regressive means, those pertaining to the pleasure principle, which take the shortest route and erase all that has been acquired in the course of development.

The father figure is in fact chased away, excluded from the group, as is the superego. It is as if the group formation represented of itself the hallucinatory realization of the wish to take possession of the mother by the sibship, through a very regressive mode, that of primary fusion. It is the case, however, that there may be a leader (one has only to think of the Nazi groups). But he cannot, to my mind, be equated with the father. In this instance the leader is the person who activates the primitive wish for the union of ego and ideal. He is the promotor of Illusion, he who makes it shimmer before men's dazzled eyes, he who will bring it to fruition. Times will be changed, the Great Day (or the Great Eve) will arrive, a heavenly Jerusalem will offer itself to our astonished gaze, our needs will be met, the Aryans will conquer the world, the day will dawn, the future yield its promise, etc. The group thirsts less for a leader than for illusions. And it will choose as leader whomsoever promises it the union of ego and ego ideal. The leader is Cagliostro. There is no absolute ruler who is not the bearer of an ideology. He is in fact the intermediary between the masses and the ideological illusion, and behind the ideology there is always a phantasy of narcissistic assumption.

Therefore the ruler partakes more of the omnipotent mother than of the father. He is like Moses returning from Sinai having seen God; his face is radiant because some of the splendour of the divinity has touched it. (Freud, commenting on this episode from the Bible writes that 'some of the *mana* had been transferred on to him, just as happens with the intermediary among primitive people'.) Nazism has often been compared to a religion, the mass rallies at Nuremberg to the celebration of Mass and Hitler to a high priest. In fact such a cult takes as its object the mother-goddess (*Blut und Boden*) rather than the father. In this kind of group one is witness to a real eradication of the father and the paternal world as well as of all oedipal derivatives. As far as Nazism is concerned, the return to nature, to ancient Germanic mythology represents an aspiration to fusion with the omnipotent mother.

Given this perspective, it is easier to understand how the superego, as indeed the mature ego ideal, may be so violently and completely set aside, whenever the Illusion has been made operative within a human grouping. If the reunification of ego and ideal is possible, all that has been acquired in the course of development becomes of no use, even a positive liability (because it has been acquired over time, by reason of the gap separating ego and ideal). Joseph Sandler, in his paper on the superego (1959), notes that

> situations do exist in which the ego can and will totally disregard the standards and precepts of the superego, if it can gain a sufficient quantity of narcissistic support elsewhere. We see this impressive phenomenon in the striking changes in ideals, character, and morality which may result from the donning of a uniform and the feeling of identity with a group. If narcissistic support is available in sufficient quantity from an identification with the ideals of a group, or with the ideals of a leader, then the superego may be completely disregarded and its functions taken over by the group ideals, precepts and behaviour. If these group ideals permit a direct gratification of instinctual wishes, then a complete character transformation

may occur; and the extent to which the superego can be abandoned in this way is evident in the appalling atrocities committed by the Nazis before and during the last war.

I cannot but be in agreement with Sandler, since I would emphasize the narcissistic return which serves to underlie the 'project' of groups that are based on an ideology. On the other hand, it seems to me that the capacity for committing atrocities (in so far as they represent an instinctual gratification) is not only the result of adopting the moral criteria of the group (which take the place of a personal superego), but the necessary consequence of the ideology of the group. Whatever stands in the way of attaining the Illusion must disappear. Now, since the goal of the Illusion is the idealization of the ego and there can be no idealization of the ego without projection, the objects receiving the projections must be hunted down and annihilated. I do not think it sufficient to say that the murder is then committed in the name of the superego and hence it becomes legitimate. I think that it is undertaken above all in the name of the ideal, as in the case of the Infidels murdered by the Crusaders on the road to Jerusalem. Any reactivation of the Illusion is thus ineluctably followed by a blood bath, provided only that the group has the means to match its violence. The principle of political machiavellism that 'the end justifies the means' is indeed an idealist principle that is applied each time the Illusion is reactivated. The end (the coming together of ego and ideal) justifies the means (annihilates the superego). 'Liberty, how many crimes are committed in your name!' is a cry that still resounds. (One has only to think of substitutes for 'liberty' such as Purity, Happiness, Greatness, Justice, Equality, Revolution, etc.)

It is important to emphasize that the members of the groups I have in mind are not necessarily together in the same place. It is not just a matter of actual groupings but also of individuals (constituting potential gatherings) united by an identical political, mystical or politico-mystical conviction (a religion in its etymological sense) that reaches beyond times when they are actually met together. The regression that operates in these groups is not therefore entirely prompted by particular physical conditions (those Anzieu describes in his article: being in an enclosed space, cut off from the outside world, etc.) although these may encourage it. For example, in May, 1968, Girod de l'Ain entitled an article in *Le Monde* on the occupation of the Sorbonne by students: 'Le Bateau ivre'. His metaphor demonstrates his intuitive sense of the intra-uterine (the boat) and elated (drunk) nature of the group regression.

The regression seems to me, on the other hand, to be very closely linked to the Illusion whose arrival is promised by the leader. If one considers that this promise stimulates the wish for the fusion of ego and ideal by way of regression and induces the ego to melt into the omnipotent primary object, to encompass the entire universe — Federn's cosmic ego (1952) — one can understand, in a general way, that the propensity to a loss of the ego's boundaries makes the individual particularly liable to identify himself not only with each member of the group but with the group formation as a whole. His megalomania finds its expression in this, each person's ego being extended to the whole group. The members of the group lose their individuality and begin to resemble ants or termites. This loss of personal characteristics is all the more necessary, because it contributes to the homogenization of the group as a whole. It thus allows each member to feel himself to be, not a minute, undifferentiated particle of a vast whole, but, on the contrary, identified with the totality of the group, thereby conferring on himself an omnipotent ego, a colossal body. The sports meetings of young people in totalitarian countries where, with the help of streamers or coloured placards a group of individuals create immense slogans or gigantic portraits, is a manifestation of this fusion of the individual ego in the collectivity. But whereas an observer who is stranger to the group would suppose that a narcissistic loss must accompany the fact of being reduced in this way to representing only a miniscule fragment of a monumental design, the exaltation of the participants (and of the crowd of spectators who also share the same illusion) indicates that, unconsciously, the psychic ego of each individual has been extended to the entirety of those who make up the crowd.

This extension of the ego to the group allows the individuals who constitute it to taste in anticipation (or rather through a sort of hallucinatory wish fulfilment) the joy of the reunification of the ego and the ego ideal. The group is at one and the same time ego, primary object, and ego ideal finally intermingled.

In *Group Psychology and the Analysis of the Ego* (1921) Freud attributes reality testing to the ego ideal. In *The Ego and the Id* (1923) he attributes it to the ego. It seems, however, that in the group situation this reality testing may be entrusted to the ego ideal, as represented by the group and the leader, who are charged with the promotion and maintenance of the Illusion. The individual ego (which, as I have just tried to show, has in any case fused with the group) makes over its prerogatives to the group. What the group as a whole deem to be true and just, becomes true and just. Anyone who does not think like the group is excluded, driven off, killed or declared mad.

In *L'Incinérateur de Cadavres*, which I mentioned earlier, a distraught woman makes episodic appearances accompanied by her husband who attempts, in vain, to restrain her outbursts. Thus one sequence of the film — an allegorical representation of the concentration camps — shows a fair in which wax figures play out bloody historical scenes in dumb show (as in the Musée Grevin). One of these figures holds a knife which he plunges into the back of another wax model with a jerky movement of the arm, as if operated by a clockwork mechanism. At this moment the woman begins to scream, 'It's blood, real blood ; I said it was!' Her husband tries to silence her and promptly leads her away, saying to the crowds gathered round the wax figures, 'She's completely mad.' It goes without saying that the wax figures represent the deportees who have been stripped of their humanity. More exactly, it is the victim-executioner relationship that is thus made unreal (Cf. Anna O . . ., in Freud and Breuer, 1895: 'All the people she saw seemed like wax figures without any connection with her.') Only the woman sees them as beings of flesh and blood. She represents the isolated individual whose ego has not delegated its reality testing function to the group. But reality, at that point, becomes the reality of the group as representative of the ego ideal, and it is then the person who has not made over to it the function of reality testing who is considered to be mad. (I would not like this example to be considered as lending support to the anti-psychiatry movement, whose aim is itself deeply ideological, in the sense of 'seeking to promote the Illusion'.) As the film gradually unfolds, the woman's appearances become more and more infrequent and towards the end she disappears whilst her husband tries desperately to find her, an indication that reality testing has passed entirely into the hands of the group. Everybody has become 'rhinocéros', as in Ionesco's Rhinocéros, a play in which he shows the establishment of totalitarianism. And the group will only accord the seal of reality to that which tends in the direction of Illusion.

It is indeed impossible for a group based upon an ideology not to be proselytising and not to seek to destroy not only its enemies, not only the objects of projection mentioned earlier, but also all those who remain outside it. Since they do not enter into the game of those who uphold the illusion, they represent a fault in the illusion itself. Since they do not abandon reality testing to the incense-bearers of Illusion, this is *ipso facto* thrown into question ('those who are not with us are against us'). It is thus essential to reduce those who are indifferent (and the sceptics) and to oblige them to cede to the 'believers' the function of reality testing (*Der Führer hat immer recht*, 'The party is always right'.)

Even under ordinary circumstances we can very easily cede reality testing to the group or at least to another: when we 'don't believe our eyes', we then readily ask a companion, 'Do you see what I see down there?' pointing out the object the sight of which we find disturbing or surprising. This is done as a control of the external (real) character of our perception (Cf. Freud, 'Negation', 1925). But it only works in the absence of 'group madness', of induced or shared hallucination.

In *The Gold Rush* a comic effect is drawn from the reverse tendency, leading to the absolute maintenance of reality testing by the ego, when the cabin, having slipped during the night, finds itself in the morning perched on the edge of the precipice and beginning to tilt dangerously. Chaplin then blames his hangover. (Thus he attributes his external perception to an internal perception, the reverse process to what generally takes place when reality testing is failing.) When his companion tells him anxiously, 'The house is moving,' he replies calmly: 'I know, it's my stomach' (this is the post-synchronized version).

Reality testing as effected through confirmation by the group of an individual perception is implicit in the description of the affect experienced by Freud at the time of his journey to America (*An Autobiographical Study*, Freud, 1925): 'As I stepped on to the platform at Worcester to deliver my *Five Lectures on Psycho-Analysis* it seemed like the realization of some incredible day-dream: psycho-analysis was no longer a product of delusion, it had become a valuable part of reality.'

It is understandable that it is both dangerous and wearing not to submit oneself to the rule of the group, to be a 'spoil-sport'. If it isn't always life that is put at risk, one does see one's supply of narcissistic gratification drying up and becomes a pariah condemned to solitude, who no longer has any right to the love of his own kind. However, there is always someone who will say: *Eppur si muove*, or 'that doesn't mean it can't still exist'. One might well think that such a person has not only a much more firmly rooted oedipal superego but that, as I have attempted to describe in the chapter on the development of the ego ideal, his ego ideal has cathected maturation itself. Despite the suffering that lack of love would mean to anybody, he finds some narcissistic gratification in the very fact of not having succumbed to the seduction of Illusion.

As I have said previously, the point of the psychoanalytic process is not to promise fulfilment of the Illusion. Grunberger has shown (1956) that the co-ordinates of the psychoanalytic situation induce narcissistic regression and the projection of the patient's narcissism (his ego ideal) onto the analyst. This can only refer to the maturative ego ideal, since if the patient remained attached to resolving the fusion of ego and ego ideal via the mode of illusion, the analytic process would remain blocked. Instinctual integrations could never be achieved and narcissism, far from constituting a driving force in the process, would represent the main brake.

A study of 'analyzability' could legitimately be based upon the quality of the ego ideal in candidates for analysis. Even the selection of future analysts could benefit from taking account of this criterion, for want of which the analysis, experienced initially as promising fulfilment of the Illusion, would be decathected at the first occasion in favour of any mysticism whatsoever, or of any dissident form of psychoanalysis itself (all dissensions sharing in the Illusion).

I think that by taking this factor into account, we are in a better position to understand the motives underlying Freud's painful experience of the dissensions he describes in 'On the History of the Psycho-analytic Movement (Freud, 1914):

> The disappointment that they caused me might have been averted . . . I knew very well of course that anyone may take flight at his first approach to the unwelcome truths of analysis; I had always myself maintained that everyone's understanding of it is limited by his own repressions (or rather, by the resistances which sustain them) so that he cannot go beyond a particular point in his relation to analysis. But I had not expected that anyone who had reached a certain depth in his understanding of analysis could renounce that understanding and lose it. And yet daily experience with patients had shown that total rejection of analytic knowledge may result whenever a specially strong resistance arises at any depth in the mind . . . I had to learn that the very same thing can happen with psycho-analysts as with patients in analysis.

Furthermore, in those moments when the illusion is activated by the social context, analysis becomes impossible for certain patients in so far as the competition between the long road that psychoanalysis offers as a way of achieving the — very relative — fusion of ego ideal and ego (the gap can never be closed entirely) and the short route offered by any mystic is to the disadvantage of psychoanalysis. The ego ideal of the patients in question will not cathect (or only very little) the analysis and the analyst, but will attach itself to the ideological group that the patient belongs to.

In his book on groups, Bion (1961) writes about the hostility of the (dependent) group towards the aims of the group: 'The nature of this hostility can be best apprehended if it is considered as a hostility to all scientific method and therefore as hostility to any activity that might appear to be approaching this ideal.' He also mentions the demand for magic in this type of group (and that the leader be a magician). I think that this is true for any group in which the Illusion has been re-activated.

Gustave Bychowski (1969) has shown — through clinical examples — the impact of the 'social climate' on the resistances of certain patients. According to the author, adherence to a political group, independent of its ideology and motivation —however noble this might be — allows the individual in analysis to idealize his own inclinations and phantasies. (This idealization might be compared to the perverse process described earlier.)

The use of the social climate to rationalize resistance to analysis can be observed from time to time in the treatment of homosexuals: 'Their tendency to organize themselves and to claim public approval helps many individuals to consider their perversion not as an illness but as a different or even superior form of human existence.' (In other words, the group confirms the patient's avoidance of development and the identifications he has made and helps him idealize his pregenitality. It is certainly no coincidence if the examples chosen by the author all relate to the perversion in which, as I have suggested, there is a particular difficulty at the level of the ego ideal.)

Bychowski considers that it would have been impossible to

analyse certain individuals at periods in history that would have supplied ample fuel to their resistances, particularly those who would have been involved in wars of religion or fanatical political movements. If there is a concordance between individual regression and that of the group, says the author, and if the system of values of the one and the other are analogous, the individual's regression and system of values find support in the group and their reversibility is brought into question. It becomes difficult to establish a therapeutic alliance. Serge Lebovici, in a spoken contribution to an advanced seminar in January 1970, told of difficulties of the same order that came up in certain treatments, in particular of adolescents. I think that an examination of the role of the ego ideal in these phenomena permits, not a resolution of the difficulty the analyst finds himself faced with, but, at least so I hope, the chance of understanding it better. Contrary to what is said, not everything can be analysed, and the possibilities are infinitely reduced for the analyst whose patient has not projected his narcissism on to him.

It goes without saying that the structure of the collective groupings that I am attempting to describe in this chapter is particularly regressive, and is a structure that is not found in those groups that do not depend upon an ideology. I would not include as an ideology those systems of thought that do not promise fulfilment of the Illusion. A group of ideas (a government policy for example, a programme having limited objectives) does not, in this perspective, constitute an ideology in the full sense of that term. Thus, in other groups, the leader may have the role of a father, as in the Freudian schema, or even that of simply a delegate of the sibship who, in the collective phantasy, may take on the figure of father or hero (in the sense that Freud, after Rank, uses this in *Group Psychology and the Analysis of the Ego* [1921]: he who has vanquished the father and taken his place, a strong support for everyone's ego ideal). On the other hand, in groups based upon 'the Illusion', the leader fulfils, in relation to the members of the group, the role that the mother of the future pervert plays in relation to her child when she gives him to believe that he has no need either to grow up, or to identify himself with his father, thus causing his incomplete maturation to coincide with his ego ideal.

Following my paper on 'Le Rossignol de l'Empereur de Chine', E. Kestemberg pointed out to me that I had not spoken about the role of the music master (the authority who declares 'that the artificial bird was much better than the real nightingale, not only as regarded the outside with all the diamonds, but the inside too'; and who 'wrote five and twenty volumes about the artificial bird; the treatise was very long, and written in all the most difficult Chinese characters. Everybody said they had read and understood it, for otherwise they would have been reckoned stupid and then their bodies would have been trampled upon'). Today I would reply to her perceptive comment that the music master, who incites the crowd to prefer the 'fake' (the illusion) to the 'real', plays precisely the role of leader as I am attempting to define it here.

In his book on groups, Bion writes about groups which show 'an aggressive rejection of the process of development . . . In the group one notices that what the members would wish to substitute for the group process would be to be able to arrive perfectly equipped, like adults who would know instinctively, without the need for any development or learning, how to live, act and take up a position in the group.' In my view this rejection of the process of maturation does not only apply to group processes, but also reflects the desire to evade personal development through the magic of the leader-magician (Cf. above). Therefore, rather than classify groups according to their size or their level of organization, I would propose a classification that took account of their relationship to the Illusion. One could in this way make an essential distinction between ideological groups and others, the latter retaining to a greater or lesser degree the oedipal dimension of the psyche, whilst the former tend towards primary narcissism and hence to an eclipsing of that which has been gained in the course of development.

A. Besançon (1971) has compared ideology itself to perversion:

Perverse knowledge is based upon a denial that permits the avoidance of an unbearable perception (the sight of the female genital organs) . . . In order to keep open the road to pleasure, knowledge has become false knowledge. It is demanded of it that it affirm that castration is a lie, that the law of separation attaching to the father, in the oedipal triangle, has no force, no existence, such that the mourning of infantile pleasure may be avoided . . . To be able to carry the motion of the wish immediately without the delay imposed by mourning, temporary renunciation, the changing of object and material and cognitive action; to spare oneself knowledge of the danger through a false knowledge that presents the danger as non-existent, such would be the initial manoeuvre that develops subsequently in the intellectual perversions of the adult.

That ideology functions as a perverse equivalent of, and is at the same time synonymous with, Illusion (that is to say, with a fallacious promise of fusion between ego and ideal) may perhaps allow us to illuminate somewhat the difference between sublimation and idealization, introduced by Freud in his 1914 paper.

5. The Ego Ideal, Sublimation and the Creative Process

Mme A. D . . . had been sold a tiny dog on the street. She went home and put the dog down to go and fetch some water. She came back to find the dog perched on a picture frame. It was a rat in the skin of a dog.

Jean Cocteau, *Opiums*

We are naturally led to examine the relation between this forming of an ideal and sublimation. Sublimation is a process that concerns object libido and consists in the instinct's directing itself towards an aim other than, and remote from, that of sexual satisfaction; in this process the accent falls upon deflection from sexuality. Idealization is a process that concerns the *object*; by it that object, without any alteration in its nature, is aggrandized and exalted in the subject's mind. Idealization is possible in the sphere of ego-libido as well as in that of object-libido. For example, the sexual overvaluation of an object is an idealization of it. In so far as sublimation describes something that has to do with the instinct, and idealization something to do with the object, the two concepts are to be distinguished from each other.

The formation of an ego ideal is often confused with the sublimation of instinct, to the detriment of our understanding of the facts. A man who has exchanged his narcissism for homage to a high ego ideal has not necessarily on that account succeeded in sublimating his libidinal instincts. It is true that the ego ideal demands such sublimation, but it cannot enforce it; sublimation remains a special process which may be prompted by the ideal but the execution of which is entirely independent of any such prompting ('On Narcissism: an Introduction', Freud, 1914).

I have tried to show in the chapter on the relationship between the ego ideal and perversions that the pervert idealizes his instincts; and, indeed, in 1905 Freud had emphasized precisely this idealization of instinct by the pervert. The concept of idealization of instincts is also present in Fenichel (1934), who called one of the chapters of his work, 'Rationalization and Idealization of Instinctual Impulses', and refers to 'perverted ideals'. The same author also writes about 'a type of instinctual idealization' in relation to asocial behaviour and acting-out. M. Balint, in the article referred to above (1948), has no hesitation either in applying the concept of idealization to the instincts, as also Mark Kanzer (1957), who refers to 'the adolescent's attempt to idealize his erotic impulses' (similarly G. Bychowski, 1969). However, this concept of an idealization of instinct does not, to my mind, fundamentally alter the distinction introduced by Freud in 1914 between sublimatory processes and those governed by the ego ideal without concomitant sublimation. Indeed, even if idealization can apply equally to instinct and object, idealization cannot of itself modify the nature of the instinct. This is what Freud already seemed to be arguing in 1914, although it should be recalled that the theory of sublimation was far from being fixed by this time — if indeed it ever was subsequently. (Here I am only concerned with sublimation in so far as it relates to the ego ideal. It would require a separate work to undertake a more complete study of this concept, one of the most interesting and most ill-defined in psycho-analytic literature. At the end of the present work the reader can find a bibliography of Freud's writings on sublimation compiled by Paulette Letarte, who has also written an interesting, though unpublished, review of the concept.)

Until 1914 sublimation is essentially defined by Freud as a 'diversion of sexual instinctual forces from sexual aims and their direction to new ones' (*Three Essays*, 1905). The accent is immediately put on the alteration of the aim of the instinct in this process. In 1908 Freud repeats this definition but makes it more precise:

> The sexual instinct . . . places extraordinarily large amounts of force at the disposal of civilized activity, and it does this in virtue of its especially marked characteristic of being able to displace its aim without materially diminishing in intensity. This capacity to exchange its originally sexual aim for another one, which is no longer sexual but which is psychically related to the first aim, is called the capacity for *sublimation* (' "Civilized" Sexual Morality').

It is however, fairly clear that the idea of an 'alteration of the aim' of the instinct leaves open the question of whether the instinct itself undergoes any real modification. The 1914 text, by underlining the difference between idealization and sublimation, hints at the possibility of a transformation of the actual nature of the instinct in sublimation and hence the need for a complement to the theory of sublimation, a complement which was not in fact to be introduced until *The Ego and the Id* (1923).

However, as from 1911, in the Schreber case, Freud is already writing about a 'resexualization' of the social instincts as a precipitating factor in paranoia, implying a preceding desexualization of the homosexual instinct. But Freud does not as yet describe the actual process of desexualization and its relation to narcissism. It is only, in fact, in 1923 that Freud shows the process of sublimation to be linked to the desexualization of the instinct itself (and no longer simply an exchange of a non-sexual aim for a sexual one). This desexualization is made possible by the transformation of sexual libido into narcissistic libido, via a phase in which the libido is withdrawn into the ego.

Indeed it was precisely the introduction of the concept of narcissism which gave Freud the basis for his hypothesis of the existence, in the course of the process of sublimation, of a phase of withdrawal of libido into the ego. However, although this argument seems to be directly deducible from the text, it does not seem to have been clear to Freud by 1914, and the distinction that he draws at that time between sublimation, involving the instinct, and idealization, involving the object, seems to my mind to be the result of his not having at his disposal the concept of desexualization. It is this which allows the distinction to be made between idealization and sublimation of an instinct, according to whether there has been sufficient desexualization or an absence of real desexualization. The important point for our present topic seems to me to be the role which is henceforward accorded to narcissistic libido in sublimation, although it is not to be forgotten that the instinct in question does have its origin in the id and that, after transformation in the ego, it continues on towards an object.

The process of creativity does not seem to differ at all, in terms of the ends pursued, in cases where the impulse to creativity comes from the ego ideal, without any corresponding sublimation of the instincts, and in those where an adequate sublimation has been achieved. Indeed, in all instances the creative act is prompted, in my opinion, by the (narcissistic) desire to rediscover a lost sense of unity (see Chasseguet-Smirgel, 1963) and represents therefore, at a certain level, a means of accomplishing the bringing together of the ego and its ideal. The deeper the wound resulting from the lack of equation between narcissistic aspirations and the real ego's situation, the more imperious will be the necessity to put into action efforts to bridge this fatal gap. It can immediately be inferred from this that problems of identification will occupy a central position. Indeed, as we have seen, the development of the ego takes place through projection of the omnipotence which has had to be surrendered onto the object, who thus becomes the personification of the child's first ego ideal. The object (the mother at this stage) has the formidable task of helping the child move on from this first ideal to other increasingly evolved ideals by an integration of the different phases of development, an integration achieved through identification with the object carrying the ego ideal at the stage in question. I have underlined how necessary it is to dose frustration and gratification so that the child is neither tempted to regress nor to remain at the level he has reached. Each stage of development must offer sufficient satisfaction for the child to sense that the next will offer yet more, but not too much, so that his interest in, and curiosity about, new pleasures will be retained. The search for this balance constitutes the essence of education. The child's ego is thus enriched with successive introjects and (secondary) identifications which then militate against a regressive bringing together of ego and ideal through primary identification. These identifications serve to reduce the gap that exists between the ego and its ideal through the new acquisitions they bring. At the same time, introjection of the qualities of the object that the child wishes to resemble, and identification with the object carrying the ego ideal, allow the ego to be loved by the id: 'Look, you can love me too — I am so like the object' (Freud, 1923). It also enables regulation of what Anglo-Saxon authors call 'self-esteem', in other words, the affect that results from the greater or lesser discrepancy between the ego and its ideal.

Once at the oedipal stage the male child projects his ego ideal on to his father, as Freud describes in a well-known passage: 'A little boy will exhibit a special interest in his father; he would like to grow like him and be like him, and take his place everywhere. We may simply say that he takes his father as his ideal.' And also: 'We can only see that identification endeavours to mould a person's own ego after the fashion of the one that has been taken as a model' ('Identification', in *Group Psychology* . . . , Freud, 1921). Two years later Freud will stress the dual identification that takes place and the links between these identifications and the emergence of the superego:

> The child's parents, and especially his father, were perceived as the obstacle to a realization of his Oedipus wishes; so his infantile ego fortified itself for the carrying out of the

> repression by erecting this same obstacle within itself. It
> borrowed strength to do this, so to speak, from the father, and
> this loan was an extraordinarily momentous act. The
> superego retains the character of the father . . .

And again:

> But now that we have embarked upon the analysis of the ego
> we can give an answer to all those whose moral sense has been
> shocked and who have complained that there must surely be a
> higher nature in man: "Very true" we can say, "and here we
> have that higher nature, in this ego ideal or superego, the
> representative of our relation to our parents. When we were
> little children we knew these higher natures, we admired
> them and feared them; and later we took them into ourselves"
> ('The Ego and the Superego', in *The Ego and the Id*, Freud,
> 1923).

It should be recalled that when Freud introduced the concept of
the superego, in this very text, he did not differentiate it at all
from the ego ideal (or ideal ego).

The role of the latency period in the acquisition of the capacity
for sublimation is well known. Freud first writes about it as early
as the *Three Essays* (1905). He takes it up again subsequently, in
particular in 'The Dissolution of the Oedipus Complex' (1923).
As can be seen, oedipal identifications and the setting up of the
superego will have an important role to play in the process of
sublimation and hence in the creative act. Most of the analysts
who have studied the creative process — and in France I am
thinking particularly of Pierre Luquet (1963), Michel de M'Uzan
(1965), and Gérard Mendel (1964) — stress the importance of the
artist's identifications. Indeed, Mendel says, '*Artistic sublimation and
identification are indissolubly linked*' (his italics).

There is no 'great man' — artist, scholar, writer or thinker —
who has not had some model, some mentor, some spiritual father.
It is as if, in the realm of creativity, the most beautiful and most
unusual flower is that which also has its roots deep in the soil of

tradition. The great innovators have known the inspiration of being with those on to whom they have projected their ego ideal and whom they wish to resemble. Homosexual libido plays an important role here, and behind the exalted and admired figure it is easy to discern the father of either side of the oedipal phase. Freud's own work is the very epitome of originality, yet it owes much to influences that he never seeks to deny:

> At length, in Ernst Brücke's physiological laboratory, I found rest and full satisfaction — and men, too, whom I could respect and take as my models . . .

> The turning point came in 1882, when my teacher, for whom I felt the highest possible esteem, corrected my father's generous improvidence by strongly advising me, in view of my bad financial position, to abandon my theoretical career. I followed his advice . . . I was soon afterwards promoted to being a House Physician and worked in various departments of the hospital, among others for more than six months under Meynert, by whose work and personality I had been greatly struck while I was still a student . . .

> In the distance shone the great name of Charcot; so I formed a plan of first obtaining an appointment as University Lecturer on Nervous Diseases in Vienna and then of going to Paris to continue my studies . . .

> I became a student at the Salpetrière, . . . One day in my hearing Charcot expressed his regret that since the war he had heard nothing from the German translator of his lectures; he went on to say that he would be glad if someone would undertake to translate the new volume of his lectures into German, I wrote to him and offered to do so . . .

These few quotations from *An Autobiographical Study* (1925) show clearly the nature of Freud's relationship to his masters, a relationship in which he was not afraid of submitting himself to their authority. By projection on to the homosexual object, the ego ideal can in this way allow the object's qualities to be taken over.

Fain and Marty (1959) have given a brilliant description of the role of the homosexual drive both in development and in the analytic process, demonstrating how it favours identification with the object carrying the ego ideal, through an acceptance of the passive position. Nor did they fail to underline the impediments to this process of enrichment of the ego, emphasizing those cases in which the object is felt to be dangerous: 'If there is too much projection, the possibility of converting the object into something hopeful, an ego ideal, is ruined, since the field of consciousness is exclusively occupied by the menacing aspects of the object.' Such a situation implies a 'libidinal poverty of identifications'. The authors consequently consider the homosexual drive to be a 'drive connected with growth'. It might be noted at this point that, whilst the homosexual drive makes its appearance relatively late in the course of development, it has an important prehistory linked to the earliest identifications and introjects, having the breast and the mother as their object.

Fain and Marty also stress the consequences for the future development of the homosexual drive of a lack of narcissistic input from the primary object. Thus one can, to my mind, consider the beginnings of a synthesis of the component instincts as taking place at the time in the oedipal phase when the homosexual instinct comes into play, a synthesis which has not taken place in cases of manifest homosexuality.

If homosexual libido plays a decisive role in relation to the ego ideal, as the authors demonstrate, developing a point made in 'On Narcissism: an Introduction' (1914), if it assists the achievement of oedipal identifications, its role is no less decisive in relation to the setting up of the superego (in as much as this represents the internalization of the incest taboo) as we have noted earlier. I would like, then, to propose the following working hypothesis: those who have not succeeded in projecting their ego ideal on to their father and his penis (I am thinking here of the development of the male child) and whose identifications are, in consequence, defective, will be driven — for obvious narcissistic reasons — to attempt to acquire the identity they are lacking through various means, the creative act being one of them. The work created in this way will symbolize the phallus, the missing identity being equated with castration. The non-possibility of an identification with the father (or with paternal substitutes) will, however, mean that the person in question *fabricates* his work rather than *creates* it, and that it will, like himself, therefore not be bound by any family tie. The introjection of the father's qualities — symbolized by the introjection of his attributes — not having been effected, and the desires related to this process having been repressed and counter-cathected, the person will not have at his disposal the desexualized (sublimated) libido necessary for the creation of his work. The prime mover for this will therefore be the ego ideal, but the raw material employed will not have undergone any fundamental modification. *Nobody's son*, the person I am describing cannot 'father' an authentic work, drawing his life force from a rich and full libido. The identity that he assumes will necessarily be usurped since it will be based on a denial of his lineage. The symbolic phallus created in this way cannot but be itself factitious, that is to say, a fetish.

Here I would like to take up again, and expand, some of the propositions that I put forward in 'The Emperor of China's Nightingale' (1968), as I believe they are closely connected to the present subject. Idealization, viewed from the perspective that I then took, superimposes itself on the 'fake', whereas 'authentic' creativity implies a sublimation of the instincts. In an earlier work (1962) on the film of Alain Resnais and Alain Robbe-Grillet, *Last Year in Marienbad*, I attempted to delineate the essence of the 'fake'. The baroque decor (in Eugenio d'Ors' sense, most scenes from the film having been shot in the castles of Louis II of Bavaria) and Robbe-Grillet's directions in the film script, lend themselves particularly to a study of Illusion. The heavily worked mouldings, the complicated and convoluted cornices, the friezes, the sculptures filling the most insignificant parts of the walls and ceiling, the whole riot of stucco, earns the following commentary in Robbe-Grillet's scenario: 'As if all these mouldings and carvings were not enough to occupy these immense surfaces, there are "fake columns", "false doorways", "false pillars", "false perspectives", "false exits" added on to this orgy of ornamentation' (*L'Année dernière à Marienbad*, ciné-roman, Ed. de Minuit, quotation marks Robbe-Grillet's). I said then, in the light of the essay as a whole, that the use of trickery, of fakery, of trompe l'oeil, could be seen as an attempt at an evasion of obstacles (resulting from difficulties in object relations) by substituting the *form* of an artificial cathexis for *quality* of cathexis, any authentic cathexis remaining unattainable.

What I now want to underline is that we also find in the process of idealization an attempt at an evasion of obstacles, whereas sublimation implies a modification of the actual *quality* of the instinct. If I might be allowed a culinary metaphor which I think eloquently captures the difference between these two processes: the knowledgeable gourmet knows how to distinguish 'brilliant' cookery, of which he is suspicious, from authentic good cooking. The former generally consists of 'exotic' ingredients prepared in a complicated sauce, often flambéed in some expensive alcohol and served on a richly chased silver platter. In the case of wine, it might have bisulphite added or be tampered with in some other way, but whatever the case it will have been put into some special kind of glassware whose label — preferably in black and gold — bears some imaginative name with a good ring to it, either picturesque or pretentious: we are in the realm of idealization. We have had our eyes deceived, been dazzled, but what has actually been served up leaves much to be desired: it is 'mutton dressed as lamb', as the saying goes. One might also draw a parallel between this simple camouflaging of a substance that otherwise remains unchanged, and the name of the well-known Italian banking house 'Banco di Santo Spirito' (cf. equally the expression 'to sugar the pill').

In the case of sublimation it is the flesh of the animal itself that has been transformed, the preparation and the cooking of it that have made it delectable. It may well be that the plate on which it is brought is of humble earthenware and that the 'honest' wine that accompanies it makes do with an ordinary pitcher or bottle. In fact, the odds are high that it will be so: when the substance itself has undergone some intrinsic change there is that much less need to be concerned about appearances; whereas in the case of idealization this is all one has.

Of course the idealization of an object in the sense in which Freud uses the term in 1914, that is to say, the projection on to it of the ego ideal, is not to be confused with the creative process as I am seeking to define it here in relation to the 'fake', to Illusion. Indeed, the projection of the ego ideal on to an object does not constitute an act of creation and does not necessarily imply a desexualization of the instincts. In love it is, on the contrary, the repression of sexuality (which is in any case not the same as true desexualization) that constitutes a pathological process. When the ego ideal is projected on to a homosexual object choice, desexualization might take place, but this is still not the same as something being created, and the categories of 'authentic' and 'fake' cannot be applied in such an instance. It is, therefore, a matter of trying to make ego and ego ideal coincide whilst by-passing the process of sublimation which, as I have said, would imply an identification with the father. In other words, it is a matter of trying to spare oneself the conflicts linked to introjection.

I now want to turn to an examination of the different types of individuals — and hence the different psychic structures — who seek to do just this. In the chapter devoted to the problems of the pervert in relation to his ego ideal I tried to show how, abetted in this by his mother or by the particular circumstances of his personal history, he had come to project his ego ideal on to his pre-genital instinctual impulses and part objects, instead of projecting it on to his begetter with a view to identifying himself with him. The pervert has to maintain the deception that he need neither grow (since, such as he is, he is loved by his mother) nor take over his father's place (for he already has). If this deception is to be preserved it would require the non-existence of genitality.

Then the illusion of having taken his father's place — and of therefore having no cause to feel envious of him — would be quite in accordance with the truth. One would then end up with a situation in which all distinctions had been eroded — between the child and his father, between the child's small penis and the father's genital organ. Moreover, as we have seen, the refusal to acknowledge the difference between the generations is closely linked to the refusal to acknowledge the difference between the sexes. (If the mother has a penis and no vagina then she is complete and has no need of the father's penis, as J. McDougall has rightly emphasized.) The pervert is never entirely deceived about the fact that the father does possess a penis with prerogatives and capacities that the child himself lacks. Consequently, to maintain the illusion, he has to try and pass off his small pregenital penis as a genital penis by idealizing it. As I see it, the pervert's 'creation' achieves this end: it represents his own glorified phallus which, for want of an adequate identification with the father, cannot but be factitious, that is, a fetish.

This process can also be seen in other instances besides perversion. It occurs wherever there is a major difficulty in identification at the oedipal level, accompanied by a projection of the ego ideal on to primitive pregenital imagos and an absence of an ego ideal that encourages maturation (for specific historical reasons). All of this pushes the person into opting to maintain an illusion — a pretence — rather than attempting to do something about reducing the discrepancy, as the neurotic or the 'normal' person hopes to do. At one level it is legitimate to differentiate the perverse structure as such from other entities in which perverse sexuality is a feature, although the ego does not show all the characteristics of the pervert (as defined by J. McDougall). As regards our present subject it may, on the contrary, be of more interest to try and delineate the nucleus common to different nosological entities ranging from perversion itself through to certain character types including the psychopathic and even the addict. Close examination reveals them to be pathological manoeuvres in which acting-out is invariably a feature and in which the created 'work' itself can be seen as a form of acting-out serving to miraculously eliminate the divide separating water from wine, pregenital penis from genital penis, child from father.

Mark Kanzer (1957) has shown just how acting-out and sublimation differ in respect of identifications:

> In sublimation . . . we are accustomed to discover strong identifications and a greater ability to tolerate tensions — sublimations in themselves serving (1) as substitute satisfactions (2) as delay mechanisms and (3) as ultimate purveyors of objects for instinctual gratification. Where acting-out regresses from thought through fantasy to action, the reverse is the case in sublimation which, depending on identifications rather than immediate object possession for security, favours the internalization of motor discharge — i.e. a binding of energy that makes it an important influence in superego formation. The internalizing process is correlated with a replacement of external objects by symbols which are ultimately found on analysis to represent impersonalized parental figures.
>
> The creative intellectuality of sublimation marks the ability of the ego to integrate successfully on a complex level of development; acting-out on the other hand is characterized by disintegrative tendencies . . . From the standpoint of identification, there is assimilation of an idealized parent in sublimation, projection and destruction of the bad parent in the case of acting-out.

Summarizing his paper, the author writes: 'Faults in identification dispose to acting-out; successful identification strengthens internalizing and sublimating tendencies.' In an article written in 1956, Melitta Schmiedeberg presents a point of view similar to my attempt to define the nucleus common to a series of nosological entities which lie outside the neurotic and psychotic when she writes that, 'Certain delinquent acts can be classed wholly or partly as perversions or fetishisms.' These structures are precisely those which constitute a contra-indication for classical analysis, Julien Rouart (1968) having shown, in his important paper on acting-out, their 'anticathartic' nature. Sauguet's (1969) fruitful idea might also be thought of in this context, likening as it does the analytic process and the neurotic process, these structures falling outside the domain of both.

The work created by someone presenting the structural nucleus that I have been attempting to describe — however cut off it may be from its paternal roots (indeed for this very reason and however original it may claim to be) — will be essentially an imitation, a copy of the genital penis. This imitation is linked to the nature itself of the primitive identifications involved and to the absence of more evolved identifications, both oedipal and post-oedipal. The works of a number of authors, many of them noteworthy, will help me support my hypothesis. It is already quite some time since Hélène Deutsch, in her paper on the 'As if' structure (1934), described 'a relationship to life ... which is lacking in genuineness and yet outwardly runs along "as if" it were complete'. The first clinical example she gave was that of a young girl who was very gifted in art and who, during the course of her analysis, entered art school. The analyst received a report in which her teacher was impressed by the speed with which she had adopted his technique and manner of artistic perception, but there was an intangible something about her which left him uneasy and perplexed. He added that the girl had gone to another teacher, who used quite a different teaching approach, and that she had oriented herself to the new theory and technique with striking ease and speed. The 'as if' person's facility in swapping identifications is found again in their 'over-enthusiastic adherence to one philosophy being quickly and completely replaced by another contradictory one without the slightest trace of inward transformation'. Another patient with an analogous personality structure 'got drunk in low dives, participated in all kinds of sexual perversions, and felt just as comfortable in this underworld as in the pietistic sect, the artistic group, or the political movement in which she was later successively a participant'. A third patient, also artistically gifted, came into analysis with the (secret) hope of becoming an analyst. In fact, although she frequently spoke of her tremendous interest in child psychology and in Freud's theory and read widely on these subjects, her understanding of them was extraordinarily superficial and her interest entirely unreal. Her plan was to become an analyst by identification with her analyst. At the same time she acted out prostitution fantasies and indulged in a variety of sexual perversions. 'She emerged from these debauches by identification with some conventional person and achieved by this means a kind of sublimation, the form dependent on the particular object.'

A young homosexual who appeared to be quite gifted turned out, in fact, to be lacking in originality: 'Everything he wrote and said in scientific matters showed great formal talent but when he tried to produce something original it usually turned out to be a repetition of ideas which he had once grasped with particular clarity.' The author stresses that the apparently normal relationship of these people to the world corresponds to the child's aptitude for imitation and is only a mimesis. 'Common to all these cases is a deep disturbance of the process of sublimation which results both in a failure to synthesize the various infantile identifications into a single, integrated personality, and in an imperfect, one-sided, purely intellectual sublimation of the instinctual strivings.' Again according to Deutsch, 'the etiology of such conditions is related first, to a devaluation of the object serving as a model for the development of the child's personality'. The superego in such cases has been very inadequately internalized, the 'as if' person adopting the moral criteria of the object with which they are identified at the moment, for want of any independent internal criteria.

In a subsequent work (1955), the same author studied the case of 'The Impostor'. This is the account of the psychotherapy of a young man. Born ten years after his elder brother and eleven years after the eldest, he was adored by mother and brothers and was their 'darling toy'. The father, a powerful and formidable man, did not concern himself with the boy, leaving him entirely in his mother's hands. The two eldest having left home as a gesture of defiance, the father turned to the youngest, aged about four at the time, investing all his hopes in him, and lulling him with dreams of grandeur. He subsequently fell gravely ill, became a complete invalid, and died, separated from his son, five years later. Both before and during his treatment the young man took up a whole series of different activities. In all of these he played a role, dressing in a particular style and tinting his hair and eyebrows when being the gentleman farmer, playing the intellectual when he had a literary salon, etc. At times the imposture became quite evident, as when he altered his name in such a way that it was almost identical with the name of a celebrity. He was perpetually 'in pursuit of an identity . . . this denial of his own identity appears to me to be the chief motive for his actions, as is true in the case of other impostors'.

Having made a study of some well known impostors, the author shows that, whilst in certain cases they could have acquired prestige in their own names, they always chose someone else's, those of men whom they would have liked to resemble. Since one's name establishes which family one belongs to, it seems to me that a change of name is equivalent to a rejection of one's origins, that is to say of one's father and his attributes. The author suggests that because he was unable to sublimate, her patient 'was able to satisfy his fantasies of grandeur only in naive acting out, pretending that he was *really* in accordance with his ego ideal'. Amongst the activities the patient took up some were creative. Thus he started to write, to pursue some scientific research, to develop inventions.

Here again is an example of the creative process operating uniquely under the aegis of the ego ideal, with an absence of subsequent sublimations *because of* faults in identification, such that we find ourselves faced with the following paradox: the more a person experiences the gulf between the ego and its ideal as something painful, or fears its exposure, the more they will be tempted to use creativity as a way of healing what they experience to be a deep wound. For some people the gulf between ego and ideal is that much greater (although at times illusorily denied), because they have not been able to really integrate their identifications. The lacunae in the ego caused by these faulty identifications lead precisely to a disturbance of the capacity for sublimation. The 'work' created, having then the function of magically filling up these lacunae, it follows that for a considerable number of works — in diverse fields — the creative process will have been under the aegis of the ego ideal and that there will have been no fundamental modification of the instincts.

For Phyllis Greenacre (1958) there are three essential characteristics of the impostor:

(1)   there must be a dynamically active family romance;
(2)   there is a disturbance of the sense of identity and of reality;
(3)   there is a malformation of the superego involving both conscience and ideals.

Now, however overdetermined, one of the implications of the family romance is nonetheless often that of a rejection of one's family, of an attempt to break with the chain of generations and hence to take on a new (and false) identity. (These implications have been highlighted by Michel Soule in his lively work on adoption, 1968.) Samuel Novey defines it as follows: 'In this light the "family romance" would represent not only an attempt to protect against the oedipal dilemma through phantasy production, but would represent an attempt to establish one's own uniqueness and to underwrite the special purposefulness of one's existence. It represents a central example of man's flight from the idea of an existence bound to biological necessity.' As for the family constellation of the impostor, Phyllis Greenacre describes it in very similar terms to that of the pervert, the mother being very attached to her child, as if he were part of herself. The father ceases to exist. 'The child is placed in a position of definite superiority to the father.' Furthermore, Greenacre writes, 'I have elsewhere indicated that if, under these conditions [i.e. those of the child whose family constellation is like that outlined above], the child has been exposed to the sight of the genitals of an adult male, it may produce in fantasy an illusory enlargement of its own phallus, which becomes indeed a kind of local imposture involving the organ and contributes to the already forming tendency to general imposture.'

The impostors cited by Phyllis Greenacre were often creative artists (and one can think of some well-known examples in the field of painting: Van Meegeren, de Hory, Maklat, etc.). The sexuality of the impostors she describes is generally perverse and sometimes linked to drug addiction. To my mind imposture (whether via a creative work or not) can best be understood in general terms as answering to the need felt by some, as I have tried to show, to pass off their little penis as a large genital phallus.

Abraham's impostor (1925), rather than acquire a penis through a progressive identification with his father, obtained (immediately) a symbolic phallus by denying his origins. Wanting to have a 'pencil box in multi-coloured lacquer ware', or a pencil of a particular colour, he went to a stationer's and passed himself off as the son of a general living in the area. He was immediately given the things he desired. Abraham writes of him: 'He was unable to exalt his father into an ideal figure. On the contrary we saw how from an early age the wish for another father dominated him.'

Annie Reich, in three seminal articles (1953, 1954, 1960), describes disturbances in identifications, and the relationship of these to the ego ideal and sublimations. She writes of the 'magic identification' with the idealized parent that may replace the (more evolved) wish to be like him. 'The formation of the superego is based upon acceptance of reality. In fact, it represents the most powerful attempt to adjust to reality. The ego ideal, on the other hand, is based upon the desire to cling to a denial of the ego's limitations.' In normal development the ego ideal is modified, there is a growing acceptance of reality and increasing fusion with the superego. The cases she looks at do not put before us examples of real identifications, but of superficial imitations.

The author gives an example to demonstrate the distinction between imitation and identification: it is imitation (or magical identification) when the child holds the newspaper *like* his father. It is identification when the child learns to read. Imitation means trying to *be* the envied parent and not necessarily to *become* it. This is the domain of magical achievements.

> From many points of view the child cannot be entirely like the adults. Normally a capacity for self-evaluation develops which pushes in the direction of the gradual achievement of identification . . . This is the normal ego ideal . . . In pathological cases, instead of firm identifications, there is a persistence of imitations, of the desire to be like the parent without the accompanying desire to do what is necessary in order to become it.

The megalomanic ego ideal, according to A. Reich, at times shows crude sexual characteristics that have not been subject to any sublimation. Sublimation is often deficient. The need for narcissistic aggrandisement is linked to profound fears of bodily destruction and castration. Inflation of the ego serves as a magical denial of castration. At times the narcissistic phantasies intended to deny castration are at odds with the exigencies of the superego 'since they contain numerous unsublimated instinctual elements'. This narcissism is above all a body one; and, says the author, any real modification of body narcissism depends above all on the capacity for sublimation.

In her 1954 article, Edith Jacobson also differentiates precocious, magical, preoedipal identifications, which she sees as similar to H. Deutsch's 'as if' character, from what she calls the true identifications of the ego, which are linked to representations of self and object. At first the ego ideal works in favour of the attempt to be one with the object (the mother) and only later fosters the attempt to become *like* the object. Freud, in the *Interpretation of Dreams* (chapter IV), draws a distinction between identification and imitation: 'Thus identification as not simple imitation, but assimilation.'

In his paper on early identification, Pierre Luquet (1961) describes with great subtlety this process of assimilation:

> In the absence of any obstacle assimilation is complete, the function then being taken on by the ego united with the object. The latter becomes a part of the ego. The ego, recognizing itself in the object, can see itself having the object's function. It is as if the instrumentality of the ego were revealed after this unity had been reestablished, as if the ego needed to pass via the object in order to be able to see itself as having its function. There is a sense of fusion with the object to the benefit of the ego. As I would put it, there has been *assimilation*.

The other end of the scale would be what Luquet describes as 'imago-oid introjection', when the object is internalized but not merged with the ego.

Gaddini (1969) distinguishes imitation from both introjection and identification (which for him seems to correspond to assimilation as defined by Luquet). Imitation is seen as being linked to unconscious phantasies of omnipotence. 'In my experience . . . the mechanism of imitation . . . is practically constant in character disturbances in general, and it may be found very frequently in male and female homosexuality, and also in fetishism and transvestism.' Here again one finds a number of disturbances presenting the same common nucleus as I have described previously. He suggests that the prototype of imitation is hallucinatory wish-fulfilment. In other words, it is a magical way to *be* the object. 'To imitate not only does not mean to introject, but may be a way of defending oneself from the anxiety provoked by introjective conflicts.' In the cases with which we are concerned here, however, the attempt to deal with the fault in the ego resulting from the lack of introjection and assimilation of the father and his penis — an unconscious process which implies a relationship involving love, admiration and physical proximity — does not take the form of an imitation of the father and his paternal attributes, narcissistically decathected. It involves, rather, an attempt to sever completely any filial ties. Imitation would be concerned with the essential genital phallus, as phantasied by the person. Models, in so far as there are any, would be distant and abstract. When they are personified, it would not be in someone representing an idealized father substitute but in someone, precisely, who had himself succeeded in avoiding introjective conflicts and in conferring upon himself a magic, autonomous phallus or someone who promises this to his followers whilst sparing them the painful process of development. We have already met such a figure: the 'ideological' leader such as I have attempted to describe in relation to the group. He is someone having one of the kinds of structure that we have been concerned with here and would, then, become the disciple of a 'magus' for want of (or prior to) becoming a magus himself. As I have said, the 'ideological' leader is someone who can make the illusion — the promise of a coming together of ego and ideal — sparkle. The pervert, and those with a related structure, will always be trying in one way or another to bring about a realization of the phantasy that lies behind the infantile sexual theory of sexual phallic monism, that is, the dual negation of the difference between the sexes and between the generations. The theory of sexual phallic monism is the infantile prototype of their adult ideologies. It is an attempt on their part to spare themselves the process of development. Hélène Deutsch says of her impostor that 'he could not wait for the process of growth to take place'.

In the definitions that Reich, Jacobson and Gaddini give of imitation as against identification, there is always the idea of magically being able, not to *become* big, but to *be* big immediately, thus by-passing the process of maturation. Now, the only penis one can possess without going through the process of development that leads to genitality is a fecal penis. Someone with the structural nucleus that I have attempted to delineate will *fabricate* a work that will represent an idealized fecal penis, that is to say a fecal penis that he will attempt to pass off as a genital penis, or better, as superior to a genital penis.

As it is only authentic sublimation based on oedipal

identifications that would allow a real transformation of anality, a counter-cathexis of the instincts used in the act of creation becomes necessary. One of the possible consequences of this counter-cathexis is that the work may take on a 'precious' quality. 'Preciosity' reappears periodically in art and literature if not also in the thought of the time itself. It does not, however, always enjoy the popularity that it did in Western Europe at the end of the sixteenth and in the seventeenth century, whether it be called gongorism, concettism, euphemism or marinism. In works which seek to mask anality by idealization, but which do not achieve any true metamorphosis of it in the sense Fenichel means ('in sublimation the original instinct disappears'), it is impossible to detect any trace of what M. Fain (1966) has called that 'long, backward-looking incline'. A verse of *Ulalume*, any Paul Klee or Nicolas de Staël drawing, a few chords by Bach take us in an instant through vast areas of the psyche and leave us marvelling at the wealth of emotion poured out through a whole series of condensed images that are spread before us, all issuing from primitive instinct. Like a deep-sea diver discovering a lost kingdom, the work suddenly illuminates the unconscious, and its light spreads right to the surface. Despite the immediate, global nature of the phenomenon, by breaking it down into its elements we can detect the displacements, the successive symbols and the condensed images which gave rise to the final, conscious form of expression.

One of the main sources of the aesthetic experience seems to lie in the contrast between the wealth and multiplicity of the emotions, affects and images lying along the whole length of that 'long, backward-looking incline', and the simple, allusive, even elliptical nature of the expression. In short, a part of the satisfaction for the admirer of the work comes from this economy of means. Alternatively it may be that the long, backward-looking incline ('the thread of the wish' that Freud also mentions, in relation, on this occasion, to imaginative activity and its connection with the three moments of time which our ideation involves — 'Creative Writers and Day-Dreaming', Freud, 1908) can be to some extent flattened out, secondary elaboration generally reduced, and the emotional impact can then proceed from this very exposure of the primary processes. This is one way, to my mind, of distinguishing, in rather cavalier fashion, and taking the terms in their broadest sense, between classicism and romanticism.

Both economy of means and exposure of the primary processes are missing from the work governed solely by the ego ideal. In this event the work will lack 'depth' (in the sense that there is a reduced 'backward-looking incline') and will not arouse in us the same wealth of emotions and images, arising from the primary instincts. In this case the repression and counter-cathexis to which the creator has subjected his instincts deprives us of the enjoyment of our own instincts (through a contemplation of the work) which is possible only through the intermediary of sublimation. On the contrary, the creator will often attempt to skirt round the internal obstacles that oppose the free outpouring of affects and of the dense and varied images to which they are linked, by means of an overemphasis on expressiveness, an abuse of metaphor known as bombast. This bombast is not to be confused with a flourishing of primary process. On the contrary, when the form affects what may be derived from it this represents, in fact, a real impoverishment.

In a letter to Abraham (1914), Freud reports an example of Jungian technique passed on to him by Jones who himself had it from a patient. Jung apparently interpreted the amorous transference of his patient by explaining to her 'that she wasn't really in love with the analyst but that she was beginning, for the first time, to struggle to understand a UNIVERSAL IDEA in the Platonic sense of the term.' In his reply Abraham says that he recognizes in the Jungian technique the distinction that Freud had made (in that same year) between processes governed by the ego ideal and those governed by sublimation. This technique he sees as promoting conformity to the ego ideal and avoiding sublimation.

Indeed the whole of Jung's thought can be seen as an 'idealizing' endeavour. Jung and his followers traced in detail the way in which the material of sexual ideas belonging to the family-complex and incestuous object choice is made use of in representing the highest ethical and religious interests of man — that is, they have illuminated an important instance of the sublimation of the erotic instinctual forces and of their transformation into trends which can no longer be called *erotic* ('On the History . . .', Freud, 1914).

The Jungians, as Freud shows, could not agree with 'ethics and religion . . . being sexualized'. Ethics and religion were not allowed to be sexualized, but had to be something 'higher' from the start. But as the ideas contained in them seemed undeniably to be descended from the Oedipus and family complex, it is claimed that these complexes themselves do not mean what they seem to be expressing, in order to be able to reconcile them with the 'abstract trains of thought of ethics and religious mysticism'. The Oedipus complex became something abstract and disembodied. The mother in it symbolized the unattainable (and not the unattainable the mother); 'the father who is killed in the Oedipus myth is the "inner" father, from whom one must set oneself free in order to become independent'.

In 1924 Freud also wrote: 'The suggestion that art, religion and social order originated in part in a contribution from the sexual instincts was represented by the opponents of analysis as a degradation of the highest cultural values' ('The Resistance . . .'). (In this context the other 'part' would refer to the aggressive instincts.) This article is no longer concerned with the Jungians but with the more general attacks on psychoanalysis and its founder, whose deleterious influence was ascribed to his racial origins.

I think one can recognize here a tendency to idealization, without any corresponding sublimation of the instincts, which aims at cutting culture off from its natural, physical roots. It is, of course, a view of the very essence of culture that is in question here, and it is not claimed that those individuals sharing this view are unable to produce a work of art — assuming them to be creative — demonstrating a real process of sublimation nor, on the other hand, that the adoption, at an intellectual level, of the Freudian point of view confers, *ipso facto*, a capacity for sublimation. It remains nonetheless the case that such a view of culture can play the same role in relation to creativity as the pervert's affirmation that his sexual 'recipe' is superior to the father's genital coitus (cf. McDougall, 1971). It is not impossible, moreover, that this tendency to idealization without corresponding sublimation of the instincts, is also present in another form, in the conception that a certain number of functions, amongst them the creative function, form part of an *autonomous ego*.

When I was attempting a study of the 'fake', I had in mind, of course, certain contemporary aesthetic and intellectual productions that one cannot but feel to be cut off from their living roots, from the erogenous zones and the instincts. This is the same point Marcel Roch made in his paper on the superego (1966):

> It is not unusual these days for the results of artistic creativity to show a striking poverty and stereotypy of phantasy, a sterility of the powers of the imagination, which seem to have given way to an empty exercise in technique for the purely narcissistic delight in form, completely dissociated from the sublimation of instinctual strivings.

However, I think that it is wiser, in this area, to stick to attempting to grasp the internal processes of the artist who feels driven to create by his ego ideal, without having the capacity for sublimation that is needed to be able to nourish his creation, rather than attempting to apply theoretical hypotheses to contemporary works. Moreover, nothing is more difficult to justify than personal choice in relation to aesthetics, especially when time has not yet afforded a sufficient perspective on the work. 'Time is a good judge', it is said. Above all it allows one to distance oneself from the opinion of the group.

Our own age does not, however, have a monopoly on works — be they artistic or intellectual —which are thus instigated by a narcissistic need to attain fulfilment, without any real development of the ego and the corresponding instincts having taken place; and if today the phenomenon seems more widespread, the example of preciosity that I gave earlier suggests that we are here in the presence of a permanent, though often latent, tendency in human nature.

Let us not forget that the work of Molière is dominated by a battle against the 'fake', as much in the aesthetic sphere as that of feelings. With the penetration proper to genius he was able to recognize the essential common factor in fakery, whether it be that of fake religiosity (one version of *Tartuffe* was called *Panufle the Impostor*), fake science (the doctors of his day), fake aristocrats and the assumption of titles (*Le Bourgeois Gentilhomme*), fake refinement (*Les Précieuses Ridicules*), fake culture, fake poetry, the general fakery of the world (*Le Misanthrope*). Throughout he aims to unmask the hypocrite, the 'bel esprit', the false friend, love that is self-interested and inconsistent, and to see simplicity, truth and good sense prevail. The particular quality of this idealization, which merely puts a layer of brilliant varnish on an otherwise unaltered fecal penis, is particularly in evidence in *Les Précieuses Ridicules* when the two lackeys, *disguised* as the vicomte de Jodelet and the Marquis de Mascarille, having charmed the two précieuses with their gallant words, their elegance and their facility at making up 'impromptus' (small, improvised plays) or delivering a madrigal, are beaten by their masters (the true gentlemen) who strip them of their garments and reveal the smock beneath the embroidered finery.

A patient of mine, with many perverse activities, began talking, in a session, about his wish to write, having earlier mentioned reading one of my articles. He was wondering how to set about it when he remembered the following (previously forgotten) dream:

> I was in a saw mill. There was an enormous pile of logs, all alike, and all of which I had to paint carefully in silver. I had to pay particular attention to making sure that each log was completely covered; it makes me think of the chocolate I had at tea time when I was little and also of the chocolate

cigarettes that I used to buy at a tobacconists that was also a sweet-shop.

The pervert (and this also applies to related psychic structures) seeks, then, to cover the chocolate (the fecal penis) with a silver wrapping that idealizes it but does not alter its basic nature. A similar process is operative in the American custom of putting make-up on their dead, dressing them in their finest clothes, surrounding them with flowers and perfumes, enveloping them in music, so that the decomposition that the flesh is undergoing and the unconscious equation between the corpse and excrement may be forgotten. But one has only to scratch the surface to discover, beneath the brilliant coating, the fecal nature of the phallus or, as Napoleon put it, the shit in the silk stocking (referring to Talleyrand).

It is certainly easier, as Freud indicated, to understand some of the hazards of development and their negative effects than to grasp why another individual, placed in the same unfavourable circumstances, should escape illness. Thus not all of those who present the common structural nucleus that I have been attempting to delineate are entirely devoid of a capacity for sublimation. Not only are there differences in the quantity of libido that is discharged in the perverse (or related) activities, but also the lacunae in identifications do not all have the same degree of importance. If there are, for the reasons I have indicated, many perverse creative people, there are also amongst them some who succeed in producing authentic works that occupy an important place in our cultural heritage. On closer examination, it would seem that amongst perverts it is particularly homosexuals who demonstrate the greatest aptitudes for sublimation. This does indeed raise the problem of homosexuality itself. Freud thought this scarcely merited being called a perversion, the object relations of homosexuals varying from one individual to another, from manifestly partial object-love to a full object love that is much more akin to genitality (*An Autobiographical Study*, 1925).

In fact those presenting the structural nucleus that I have just described do not have any monopoly on inauthentic creativity. And the first time I wrote about the creation of a fake phallus was in fact in relation to the paranoic (1966; cf. 1965, 1968).

I can but rehearse the points made then. The origin of the paranoic's 'fake' creation is equally to be found in the weakness of his paternal identification. However, the reasons behind this weakness are, it will be appreciated, different from those pertaining to the structures described earlier. It could be said that the future paranoic, whose phallic maternal imago is invariably bad, has not been able to find in his father, for certain specific historical reasons, any support for the firm establishment of the triangular situation. He has not been able to go through the phase of idealization of the father which is necessary, within certain limits, if oedipal identifications are to take place. The father's penis is to him an erotic and aggressive object, but not the bearer of his ego ideal. It remains a *penis* and not a *phallus*, according to the distinction made by Béla Grunberger (1963). Fears for the ego will prevent the future paranoic from introjecting the father and his attributes and will lead him to idealize his own ego, this idealization representing the first fruits of his uncontrolled megalomania. Mystic paranoia therefore represents an attempt to project the ego ideal on to a divine figure, far from the flesh and blood father, and constitutes a favourable development in the illness, as Freud showed in the case of Schreber. It allows some narcissism to be wrested from the ego and enables a degree of reconciliation with the homosexual instinct. If the paranoic has not been successful in this endeavour and has retained his own ego as his ideal (relatively, at least, in non-psychotic states), then the boundaries of his ego will be fiercely cathected at the cost of his object cathexes, all introjections being rejected as dangerous and destructive intrusions.

Cathexis of the ego represents a major defence against homosexual attraction. The subject will elaborate phantasies and acts that aim to demonstrate that he already possesses an all-powerful penis that is perfect in every respect: superior to all others, it is manifestly superior to his father's, of which he consequently has no need. Given that the existence of this penis is based on a lacuna (the non-introjection of the father's penis) and aims to mask this fact, it will possess certain characteristics. One of these is immediately apparent: this penis has been conceived 'megalomaniacally' by its 'inventor' — and it is well known that classical psychiatry itself describes *invention* as one of the activities that is often characteristic of the paranoic. The natural process for acquiring a penis having been avoided, the creation of an autonomous penis will fall outside the bounds of the reality principle and will take on a magical quality. The magical autonomous phallus will by this very fact occupy an inordinate place in his ego, inflating his pride.

It is equally well known in classical psychiatry that one finds many paranoics who are self-taught and who thus 'skip' the state of being a pupil, the knowledge that comes from a teacher being equated with the father's penis that is to be taken in. The necessity of short-circuiting the phase of introjecting the father's penis, the positive narcissistic cathexis of this penis reverting to the ego, will have as its result that the productions of the paranoic, intended to represent his penis in all its glory, will have an inauthentic quality because they mask a major fault. If they are successful at taking in others — for reasons we shall look at later — they do not suffice completely to reassure their author, who will brandish them at every occasion and who will find himself forced to inflate their proportions to an ever greater degree in order to deny the idea, perceived at some level, that they are but a hollow shell with no real content. It is in order to rid himself of this highly anxiety-provoking perception, which would run counter to all his defences, that the paranoic finds himself obliged to project it onto the external world, which then appears to him to be factitious.

There is a particularly striking parallel to this perception and denunciation of the fake in the world of the paranoic in the literary and autobiographical work of Strindberg that I have had occasion to refer to elsewhere. Here I will just recall two particularly eloquent examples. His play *The Burned House* is supposed to have been inspired by him seeing the ruins of the house in which he had spent his childhood. The Stranger, who is in reality one of the sons of the house, arrives at the scene of the fire. In fact the family who lived in the house were engaged in contraband: 'the dye-works was but a facade intended to conceal the contraband in wool which was dyed in order to make it unrecognizable.' The house was built with false walls so that the goods could be hidden. This 'honourable family' was, then, engaged in illegal traffic. But after the fire, the Stranger intends to bring 'all these old shady dealings to the light of day' (the Stranger goes over to the things that have been saved from the fire and examines some books). 'The same rubbish as when I was young. Livy's *History of Rome*, in which there isn't a word of truth . . . And what's that? The headboard of the mahogany bed in which I was born. Damn it! Item: the foot of the dining room table, *quite the heirloom, handed down from father to son* [my italics]. Ha! They claimed it was ebony, everybody admired it, and now, fifty years on, I find that it was just poplar that had been stained. *Everything was dyed in our house, everything given a coat of make-up* [my italics] . . . What a joke, the ebony table . . .' (He goes up to a clock): 'Let's see what's inside you, my friend.' (He picks it up and it falls to pieces.) 'It falls apart as soon as you touch it. Everything fell apart in this house once you touched it, everything . . .'

It is not too far-fetched to suggest that 'the heirloom handed down from father to son', as also the contents of the clock, represents the father's phallus, symbolizing the succession of generations, on to which the Stranger projects his feeling of fakery, as appears clearly in *The Ghost Sonata*:

The Colonel is equally a faker and a usurper whom the Old Man will unmask.

> OLD MAN: Everything. Everything you see. It is all mine.
> COLONEL: Very well. All that is yours. But my patent of nobility and my good name — they at least are still mine.
> OLD MAN: No. Not even those. (*Pause*) You're not a nobleman.

COLONEL: How dare you?

OLD MAN: (*Takes out a paper*) If you read this letter from the College of Heralds you will see that the family whose name you bear has been extinct for a hundred years.

COLONEL: (*Reads*) I — have heard rumours to this effect, it is true — But I inherited the title from my father — (*Reads*) No. It is true. You are right. I am not a nobleman. Even that is taken from me. I can no longer wear this ring. Take it. It belongs to you.

OLD MAN: (*Puts on the ring*) Good. Now let's continue. You're not a Colonel either.

COLONEL: Not a Colonel?

OLD MAN: No. Because of your name you were commissioned Colonel in the American Volunteers, but since the Cuban War and the reorganization of the American Army all such commissions have been cancelled.

COLONEL: Is that true?

OLD MAN: (*Puts his hand towards his pocket*) Would you like to read about it?

COLONEL: No — there's no need. Who are you, that you claim the right to sit there and strip me like this?

OLD MAN: You'll find out. Talking of stripping — I suppose you do know who you really are?

COLONEL: You have the effrontery — !

OLD MAN: Take off your wig and look at yourself in the glass; take out your teeth, shave off your moustaches; get Bengtson to unlace your corset. Perhaps then a certain footman may recognize himself; who used to sponge food from a certain cook in a certain kitchen.

The papier-mâché decorations, the false situations, the usurped functions, the artificial feelings, the made-up faces, the masks, the false walls, the hidden crimes, the misleading values, the frauds, the tricks, the plagiarisms, the lies which fill Strindberg's dramatic world and which he denounces tirelessly appear, particularly in this last scene, to stem from a profound sense of the inauthenticity of his own identification with his father. The Colonel, who is progressively stripped of his fake, narcissistic emblems and who finds himself a footman again, is he not the — no doubt unconscious — *alter ego* of he who Strindberg called 'the servant's son'? (I would remind the reader that this is the title he gave his autobiographical work as a whole.) In *Miss Julie* he gives the valet the same Christian name that he gives himself in his autobiography.

Strindberg's example demonstrates that even when identification with the father has not taken place, this does not necessarily bar the way to sublimatory processes, albeit under certain conditions, the presence of which implies a very unstable and easily destroyed equilibrium. For indeed the Swedish dramatist's literary productivity virtually dried up between 1892 and 1897. The break is sudden: in 1892 he had written six more plays. It would seem that the separation from his first wife, Siri von Essen, was the precipitating factor in this episode of literary sterility and fecundity of pathology. Married life represents a bulwark against homosexuality thanks to the indirect homosexual satisfactions that it allows through identification with the partner. The departure of his wife seems to have obliged Strindberg to recover some of his feminine wishes, though under protest. The persecutory pressure will increase. Strindberg then substitutes 'scientific' invention for literary creation. It seems to me that this scientific invention represents an attempt to evade the dangers linked to the passive homosexual instinct through the possession of an omnipotent phallus created *ex nihilo*, and therefore having something of magic about it. In 1894, after a lightning marriage, he separated from his second wife, and pursued his researches into chemistry with even more vigour, but his wife, his circle of friends and the experts having refused to confirm his 'discoveries', he decides to 'produce a decisive blow' and *to make gold*.

The old dream of the alchemists is the representation, *par excellence*, of the wish to acquire the omnipotent phallus from nothing (that is to say, outside of any genetic continuity). It may be recalled in this respect that Joseph Balsamo, who claimed the title of Cagliostro, magician, adventurer, impostor, charlatan and swindler was also an alchemist and, at the very beginning of his life, a copyist of paintings. The copy may represent an attempt to identify oneself with the Masters but also, as I have said, an impossibility: that of metabolizing the object.

In *To Damascus*, it becomes particularly clear that for Strindberg the significance of the wish to create gold is that of creating a magic, autonomous and omnipotent phallus that renders its owner invulnerable, superior to all and equal to God: 'The Stranger', the hero of the play, finds himself in the laboratory with the Mother. He wants to be able to make gold. The Mother cries out: 'But it's a defiance to God, it's black magic!' The Stranger explains to her that 'Honours are man's most lasting illusions' and that he hopes to gain these honours through his discovery, which is likened to the construction of the tower of Babel that was to reach right to the sky 'for fear of an attack by the powers above'. At the same time he would have supreme power: 'I have in my crucible the destiny of the world . . . I am he who has done that which no man before me was able to do . . .'

The wish to acquire a magic, autonomous phallus, of which the creation of gold is a prototype, is seemingly able to reverse the direction of anal persecution which tends to debase the world and render it fecal, transforming it into a 'hell of excrement'. This is the name given by Strindberg to the mad world in which he found himself during the time of his 'scientific' researches, a period described in *Inferno*. The term 'hell of excrement' is borrowed from Swedenborg, whom Strindberg was reading at that same time. This 'fecalizing' process is very often described in Strindberg's theatre.

For example, in *To Damascus* the banquet in the inn begins in an atmosphere of luxury, amidst a profusion of lights, gold and silver ornaments and crystal-ware. Little by little everything becomes poorer: 'Servants have exchanged the gold cups for dull pewter ones and now begin to remove the peacocks and pheasants etc. . . . . The tables have now been cleared; even the cloths and candelabra are gone so that the wooden boards and trestles stand bare. A big stone pitcher is carried in, and stone mugs of the cheapest kind are set out on the top table . . .' A little later still: 'A prettily decorated screen with palms and birds of paradise has been removed, revealing a squalid taproom with a bar, behind which a barmaid is dispensing drinks to down-and-outs and whores.' This scene is all the more significant in that the banquet was organized in honour of the Stranger, the hero of the piece, who is supposed to have succeeded in producing gold, but it turns out at the end of the play that the intention was to mock him and he is, finally, treated as a charlatan.

We see therefore that being unmasked as a charlatan is the same as revealing that behind all the gold and crystal, behind the screen decorated with palms and birds of paradise, there lies a squalid dive. It is to reveal the fecal world hidden behind the decorations: 'I read one day that the gold which the Devil gives his victims regularly turns into faeces; and the next day Herr E., who describes his old nurse's money-deliria to me, suddenly (by a round-about path via Cagliostro — alchemist — *Dukatenscheisser*) said that Louise's money was always faeces' (Freud to Fliess, 1897: S.E.1, p. 242). It is to negate the process that led to the fecal wand being transformed into gold; it is to strip off the borrowed finery. The persecution that forces the subject to reveal the anal character of his phallus inheres to the homosexual instinct. If his phallus has lost its magical, narcissistic characteristics, the subject is driven back to recognizing his erotic wish for the father and his penis, that is to say, his need for identification with the bearer of the genital penis through the introjection of his attributes.

The magical, autonomous phallus of the paranoic also serves, therefore, to mask the *anal* character of the phallus which seeks, through idealization, to pass itself off as equal and even superior to the genital penis. For the paranoic it is confrontation with the father's penis that is directly at issue as it is also the refusal of passive instincts, whilst in the structures described above it is the preservation of the link with the mother and the concomitant exclusion of genitality and of the world of the father. In both cases paternal introjects are set aside. Put schematically, the recognition by the pervert that there is some lack in his ego could lead to a loss of illusions and to depression; in the case of the paranoic, to persecution. Since the magical, autonomous phallus of the paranoic has also not undergone any alteration of its substance, it only requires the counter-cathexis of the instincts that served in its 'fabrication' to be shaken for the anality to reappear in its primitive form, like the poplar wood beneath the paint, and the 'old shady dealings' exposed to 'the light of day'. (Cf. the quotation from Strindberg's *The Burned House*.)

It should be added that, in both cases, the creation of the magical, autonomous phallus — the fake phallus — represents a trap into which fall those who trust to appearances (the silver paper covering the chocolate, the gold and crystal disguising the 'dive', the paint covering the poplar wood, the 'lamb' which is dressed-up mutton or, in 'The Emperor of China's Nightingale', the diamonds and the precious stones that bedeck the clockwork bird, and again the silk stockings containing the shit), the camouflage here playing the role of the foliage masking the snare or the traps. Indeed, the fabricator of the 'fake' aims to dupe the spectator, the listener or the reader, in such a way as to make him acknowledge the fetish-creation as superior to the real genital penis. It is with the paranoic that the secondary significance of a trap taken on by the 'magical, autonomous phallus' is most in evidence because of the object-relation in question here. Indeed, the defence the paranoic offers to passive penetration forces him into either a constant penetration of the other or his capture (followed by destruction and ejection) in the anal sphincter. The relationship is finally restricted to a relentless, imaginary battle: who will penetrate whom, who will manage to trap whom?

The relationship of the pervert (and those with a related psychic structure) to his 'public' is often less sadistic and destructive, unless there are, as is not exceptional, paranoid elements or wishes for vengeance against the mother, who has seduced but finally given nothing. In his case he seeks, in the manner of the illusionist and the conjurer (though in their case the relationship is embedded in the context of a pre-established convention) to amaze the spectator, listener or reader by such intellectual or verbal gymnastics, by such technical virtuosity and such a degree of ingenuity and artfulness in respect of formal expression as will earn him the kind of doting admiration his mother once lavished on him, thus confirming his role as an adequate sexual partner and the father's corresponding lack of value. By taking in the public with his illusions, the illusionist endeavours to maintain his own illusion. The Americans have a significant expression for a certain type of individual who attempts to 'show-off': *'Look mum, no hands'*, alluding to the little boy showing his mother how well he can perform on his bicycle and how, with the feeble means at his disposal, he can manage acrobatics that are beyond the grown-ups, or so he imagines.

The most perfect example of a process of idealization not involving any concomitant transformation of the materials involved, seems to me to be the following work, on display at the time of writing at the Grand Palais — *Twelve Years of Contemporary French Art* organized by the Ministry of Culture. This consists of a jar containing a greenish liquid, and bearing the title: 'My urine in 1962'. Certainly the practical joke (the French word for this has the same stem as that of cannula) can have a liberating effect, but Dada dates from the First World War, and the urinal put on display by Duchamp from the Twenties. It is therefore a practical joke that is rather old hat and is now but a plagiarism. Furthermore, it is to be feared that a number of people — including the selection committee itself — may have the idea that this represents a genuine work of art (in line with the title of the exhibition).

This example is all the more significant in that the quality of the object as excrement is no longer even masked and it is put forward as a 'work' solely by magical virtue of the wish of its author and the complicity of the spectator. (A pure black canvas similarly bears the title: 'I am black and I am beautiful', the 'aesthetic' value of the object residing uniquely in the 'artist's' affirmation, paraphrasing the Sulamite. Some time ago I saw a number of urinals in a gallery, identical to the original made famous by Duchamp, and all being sold at a price considerably above that in the Armitage-Shanks' catalogue.

We have to ask ourselves where the libido employed in idealization comes from, since we have seen that idealization here implies an absence of desexualization. All the masks worn by the fecal phallus themselves refer us back to anality: gold, silver, precious stones, the showy and the brilliant, are all of an anal order. We have known since Freud that 'the connections between the complexes of interest in money and of defaecation, which seem so dissimilar, appear to be the most extensive of all' ('Character and Anal Erotism', Freud, 1908). Freud attempts to explain these connections:

> It is possible that the contrast between the most precious substance known to men and the most worthless, which they reject as waste matter (*refuse*), has led to this specific identification of gold with faeces.
>
> Yet another circumstance facilitates this equation in neurotic thought. The original erotic interest in defaecation is, as we know, destined to be extinguished in later years. In those years the interest in money makes its appearance as a new interest which had been absent in childhood. This makes it easier for the earlier impulsion, which is in process of losing its aim, to be carried over to the newly emerging aim.

Freud thus demonstrates the manifest contrast between, on the one hand, the original object (faeces) and the derived object (money) and, on the other hand, the apparent hiatus between the interest in money and defaecation, whilst at an unconscious level there is identity and continuity.

However, in this text the precious quality of gold seems to be accepted as an intrinsic fact. It was Ferenczi (1914) who subsequently demonstrated the link between the original interest in faeces and the later interest in money, precious stones and other brilliant materials, emphasizing the course of development that leads from excrements with all their particular characteristics (smell, consistency, appearance) to materials apparently at the furthest remove from the original object (clean, solid, dry, brilliant), through all the intermediary stages that the observation of children and their games can show us (mud, sand, pebbles, shells, buttons, marbles, etc.). It is the process of reaction formation that brings about this apparent reversal of values. 'Thus shining pieces of money are nothing other than odourless, dehydrated filth that has been made to shine. Pecunia non olet.'

One could quote here the saying 'clean as a new pin' (in French it is a coin: 'Propre comme un sou neuf'). Furthermore, for Ferenczi the roots of aesthetics also lie in repressed anality. A study of the effect produced by the loss of omnipotence and of the value originally attached to faeces by the child would also seem to be appropriate. This omnipotence and value, like all the satisfactions that man has once enjoyed and that cannot, according to Freud, disappear, but only be exchanged for others, seem not to be transferred entirely on to the satisfactions inherent in subsequent phases of development. They require apparently new substitutes, with characteristics opposite to those of the original object. These opposing traits make them acceptable to the ego, which then cathects them with the potency and value originally attaching to excrement.

In the initial stages of this process any material having attributes unlike those of the original object could serve: a coloured pebble, a glittering stone, a particle of metal, etc. Little by little, I imagine, man has attempted to reconcile the pleasure principle, which the possession of substitutes for the original object implies, with the reality principle, by cathecting materials whose intrinsic qualities justified — in part at least — the interest he took in them. It is not only their rarity that is implicated here — a property which, whilst it is in contrast to the banal and common nature of faeces, takes us beyond the issue of anality. Each human being is rare, and even unique, as is the oedipal penis and object. A number of obvious qualities (such as their unchangeability, for example) also make gold and certain precious stones satisfactory guarantors of value. Social convention makes of them a standard resting on elements that are linked to the pleasure principle as well as the reality principle. In other words, at the beginning of the process that transfers the cathexis of the original anal object on to objects that match it with opposite characteristics trait for trait, it is only reaction formations that are involved. Ferenczi does not distinguish in his work between sublimations and reaction formations, in like manner to Freud in 1905 (*Three Essays*) and 1908 ('Civilized Sexual Morality', 'Character and Anal Erotism'). However, it seems necessary to follow Freud's later formulations where he stresses the absence of repression and counter-cathexis in sublimation, in opposition to reaction formation (despite the difficulty there can be at times differentiating certain phenomena in this sense). It is indeed impossible to imaging desexualization intervening in reaction formation.

Thus when the ego ideal is in sole charge of the production of a work, it can only modify anality by subjecting it to diverse incarnations linked, not to sublimation, but to displacement and to reaction formation, according to the model proposed by Ferenczi for the ontogenesis of the interest in money. I would therefore be most inclined to think that the wrapping that seeks to pass off the fecal phallus as an object of great value is never itself made of pure gold or precious stones, but of pasteboard, shinier than the real gem: diamonds cut in the old style have a dull and discrete lustre that any piece of glassware infinitely surpasses in intensity. Vauvenargues wrote: 'The false presented with art surprises and dazzles.'

Without doubt, therefore, it is because the anal instinct or the excrement have simply been camouflaged as their opposite — and because the opposite always bears the indelible stamp of that which it seeks to deny — that it is possible to recognise the anal character of the phallus not only *behind* the brilliant trappings that veil it, but in *their very brilliance* (Cf. 'Negation', Freud, 1925). Thus the village of 'Moncul' (literally 'My arse') has just asked for its name to be changed to 'Monrosier' ('My Rose-tree').

In relation to this one might recall Alceste's reply to Oronte's sonnet in Molière's *The Misanthrope*:

Frankly — the only thing to do is to put it away and forget it. You have formed your style on bad models. The expressions you use are not *natural*. What's the meaning of 'and for a while brings consolation'? or 'be followed by frustration'? and 'kinder had been the cruel word'? or 'hope deferred begets blank hopelessness'? This *figurative style* people pride themselves so much on is *false* and meretricious. *It's just play upon words — sheer affectation! It isn't a natural way of speaking at all.* I find contemporary taste appalling in this respect. *Our ancestors*, crude and unpolished as they were, did very much better. I prefer to any of the stuff people admire so much nowadays an old ballad such as: . . .

The rimes may be crude and the style old fashioned but don't you see how much better it is than all this *trumpery stuff* that's so revolting to one's common sense? Don't you feel that this is the voice of true love speaking? . . .

Yes Sir, you may laugh, *but whatever your wits and your critics may say I prefer that to the solemn flourishes and superficial polish that everyone makes such a fuss about* [all italics mine].

If Alceste has no time for such trumpery stuff and prefers 'truth' and 'nature', many are those who do make a fuss about, and admire, the display of 'superficial polish'. Why?

Abraham's study of an impostor contains numerous items which demonstrate the ascendancy exercized by this character on all those about him: 'It should be mentioned here that N. knew how to gain the confidence of people of any age, status or sex, only to betray such confidence immediately.' N. succeeded in duping all his warders. Abraham recounts the following episode:

When I explained this to the court, it was ordered that N. should be put in a room on the top storey. Special measures were taken to prevent his escape. Three particularly reliable and intelligent sergeants were detailed for guard duty outside N.'s room. To avoid their being influenced by N. the guards had strict instructions not to enter his room or to hold any conversation with him.

Consequently N. was transferred with his three guards to the military hospital, and this move was accomplished without difficulty. Ten minutes after his admission I went to make sure that he was being accommodated and guarded as the court had ordered. To my amazement I found no guard outside his room; only three empty chairs. On entering the room an astonishing sight met my eyes. N. was sitting at the table drawing; one of his guards was posing for him, and the other two were looking on.

Hélène Deutsch's impostor exerts no less a fascination on those around him: 'This time he chose as his collaborator an experienced physicist, and within a short period succeeded in making this man believe that Jimmy was a genius. With uncanny skill he created an atmosphere in which the physicist was convinced that his own achievements were inspired by Jimmy the genius.' And also: 'His success in temporarily impressing his teachers as an outstanding student of philosophy was almost a farce.' It might well be thought that the obligation the impostor (or the creator of the 'fake') finds himself under to gain recognition for the identity he has conferred upon himself in order to resemble his ego ideal, plays a determining role in his diabolical capacity for seduction and powers of persuasion, and certainly this is a most important element for understanding his relationship to his 'public', but this relationship involves two parties and without the complicity of the other there would be no impostor.

Phyllis Greenacre stresses the fact that the impostor plays on the public's appetite for illusions. 'In some of the most celebrated instances of imposture, it indeed appears that the fraud was successful only because many others as well as the perpetrator had a hunger to believe in the fraud, and that any success of such fraudulence depended in fact on strong social as well as individual factors and a special receptivity to the trickery.' I am of the opinion, in fact, that 'the fake' exercises over all of us, to varying degrees, a very real fascination.

In *Jokes and their Relation to the Unconscious* (1905), Freud emphasises the notion of the 'economy' that the joke allows the hearer to make:

> He might be said to have been presented with it [i.e. the pleasure of the joke]. The words of the joke he hears necessarily bring about in him the idea or train of thought to the construction of which great internal inhibitions were opposed in him too. He would have had to make an effort of his own in order to bring it about spontaneously as the first person, he would have had to use at least as much psychical expenditure on doing so as would correspond to the strength of the inhibition, suppression or repression of the idea. He has saved this psychical expenditure.

This view of the joke may be superimposed on that which Freud gives, on several occasions, of the work of art and its effects on the public. Thus, writing about literary creation: 'Our enjoyment of an imaginative work proceeds from a liberation of tensions in our minds. It may even be that not a little of this effect is due to the writer's enabling us thenceforward to enjoy our own day-dreams without self-reproach or shame' ('Creative Writers . . .', Freud, 1908). As for aesthetic pleasure, this would constitute a 'bonus of pleasure' intended to open the way to a higher enjoyment emanating from deeper psychic sources. For my part, I do not think that one can thus dissociate aesthetic pleasure from the work as a whole and reduce it to a bait.

If the attraction exercized by a work of art (or a joke) lies, in part at least, in a saving of energy that would otherwise be used for repression, what sort of saving results from the 'fake' work, that which is a product of idealization and not of sublimation, such that it evokes an infatuation that is often greater than that evoked by the real article? To my mind, it allows us the illusion that our own conflicts relating to introjection, our own development (and whatever our age and structure, this is always unfinished and incomplete) may be side-stepped or avoided (as by a conjuring trick) and narcissistic fulfilment — the abolition of any gap between our ego and our ideal — attained at less cost.

The admirer of the 'fake' is thus brought up against the possibility of acquiring the phallus immediately, divorced from any area of conflict, and for all time in a world that excludes castration. The fecal phallus cannot be castrated because it is permanently renewable; it is by definition the only indestructible penis, both dead (castration and life are as inseparable as death and anality in the unconscious) and eternal. Like the phoenix, it rises from its ashes or recreates itself by self-fertilization. Like the phoenix it is decked in brilliant colours that 'make it more handsome than the most splendid peacock' (Grimal). The myth of the phoenix thus seems to me to represent the phantasy of the uncastratable phallus (it rises again from its ashes) obtained without reference to its procreator (it fertilizes itself), its nature — necessarily anal on the one hand and idealized on the other — being represented by the ashes and the brilliancy of its colours.

If, during the course of development, the fecal phallus prefigures the genital penis, afterwards it becomes an imitation of it (prostheses, orthopaedic aids to replace a limb or supplement one that is deficient are unconsciously identified with the fecal phallus, and often chosen as a fetish). By virtue of idealization the fecal phallus represents itself as a genital penis. Masking the characteristics of the excrement which is its essence, it is able to preserve the invulnerability inherent to it, thereby operating on two fronts, so to speak. The person brought up against the 'fake' is thus at the same time brought up against a particular success in avoiding conflict and castration, that is to say against Illusion itself. Equally Marcel Roch, in his paper, mentions the success won by someone whose work was, however, to culminate in a drying up 'into a narcissistic complaisance that alienates him' from a public 'in search of any exhibition that stands guarantor for the needs of narcissism'.

There are also works whose (avowed) intention is to imitate

the living, the real. It is thus with paintings that make use of 'trompe l'oeil' and automatons. I do not think that these can be equated with the 'fake' that I have been writing about, even though the phantasy presiding over their creation may in part involve a wish to 'fabricate' the real or, in the case of the automaton, a human being, rather than to 'beget' it. (Automatons are in fact experienced by the unconscious as phalli and animation as an erection, as various dreams have seemed to show me.) To Freud's interpretation, according to which Olympia would stand for Nathaniel's feminine double and represent his passive attitude towards his father, one might add that the doll, a creature that has been fabricated and not begotten, is entirely dependent on its creator who animates or immobilizes it at his pleasure. This feminine double of Nathaniel's is thus entirely possessed by its creator and given over to him in a way that is analogous to that which is at the heart of delusions of influence. Olympia may be seen as Nathaniel's 'influencing machine'. Nathaniel does not belong to himself; he escapes his own control, in the same way that little boys feel that erections happen without their egos having any part in it. The impression of something 'uncanny' (Freud, 1919) produced by madness and epilepsy, linked by Freud to a manifestation of mysterious forces obscurely sensed by the observer to exist within his own person, applies equally to erections and perhaps it even owes its origin in part to this phenomenon. At another level, the appeal that automatons have for many people is very likely linked to the arousal of the Illusion which is prompted by the magical sight of a life created without flesh-and-blood parents, and hence to the exclusion of castration and conflict. Thus I once visited a marvellous exhibition of automatons put on by a collector, an old man with fair hair, powdered and curled, but the number of visitors and their passionate attention bore witness to the fact that the interest in automatons is not confined to those who have flagrant problems of identity.

The creative process in the case of the makers of automatons cannot be superimposed on that of the producers of the 'fake', for not only is artifice sought openly but its success requires immense technical skill and artistic aptitude. The precise regulation of the clockwork mechanism that controls these artificial creatures is seemingly accompanied by a great wealth of sublimations. If, in Andersen's tale, a clockwork nightingale is opposed to a 'real' nightingale, it is because the essence of the 'fake' is immediately revealed in this instance, whereas the construction of an object with the conscious and avowed task of imitating nature may perfectly well involve authentic creativity. It is thus with the artificial perspectives of Andrea Palladio the sight of which can give a genuinely poetical pleasure.

The fascination exercised by the 'fake' is fairly similar to that exercised by ideologies. In both cases it is the hope of a reuni-fication of the ego and the ego ideal, by the shortest route, that is aroused, that is brought to life once more. Here again, however, the attraction does not act on everybody in the same manner. In Andersen's tale, those who accept themselves as they are (who do not experience the gap between their ego and their ideal as too painful or, to put it another way, whose self-esteem is well regulated) — the poor fisherman and the kitchen maid — value the modest, grey little bird (the 'real' nightingale) higher than the bird covered with shimmering gems (the 'fake' nightingale). The music master, the knight and the courtiers — whom Andersen portrays in a very similar light to Molière's Oronte and his petty nobles — succumb to the contrived charms of the clock-work bird, in which they recognize their own idealized egos. There will always be those who prefer the real to the 'fake'; moreover, the appeal exercised by the 'fake' is often only transitory, just as adherence to an ideology may be. As was said of the Germans, after the defeat of Nazism, they seemed as if they were coming out of a dream. Both a 'fake' and an ideology can be seen, by the same token, to be like a dream in which the wish for a reunification of ego and ideal — and hence the realization of incestuous fusion — attains fulfilment.

One might think, on the contrary, that sublimation represents one of the essential post-oedipal outcomes of the old wish for the uniting of ego and ideal — that is to say, following the setting up of the incest barrier. I previously emphasized the fact that Freud, who in other respects so often modified his theory of sublimation, had immediately linked this to the latency period. Nearly all those authors who deal with the problems of identity and identification that I have mentioned describe the difficulties in sublimation experienced by those they are writing about and refer to their primitive ego ideal and their inadequately internalized superego (Cf. M. Kanzer, Phyllis Greenacre, Annie Reich). Karl Abraham (1925) states clearly in relation to his impostor:'. . .Those processes of sublimation which *evidence a successful overcoming of the Oedipus complex* [my italics] . . . could not take place.'

If the superego, as an anti-instinctual entity, is always in contact with the id (it has 'intimate relations with the unconscious id', writes Freud in 1923) it is nonetheless the product of the introjection of an essential element of reality, represented by the father, who personifies the incest barrier.

Annie Reich (1953) says very firmly that 'the formation of the super ego is based upon acceptance of reality. In fact, it represents the most powerful attempt to adjust to reality.' This is particularly true if one considers that the ego ideal, on the contrary, promotes union with the mother, and hence the transgression of the incest barrier. In fact, I do not believe that the superego represents a real attempt to accept reality since I would agree with Grunberger in seeing the superego as still representing some attempt at a recouping of narcissism by holding an interdict responsible for that which actually stems from the child's sexual impotence, and which is the result of the discrepancy between oedipal wishes and the capacity to satisfy them. Seen in this light the superego is a compromise formation, doubtless relatively the most acceptable.

Following the setting up of the superego, the economics of the individual's narcissism will find itself profoundly altered. I would agree with all those who insist on differentiating the heir to the Oedipus complex from its possible precursors. Thus even if one agrees with Melanie Klein's view that the superego is established along with the very first introjects, it still seems necessary to me to distinguish the internalization of the incest barrier from other interdicts internalized previously (and from interdicts in general), particularly in relation to the present topic. Indeed the possibilities for the individual's narcissistic growth will henceforth encounter precise limits, and any work that is a product of sublimation will have the particularity that it symbolizes a fulfilment obtained through very precisely defined means, and through very narrow channels.

I am taking up a position here that is, I think, close to that of Marcel Roch when he asks the following question:

> Cannot the superego be seen to play a determining role in creative activity in two opposing senses:
>
> 1. By its selective function, fostering creativity through setting limits within which the active forces of the artist or inventor may have complete freedom of expression.
>
> 2. By an inverse selectivity, operating when the superego is functioning regressively, which prevents the artist precisely from making use of all that he has within himself that is most valuable and talented in the production of his work? (Roch, 1966).

In his work on 'A Variant of the Narcissistic Phallic Position' (1962), André Green stresses equally the links that are maintained between sublimation and the superego and the ego ideal, sublimation making its appearance, according to him, at the time of the castration complex. However, I do not share his opinion that there is a phase of phallic, genital organisation that is based on an ignorance of the difference between the sexes, at even an unconscious level. In the case of creativity that is linked to the post-oedipal acquisition of sublimatory capacities, the necessity of finding substitutes for the forbidden incestuous objects seemingly favours symbolic activity, as noted by Kanzer (Cf. above). Ferenczi described the beginnings of symbolic activity in the child as follows:

> The child's mind (and the tendency of the unconscious in

adults that survives from it) is at first concerned exclusively with his own body, and later on chiefly with the satisfying of his instincts, with the pleasurable satisfactions that sucking, eating, contact with the genital regions, and the functions of excretion procure for him; what wonder, then, if also his attention is arrested above all by those objects and processes of the outer world that on the ground of ever so distant a resemblance remind him of his dearest experiences.

Thus arise those intimate connections, which remain throughout life, between the human body and the objective world that we call *symbolic*. On the one hand the child in this stage sees in the world nothing but images of his corporeality, on the other he learns to represent by means of his body the whole multifariousness of the outer world ('The Onto-genesis of Symbols', Ferenczi, 1913; cf. A. Balint, 1953).

We may infer from this text that as the formation of symbols ultimately constitutes an extension of one's own body into external space, it represents an attempt to regain the cosmic ego. This process is not unrelated to primitive animism and magic; in the schizophrenic one can observe a reappearance of the confusion between the individual's own body and nature, between micturition and rain, for example (cf. Sechehaye, 1950). At this point the attempt to regain the cosmic ego is not regressive, since it is based on the first effects of the recognition of the distinction between the 'me' and the 'not-me'. This is the attempt to take a hold of one's own body and the corresponding attempt to take a hold of the external world. It involves the appearance, also, of wishes brought about by the rupturing of the primary sense of fusion which entails a search for an identity of perception capable of providing satisfaction (the parts of the body being auto-erotic objects).

Melanie Klein's views on symbol formation are well known (1930). She links this process to the anxiety aroused by fears of retaliation from part objects that have been attacked in phantasy, impelling the child to seek equivalents for them. The views she expressed in 1923 are perhaps less well remembered. Then, with reference to Freud, she attributed symbolic activity to the discrepancy between the wish and the satisfaction of it that could be obtained in reality. Ferenczi's view, and that of Melanie Klein in 1923, therefore lay emphasis on symbolic activity as an attempt to restore a lost sense of fulfilment. That conflicts within the object relationship should reinforce and complicate the process — and in particular drive the symbolized object into the unconscious — would seem fairly obvious. It is nonetheless the case that symbolic activity, as a creator of substitutes, results from man's most fundamental sense of non-satisfaction, which is linked to his immaturity. This activity knows an upsurge during the latency period because of the necessary abandoning of incestuous cathexes in their direct sexual form. The setting up of the superego signs the renunciation of the reunification of ego and ideal through genital union with the mother, within which primary fusion is 'contained'. The symbol, says Melanie Klein, constitutes 'the basis of all phantasy and of all sublimation'. We have an example, there, of the way in which the superego, and the strait way which henceforth the creative process must take, act upon the work. Creativity, instead of having an unlimited field for expansion, will find itself having to wrest its materials from a thin strip of ground bordered by precipices. It must satisfy several masters at once, and no longer only narcissism allied to the instincts. The contrast I am suggesting here is, after all, a fiction, since the individual creating a work under the sole aegis of the ego ideal is nonetheless obliged to take account of external reality, though to a diminishing degree (the latter today being easily bent to his will).

Freud considered that art reconciled the pleasure principle and the reality principle.

An artist is originally a man who turns away from reality because he cannot come to terms with the renunciation of instinctual satisfaction which it at first demands, and who allows his erotic and ambitious wishes full play in the life of phantasy. He finds the way back to reality, however, from this world of phantasy, by making use of special gifts to mould his phantasies into truths of a new kind, which are valued by men as precious reflections of reality. Thus in a certain fashion he actually becomes the hero, the king, the creator, or the favourite he desired to be, without following the long roundabout path of making real alterations in the external world. But he can only achieve this because other men feel the same dissatisfaction as he does with the renunciation demanded by reality, and because that dissatisfaction, which results from the replacement of the pleasure principle by the reality principle, is itself a part of reality ('Formulations on the Two Principles', Freud, 1911).

The setting up of the superego and the commencement of sublimatory processes vouchsafe a greater role to the reality principle, and the admiration the public accords to the artist relates, to my mind, to the feeling that, like the tight-rope walker on a high wire, he has succeeded, despite the obstacles, in achieving a symbolic narcissistic fulfilment. There is a particular satisfaction in overcoming obstacles, in obtaining pleasure despite the difficulties and the detours imposed by reality, rather like the pleasure to be gained from being able to nip in and out of a traffic jam. I have had occasion to try and show the mechanisms that are at work in this case ('A propos de . . .', 1967). It can be most reassuring to the ego to be able to overcome that which is ugly, difficult, bad, discordant, defective, and to be able to make up for that which is missing, to close up wounds, to seal the breach and hence attain mastery over bad objects and the disappearance of castration. The confidence of the ego in its capacity to repair itself (and to repair its objects) is thus enhanced. And it is not pure masochism if certain authors and poets impose restrictions upon themselves, if certain artists choose to work with intractable materials, thus voluntarily adding external difficulties to their internal obstacles, and at times giving the impression of 'making difficulties' the better to 'make light of them'. The artist thereby furnishes himself with proof that narcissistic or object-related difficulties can be mastered. Certainly the path he chooses is shorter, as Freud states, than that which would involve a modification of external reality, but the authentic work does not avoid all obstacles in the way that the 'fake' does. It could be said that the former manages to pick its way through development — in spite of it —whereas the latter aims at an abolition of development.

In 'Le Rossignol . . .' (Chasseguet-Smirgel, 1968), I followed the vicissitudes of creativity in the case of a number of neurotics who could only imitate or copy without being able to express themselves in an original way. Their inhibitions are very different from those of the pervert or the paranoic. The conflicts appertaining to introjection, which prevent him from metabolizing the object are essentially linked to fears for the object (and not for the ego) and relate to Oedipal problems. The lifting of these inhibitions is, by and large, relatively easy. In the case of Carine (Diatkine and Simon, 1972), the authors show very clearly the development of this little patient from imitation of her mother ('to be like her mother . . . by "pretending", that is to say demonstrating at the same time her lack of capacity for identification') to an identification with her, following the integration of her sadism.

The proof that the artist thus gives himself (and hence his public) is, however, generally linked to profound unconscious doubts. This implies a difficulty in the regulation of self-esteem linked to narcissistic and object-related conflicts and to a painful hiatus between the ego and the ideal. For my part, I am not at all convinced that creativity depends upon a surplus of libido — the monopoly of those individuals who are perfectly well integrated and balanced. The fact that oedipal identifications and the superego have a preponderant role to play in creativity, that likewise the ego ideal has that maturative aspect that I spoke of earlier, does not imply an absence either of fixations or of regressions. Michel de M'Uzan (1965) shows clearly that the creative process is not idyllic: 'Thus this is no idyll, but a most hazardous business, for ever under threat.' He also writes that 'the creative process is a drama'. It would be an idyll if it corresponded to the (equally idyllic) conception of it as an undertaking based upon the richness, the integration and the balance of the personality. But were it simply the expression of a surplus of energy, it would have neither the coercive quality that it does in fact possess, nor the sense of ultimate value that it holds for both artist and public. Melanie Klein (1957) said that creative capacities are the object of the greatest envy and takes this back to the mother's capacity for bearing children. Certainly, at some level, the creative process does represent giving birth, and the work represents a child-penis. But having children places one within the biological order, within the common lot, of women at least, in which men participate by virtue of their paternal role and particularly by virtue of their dual identification. And even if, as has been said, creativity were linked in men to the desire to be able to procreate like women, it is nonetheless the case that the work is a much more narcissistic product; it is, for the artist, much more of 'a child after his own heart':

> Now, considering this simple occasion for loving our children by reason of our having begotten them, wherefore we speak of them as our other selves, there is seemingly another production issuing from us which warrants no less a recommendation: for those things which we engender by way of our soul, the children of our mind, of our courage and of our sufficiency, are the product of a more noble portion than the corporeal, and are more our own; we are father and mother both in this generation. These latter cost us more dear and bring us more honour, if they prove of some good: for the worth of our other children is much more theirs than ours, our part in it is slight indeed; whilst with these all their beauty, all their grace and price is ours. In this way they do represent us and bring us return in much greater measure than the others. Plato adds that these are immortal children who immortalize their fathers, yea even deify them . . .

So writes Montaigne, 'On the Affection of Fathers for their Children' (*Essays*).

The role given to the superego in sublimation, as also the demonstration of the motives for the admiration the public bears the artist, is linked, I believe, to his success in attaining fulfilment in the midst of obstacles and difficulties. This seems to me to warrant a diminution of the importance of the social factor, to which Freud refers frequently, according to which, in sublimation, the aim becomes socially acceptable or the instinct which has undergone sublimation acquires a social value. Wilfrid Sebaoun (verbal statement) once said that the theory of sublimation would do well to forego the social explanation. Jones had already written, à propos of the 'London school' (1935), '. . . there is no danger of any analysts neglecting external reality, whereas it is always possible for them to underestimate Freud's doctrine of the importance of psychical reality'. Thus the *social* value of sublimation would stem essentially from internal factors.

CHAPTER SIX

The Ego Ideal and the Ego's Submission to Reality Testing

He would take immense pleasure in looking at the portrait. He could thereby explore the hidden recesses of his soul. It would be a magic mirror. It had revealed to him the image of his body, henceforth it would reveal to him his soul.

Oscar Wilde, *The Portrait of Dorian Gray*

. . . To produce a reaction in many, which gives you in return the feeling of having been the author of it, and hence that you exist — of which no one is, prior to this, entirely certain.

Mallarmé, *Quant au livre. L'Action restreinte*

We have seen that the aim of creativity is essentially that of reinforcing self-esteem by diminishing the hiatus that exists between the ego and the ideal, whether or not the creative process has involved the utilization of sublimated instincts. The work thus represents an image of the artist's idealized ego which, at a certain level, is confused with a phallus, the symbol of fulfilment. 'Any work of art is a portrait of the artist', said Oscar Wilde. Indeed, but only on condition that one adds that it tends to represent him in a state of primary perfection. For this reason I prefer Bazaine's (1959) formulation according to which artistic productions are 'man's marvellous double'.

In so far as the work tends to represent the projection of the artist's idealized ego it need only contain a small fault for this to evoke a painful echo in the author's own ego. Thus, according to

Miró, blood circulates through his canvasses and when there is something wrong with the circulation, when the composition is defective, he can sense something wrong with his heart. We have remarked that the person fabricating the 'fake' has an imperative need, not only to create but also to impose his creation, that is to say, to have it recognized by the public. This is true, though to a lesser degree, for any creative artist. And indeed we know that we are all, more or less, dependent upon 'opinion'. It is a point we have touched upon briefly in relation to the group and which, in reality, concerns the much greater problem of man's relationship to his own kind (his peers). Why does the regulation of our self-esteem so often depend upon others? We have noted that the superego, an agency that is something of a late-comer, might be inadequately internalized and easily swept away by activation of the Illusion. We have recalled that, according to Freud, many human beings do not know guilt but only social anxiety. However, clinical experience reveals many examples of cases in which, in addition to a rigorous superego, there is at the same time an important element of social anxiety (amongst certain depressives in particular). Social anxiety itself includes, it would seem, a number of disparate elements. When Freud described it in *Civilization and Its Discontents* (1929) he put the accent on the fear of loss of love. At the same time he writes that 'such people habitually allow themselves to do any bad thing which promises them enjoyment, so long as they are sure that the authority will not know anything about it or *cannot blame them for it* [my italics]; they are afraid only of being found out'. And Freud adds in a note: 'This reminds one of Rousseau's famous mandarin.'

I believe this definition of social anxiety to include two different orders of things (and hence of affects). To carry out a misdeed, if one is sure of not being punished, is of the order of 'so long as you don't get caught' or fear of the law, and gives rise to the affect of fear rather than anxiety (unless one is speaking of *real Angst*). In that instance there is certainly a non-internalization of interdicts, and the superego and the sense of guilt are missing. The fear of loss of love seems more complex. In 1914 Freud said that being loved increased self-regard which 'has a specially intimate dependence on narcissistic libido'. It is the 'fulfilling of the ideal' that reinforces the ego's narcissism. To be loved therefore helps in the fulfilment of the ideal. The loss of 'society's' love would consequently lead to a widening of the gap between the ego and the ideal and be the equivalent of a narcissistic injury. The consequences of this state of affairs are, it would seem to me, very different from a simple fear of being punished. And indeed in 1914 Freud concluded his article by writing about social anxiety in a way that is very close to some of the views that I shall endeavour to elaborate:

> The ego ideal opens up an important avenue for the understanding of group psychology. In addition to its individual side, the ideal has a social side; it is also the common ideal of a family, a class or a nation. It binds not only a person's narcissistic libido, but also a considerable amount of his homosexual libido, which in this way turns back into the ego. The want of satisfaction which arises from the non-fulfilment of this ideal liberates homosexual libido, and this is transformed into a sense of guilt (social anxiety). Originally this sense of guilt was a fear of punishment by the parents, or, more correctly, the fear of losing their love; later the parents are replaced by an indefinite number of fellow-men. The frequent causation of paranoia by an injury to the ego, by a frustration of satisfaction within the sphere of the ego ideal, is thus made more intelligible . . . ('On Narcissism', Freud, 1914).

The loss of love, to the extent that this is equivalent to a loss of esteem, that is to say, when love serves above all as a food for narcissism, may result in very particular affects (that we all experience in some degree) that have been linked to *shame*. Piers and Singer (1953) have endeavoured to distinguish shame from guilt. Piers recalls that Freud connected shame to exhibitionism (being seen). Nunberg also connects it with exhibitionism. Fenichel links it to the loss of sphincter (urethra) control. It is in contrast to ambition. But, remarks Piers, to control micturition means not to be seen urinating, and ambition is of a narcissistic order. Piers therefore links shame to narcissism. For the author, shame results from a tension between the ego ideal and the ego, and not between the superego and the ego as in the case of guilt. Whereas guilt is aroused when a limit (established by the superego) is touched or transgressed, shame arises when a goal (proposed by the ego ideal) is not reached. Shame accompanies defeat, guilt transgression. Furthermore, for Piers,

> There is a continuous psychological interchange between the individual ego ideal and its projections in the form of collective ideals. It is important to recognize that the images that go into the formation of this part of the ego ideal do not have to be parental ones at all. The sibling group and the peer group are much more significant.

Alexander (1938) distinguished feelings of inferiority from feelings of guilt, the former referring to narcissism and the latter, with which they may enter into conflict, to 'conscience'. He beat a path for those authors wishing to differentiate phenomena that relate to the ego ideal from those of a superego order. Nor is this distinction between shame and guilt totally absent from Freud's thought when he writes: 'The adult is ashamed of his phantasies and hides them from other people. He cherishes his phantasies as his most intimate possessions, and as a rule he would rather confess his misdeeds than tell anyone his phantasies.' ('Creative Writers . . .', Freud, 1908; cf. Appendix on Freud on the ego ideal, below p. 220). However, in 'The Dissection of the Psychical Personality', in his *New Introductory Lectures* (1932), he would refuse to differentiate feelings of inferiority from feelings of guilt, both then being associated for him with tension between the ego and the superego.

Before discussing (in the next chapter) the separation Piers proposes between ego ideal and superego, I should like to attempt to link together certain elements that have all been related to the affect of shame. That there is a connection between shame and exhibitionism seems to me to be confirmed by the exclamations to which this affect gives rise: 'I wished the ground could have swallowed me up; I wished I could have vanished', says the person who has felt very humiliated. Furthermore, Piers underlines the importance of one's 'peers' as far as the individual ego ideal and the group are concerned. Hence we could say that we fear being seen by our peers in situations that are narcissistically unsatisfactory. Our peers then play the role for us of a mirror in which is reflected our ego with all its possible faults. It is as if our sense of personal worth, our self esteem, the tension or on the contrary the harmony between our ego and our ideal depended, to a large degree, on the image of ourselves that our peers reflect back to us, as if it were through our peers that we had proof of the worth or lack of worth of our ego.

I believe we find ourselves brought to measure our ego in the mirror held up to us by our peers because of an intrinsic difficulty in evaluating it differently. Freud did indeed describe reality-testing as being based upon the distinction between internal and external perceptions ('Negation', Freud, 1925). A presentation is real when we can rediscover its object in the external world. 'What is unreal, merely a presentation and subjective, is only internal; what is real is also there *outside*.' We have practically no way of effecting reality-testing in relation to our psychic ego, since there is no external object corresponding to its internal presentation. Consequently we find ourselves obliged to find mirrors in which we can observe our psychic ego, analogous to those mirrors in which we see reflected our body ego, which we can, in addition, apprehend almost completely by direct vision, apart from the face and back.

The way in which we are seen, are perceived by others, represents an equivalent to the projection into the external world of our psychic ego and hence constitutes an essential possibility of submitting it to reality-testing. There exists, therefore, a relationship between this evaluation of our psychic ego and homosexuality; a homosexuality that is normally inhibited in respect of its aim, more or less completely desexualized, and that forms the basis for the 'social instincts'.

Freud, in studying paranoia (Schreber, Freud, 1911), assigned the role of precipitating factor in this psychosis to 'social humiliations and slights' and linked these narcissistic injuries to the homosexual instinct, 'the social feelings' having their roots 'in a directly sensual erotic wish'. Describing the line of development that leads from narcissism to homosexuality, Freud picks out the links that exist between these two stages of the libido. (Narcissism is seen, in this text, as the unification of the sexual instincts which then cathect the subject's own body. 'What is of chief importance in the subject's self thus chosen as a love-object may already be the genitals.' 'The line of development then leads on to the choice of an external object with similar genitals — that is, to homosexual object-choice.' These well-known formulations seem to me to corroborate the view according to which our perception of the way in which we are seen by our peers, our narcissistic — and hence homosexual — doubles, allows us to gauge our own ego. At the same time we are able to get closer to certain aspects of exhibitionism (as a component instinct). In 'Instincts and Their Vicissitudes' (1915), Freud, studying the fate of voyeurism and exhibitionism, showed that these two component instincts are linked to narcissism. If exhibitionism consists in exchanging an active aim (looking) for a passive aim (being looked at), and an external object for one's own ego, voyeurism, for its part, has a narcissistic origin. The voyeur's original object was his own body and his aim that of seeing himself. Fenichel (1934) considers that as a result of this origin, 'exhibitionism remains more narcissistic than all the other component instincts. Its erogenous pleasure is always linked to an increase in self-esteem.' As the psychic ego has no presentation in the external world, it often makes use of the body ego, with which it identifies, in order to represent it. I consider this to be the origin of the confusion, not only between moral and aesthetic values but between value judgements in general and aesthetics: 'he gave a *beautiful* presentation', 'It was a *beautiful* performance', etc. Reality-testing in relation to the value of our psychic ego thus tends to be confused, at some level, with the judgement that is made of our body ego.

In the course of development, the body ego must be assimilated with the psychic ego and cathected with narcissistic libido, as described by Tausk (1919). When this 'egotization' comes undone during the course of major regressions, one witnesses not only phenomena such as the institution of the influencing machine (the projection of the subject's own body or genital organs) but also a projection of the psychic ego into the body ego itself.

Thus a patient whose friend (and at the same time rival — they were in love with the same man) shouted at her, in a moment of anger: 'I suppose you imagine you have very beautiful feelings', believed she noticed, over the following days, brown marks appearing on her face. In this example, the body is experienced as a stranger to the ego, and the psychic ego (the feelings which are not beautiful) is projected on to the body ego. The gain that is obtained is the same as in all projection. That which is bad is no longer internal, and it can be mastered: the patient hoped to get rid of these marks through an external form of treatment. It seems likely that such mechanisms are also at work in the case of certain people who seek cosmetic surgery, people whom one knows to be in other respects very damaged psychically. In my view, they have in fact regressed to a level at which the body ego has become detached from the psychic ego and has become a focus for projection.

In those cases where, on the contrary, the body ego is totally identified with the psychic ego (the body ego taking the role of representative of the psychic ego) we are equally in the presence of a regressive situation, though to a lesser degree. Indeed, whilst it may be normal to 'egotize' the body ego, it is not to be confused with the psychic ego. A complete coalescence of the two aspects of the ego in fact results in an impairment of the latter function, since the psychic ego is not identical with the body in which it is housed. (The aim of this coalescence seems to me to be linked, as I have said above, to the need to be able to achieve reality testing.) A beautiful body implies neither a beautiful soul nor extraordinary abilities. It is, no doubt, a regressive confusion between these two aspects of the ego that is present in certain 'narcissistic' subjects who seem to cathect only their bodies, are intolerant of the slightest physical imperfection and cannot bear to grow old. The body is for them much more than a body. It is the very representative of their most intimate being. The myth of Narcissus, contemplating and adoring his own image, insensible to other objects (the nymphs and young people), seemingly corresponds to this confusion. By this I mean that not only does he take himself as a sexual object, but in contemplating his exquisite body it is his very soul that he is attempting to grasp. As is well known, this turning inwards to the subject's own body is common to numerous psychotic regressions, but in fact at the level of the primary process, psychic ego and body ego continue to be identified. One can recognise numerous offshoots of this throughout the lives of subjects whose development has taken a satisfactory course. Links between the psyche and the body make the body ego a 'double' for the psychic ego. Ferenczi has shown that the penis is a double of the ego in miniature. It can therefore be utilized for making an evaluation of the ego. The absence of this double in women no doubt contributes to their being more at the mercy of 'opinion', reinforcing their dependency and need for narcissistic confirmation. The 'double' is eventually a focus for projection and, hence, a persecutor. A consideration of the connection between these links and the subsequent relationship between the subject and his peers, as homosexual doubles, seems to me to show the complementary nature of Tausk's theory of delusions and that of Freud's. If one is prepared to accept that the homosexual object plays the role of intermediary in relation to the subject's own body in an evaluation of the (psychic) ego, then there is no contradiction in seeing the focus of projection (and hence the persecutors) as being at one time the body (the influencing machine), at another the homosexual object. Subsequently, the evaluation of the psychic ego will take place through an internalization of the parents who observe the child and demonstrate their pleasure or disapproval. Initially the task of supplying the child with narcissistic confirmation falls primarily to the mother (Grunberger). If the child feels himself to be loved by his mother (but not seduced by her) simply by virtue of *the fact that he exists*, then he will be able to internalize, to some degree, a capacity for self-evaluation. This will make him less dependent on those around him for the regulation of his self-esteem.

Seen in a broader perspective, the achievement of identifications with objects that support the ego ideal, will allow him to acquire a good sense of self-esteem. His ego will be identified with idealized objects, thereby coming closer to his ideal and, at the same time, being able to offer itself to love of the id (*The Ego and the Id*, Freud, 1923). His self-esteem will thereby be increased and this will make him more autonomous in relation to 'opinion'.

Generally speaking, the (belated secondary) identifications permit a better evaluation of the subject's own ego, their objects having previously been external and therefore subject to reality-testing. When — according to the distinction rightly made by certain authors — the mother does not love her child for what he *is*, but only for what he *does*, evaluation of the ego and reinforcement of self-esteem can only be accomplished through deeds. In principle, deeds permit an accurate evaluation of the ego to be made, since, as they represent a form of objectification, a projection into space and time, they can be subjected to reality-testing. But in fact the attitude of the mother has vitiated the 'objective' character of the deed, which will no longer be used as proof in itself of the ego's abilities, but as a means to gain confirmation (approval) from others, as previously from the mother.

Furthermore, these deeds are not experienced as expressing the totality of the ego, but only fragmentary aspects of it. They do not, therefore, represent a test of its overall worth. Only an act of creativity enables the ego to be evaluated in its entirety ('Your deed is always placed on paper; for to reflect without leaving any trace becomes evanescent, as for the instinct to be exalted in some vehement gesture then lost to your search' [Mallarmé], whence its significance for abolishing the gap between the ego and the ideal. We have seen that recognition of the work by others is absolutely indispensable to the author of an inauthentic work. We have said that it is conflicts linked to introjection and unrealized identifications that lead to this type of creation, and we have noted that their authors are aware, at some level, of a deficiency in their ego, even if they desperately proclaim the contrary. They thus have no autonomous capacity for regulating their self-esteem and are forced to depend upon the recognition of others.

This search for confirmation via external objects often takes a less absolute form in those creative artists whose productions have involved the use of sublimated instincts. We have seen that they have been better able to integrate their oedipal identifications, and doubtless one can see in this the origin of their greater autonomy vis-à-vis public opinion. However this is never total, and if Freud managed to forego the approbation of his contemporaries over a long period, he nonetheless communicated his discoveries to a privileged correspondent from whom he expected judgement and confirmation. The 'creator' does indeed hope to have his work recognized by others. He 'publishes' or 'exhibits' it to this effect, and it is my view that if he had a good capacity for regulating his self-esteem, a well-internalized loving mother, he would quite simply not 'create'. Why project one's idealized ego to the external world if one is intimately assured of its worth? This would seem to add support to the view that the creative artist's balance is a precarious one. I am here completely in agreement with Michel Fain, who describes, in his contribution to Gérard Mendel's paper (1964), a patient who reads out, in a session, a tale that expresses the nub of his conflicts, about which he concludes:

> The activity accompanying such a sublimated act, his exhibition, causes the whole to be genetically related to a phantasy acted out in front of the parents, whereas

integration, as an internalized phantasy activity, requires an identification with the observer, in the case cited above. To show oneself, to see the reaction of the other, to thereby gain a feeling of existing, a sequence that is characteristic of exhibitionism, demonstrates the difficulty experienced in being one's own observer, that is to say in being able to ensure the regulation of one's self-esteem.

However, I have argued previously that there was an intrinsic difficulty in submitting our ego to reality-testing and that, for this reason, we made use of our peers to reflect back our image. I think that to some extent this difficulty is never entirely resolved, even when the observer has been internalized, because as a result of projections and educational constraints this observer is never entirely good. A lack of satisfaction will result in respect of the subject's own ego, a gap between it and the ideal, such that he will then seek external gratifications. Furthermore, each stage of development seemingly requires a fresh internalization, the child showing himself to the observer with his newly realized acquisitions, and the most well-conducted education risks failing in the integration of one or other of these phases. The relationship to our peers always plays a role in the regulation of our self-esteem, to a greater or lesser degree depending on the vicissitudes of our personal development. Certainly in some cases this role is of very little significance, whereas in others it may become overwhelming.

The exhibition which then takes place essentially, as I said above, in front of the subject's (homosexual) doubles, who play the role of mirror, engenders, when it fails to achieve the anticipated narcissistic satisfaction, the affect of shame. This seems to me to be linked not only to the narcissistic injury suffered, but also to the resexualization of the homosexuality that results therefrom. Indeed, it seems to me that the narcissistic injury resulting from the lack of recognition by others (the homosexual double) is immediately sexualized, that is to say assimilated to a genital castration, experienced as being sure to lead to passive penetration. I have been struck by the fact that those authors who have written about shame — those at least that I have had occasion to consult, such as Piers and Singer (1953) and Levin (1971) — however interesting their work may be in other respects, fail to take account of the fact that shame causes a person to *turn red*. This is indicative of the presence of a sexual phantasy, whilst in another connection the links between a phobia of blushing and paranoia are well known. One patient with a phobia of blushing dreamt of a *red moon*. (In French, 'moon' is a childish word for bottom.) I do not think one could find a better condensation of anal exhibitionism, the wish for penetration attaching to it, and the redness of the face, the whole projected outside, into the sky. The fear of going red is therefore linked to that of an imminent emergence of anal wishes, wishes that, according to the patient, run the risk of being spotted by the observer and interpreted as a manner of offering himself passively to him. 'Losing face', the ultimate fear for certain people and in certain cultures (so-called 'cultures of shame') thus implies an uncovering of the behind (the anus).

The person who feels ashamed hides his face. Thus not only does he attempt to disguise the signs of the re-sexualization of his homosexual instincts (his blushing) but also the displacement, from the rear to the front, of which he is the object. He has *lost face*, and his face has become his rear (cf. the equation cheeks = buttocks). The fact of not being able to see either one's own back or one's own face (without a mirror) is probably not unrelated to this displacement. There must be some link between the wearing of the veil, homosexuality and the fear of losing face in 'the cultures of shame'.

It is evident that the 'social instincts' are often fragile, that is to say insufficiently desexualized. The passive homosexual instinct is repressed with a significant narcissistic fixation. The more this occurs, the more the resexualization of homosexuality will be violent and pathogenic, leading the subject in the direction of narcissistic regression.

It is possible that here I am in line with Jean Mallet's interesting theories about paranoia (1964, 1966), in which he emphasizes the role of the sibship for the future paranoic, and more particularly that of the elder brother, the 'reduplication of the subject in the external world'. Similarly Catherine Parat (personal communication) has mentioned the important role played by the fact of belonging to the same generation. I think this is in accordance with the role of mirror given to our *alter egos*. That the exhibition which fails in its purpose of feeding our narcissism, through the flattering image of our own ego that others would reflect back to us, should lead to a resexualization of (passive) homosexuality, can I think be inferred from Freud's analysis of 'Embarrassing Dreams of Being Naked'. Indeed, says Freud,

> Dreams of being naked or insufficiently dressed in the presence of strangers sometimes occur with the additional feature of there being a complete absence of any such feeling as shame on the dreamer's part. We are only concerned here, however, with those dreams of being naked in which one does feel shame and embarrassment and tries to escape or hide, and is then overcome by a strange inhibition which prevents one from moving and makes one feel incapable of altering one's distressing situation. It is only with this accompaniment that the dream is typical; without it, the gist of its subject-matter may be included in every variety of context or may be ornamented with individual trimmings. Its essence [in its typical form] lies in a distressing feeling in the nature of shame and in the fact that one wishes to hide one's nakedness, as a rule by locomotion, but finds one is unable to do so. I believe the great majority of my readers will have found themselves in this situation in dreams.
>
> The nature of the undress involved is customarily far from clear. The dreamer may say "I was in my chemise", but this is rarely a distinct picture. The kind of undress is usually so vague that the description is expressed as an alternative: "I was in my chemise or petticoat". As a rule the defect in the dreamer's toilet is not so grave as to appear to justify the shame to which it gives rise. In the case of a man who has

worn the Emperor's uniform, nakedness is often replaced by
some breach of the dress regulations: "I was walking in the
street without my sabre and saw some officers coming up", or
"I was without my necktie", or "I was wearing civilian check
trousers", and so on. (*Interpretation of Dreams*, Freud, 1900)

In fact, Freud does not explain why certain dreams of being naked
do not arouse shame. On the contrary, the examples he gives
are all, above all else, centred upon castration. For Freud the
painful feeling, shame, comes from the censorship. But why
should the censorship transform the wish to exhibit oneself — for
Freud indeed says that these are dreams of exhibiting — into an
exhibition of castration, particularly since according to Freud this
type of dream always ends in a *nightmare*. Now, since the theory of
nightmares implies the imminent realization of an unconscious
wish that is brought up against the preconscious, why suppose that
we have here a wish (that of exhibiting oneself) already modified
by the censorship (which would supposedly have converted it into
its opposite: what is exhibited is castration), when the essence of
the nightmare is to realize the wish, in barely disguised form? It
seems to me that the wish of the dreamer, in the examples given
by Freud, is to offer himself passively to those observing him, for
example, the officers approaching the dreamer without his sabre.
This seems to me to be confirmed by the references to paranoia
which appear on two occasions in the text. Starting out from the
pleasure children take in exhibiting themselves and the fact that
this exhibition is often prevented by adults, he says: 'In the early
history of neurotics an important part is played by exposure to
children of the opposite sex; in paranoia delusions of being
observed while dressing and undressing are to be traced back to
experiences of this kind', and also: 'Curiously enough, the people
upon whom our sexual interest was directed in childhood are
omitted in all the reproductions which occur in dreams, in hysteria
and in obsessional neurosis. It is only in paranoia that these
spectators reappear and, though they remain invisible, their
presence is inferred with fanatical conviction.'

It therefore seems to me possible to bring together a certain number of elements discovered by Freud and by those, such as Piers, who seek to differentiate shame, which belongs to the order of the ego ideal, from guilt, relating to the superego. Indeed, if the ego ideal is linked to narcissism and to homosexuality, shame seems to me to originate from the same libidinal sources. Furthermore, I have attempted to delineate the following sequence: the wish to receive narcissistic confirmation from one's peers (to diminish the margin between the ego and the ideal) leads the subject to exhibit himself to them. If this exhibition fails to ensure such satisfaction (if a narcissistic injury or a 'social humiliation' results), the resexualization of homosexuality renders the narcissistic injury equivalent to a castration, and the exhibition to an exposure of the anus. This 'about turn' (literally) of the exhibition of a narcissistically cathected phallus into an anal exhibition may be compared to that which has been described in the previous chapter in relation to the discovery of the fecal phallus beneath the gilt that seeks to mask it. An example of this 'about turn', this time applied to the object, is supplied by the play-on-words 'patriarche — *Vaterarsch*' ('A Mythological Parallel . . .', Freud, 1916).

Shame is an expression of the proximity of the sexual phantasy. In predisposed cases, as defined by Freud, a paranoid process may be precipitated. Social anxiety, seen in this light, would essentially be linked to the fear of the resexualization of passive homosexual impulses for want of narcissistic gratification from peers. That which only relates to a 'fear of the law' should be treated separately.

How is one to integrate into this whole an element that was alluded to in connection with the exhibition dream, namely the delusion of being watched? It does not strike me as overly risky to distinguish 'a commentary on one's actions' from other forms of delusions of persecution. Indeed, in 1914, Freud used the example of delusions of being watched to announce, in advance as it were, the arrival of the superego:

It would not surprise us if we were to find a special psychical agency which performs the task of seeing that narcissistic satisfaction from the ego ideal is ensured and which, with this end in view, constantly watches the actual ego and measures it by that ideal. If such an agency does exist, we cannot possibly come upon it as a discovery — we can only recognize it; for we may reflect that what we call our "conscience" has the required characteristics . . .

Patients of this sort [those subject to delusions of being watched] complain that all their thoughts are known and their actions watched and supervised; they are informed of the functioning of this agency by voices which characteristically speak to them in the third person ("Now she's thinking of that again", "now he's going out") ('On Narcissism', Freud, 1914).

It seems to me that this type of delusion can be likened to two other syndromes, one of a psychotic nature, the other encountered in certain so-called character-neuroses. The first, of which I have had an example amongst my patients, consists in imagining that acts or words are imitated or repeated ('if I lift my arm, somebody else lifts their arm. If I say "victory" somebody else during the day will say "victory" ', i.e. mental automatism).

The neurotic syndrome is described in the Anglo-Saxon literature under the name of self-consciousness. It refers to those who cannot appear before others without an acute and constant awareness of their gestures, their general appearance, which they feel is always being watched by those around them. Annie Reich (1960) writes of them: 'They feel that attention is indeed focused on them in a *negative* way: as though others, instead of being dazzled, were discerning the warded-off "inferiority" behind the false front'. The author attributes this 'consciousness of one's self' to an insufficient desexualization of the ego functions. I would see it as corresponding to an impossibility of evaluating the ego other than by exhibition to external objects, for want of an internal observer and integrated identifications, at the same time as this excessive self-awareness indicates that the ego lacks cohesiveness and, hence, a sense of identity. If one is constantly aware of being oneself, this is because one is actually on the point of losing this certitude and because the different identifications which make up the ego are very close to being dissolved. It seems to me that in fact the social instincts of these subjects have been insufficiently desexualized (or have been resexualized) since, instead of receiving narcissistic confirmation from others (who would be 'dazzled'), they are 'seen through' ('behind the false front'), their 'inferiority' (their castration) being revealed, along with the resultant humiliation, in relation to which I advanced the hypothesis that it was the equivalent of an anal exhibition (of that which is literally 'behind the front'). Here again we rediscover the fears described in the preceding chapter concerning the discovery of the fecal phallus beneath the brilliant gaudery. However, those who manifest the syndrome of self-consciousness are not necessarily producers of 'fakes' and may possess a maturative ego ideal.

For some young girls a profound sense of shame attaches to the appearance of any stain of menstrual blood on their clothing. To view this as a demonstration of castration does not seem to me to be a sufficient explanation of this affect (these same young girls can talk freely about their periods). It must be taken into account that the stain is always situated in the area of the buttocks and that the exhibition of genitality is thus replaced by that of the anal zone.

The person who believes his words and deeds to be imitated has reached a much deeper state of regression. His ego has lost its capacity for self-evaluation. The function of the other as mirror, reflecting back the image of the ego, has become a caricature. Identifications are scattered, actions and words are no longer experienced as belonging entirely to the ego. The ego is, at the same time, in the stranger who imitates it, and this stranger has taken possession of the tottering ego. For the subject, the phenomenon as a whole always has a persecutory tone.

According to Freud, the delusion of being watched is a

function of the reprojection outside of the critical agency (the future superego). But in that case the insults that the patient hallucinates, generally concerning his sexuality, and a commentary on his actions would be one and the same thing. Yet Freud describes the case of a patient who was attempting to spare herself the reproach of being a 'bad woman' by hallucinating gibes from her neighbours (following an attempted seduction of which she was the object). 'Afterwards she came to hear the same reproach from outside', says Freud,

> Thus *the subject-matter remained unaffected;* what was altered was something in the *placing* of the whole thing. Earlier it had been an internal self-reproach, now it was an imputation coming from outside. The judgement about her had been transposed outwards: people were saying what otherwise she would have said to herself. Something was gained by this. She would have had to accept the judgement pronounced from inside; she could reject the one arriving from outside. In that way *the judgement, the reproach, was kept away from her ego.*
>
> The purpose of paranoia is thus to fend off an idea that is incompatible with the ego, by projecting its substance into the external world ('Draft H . . .', Freud, 1895).

One cannot therefore assimilate the function of the projection of a reproach (externalization of the superego) to that of a commentary on one's actions which, it seems to me, represents the externalization of the observer charged with reflecting back the image of one's ego, from whom one seeks a narcissistic confirmation aimed at bringing ego and ideal closer together. We have seen that this role — and Freud was already saying this in 1914 —, which fell to the parents, is subsequently taken over by the 'peers'. Now, the paranoic tends, as we know, to regress to narcissistic megalomania, that is to say to the stage at which he was his own ideal. If he achieved this completely he would have no need of any object in order to evaluate his ego. The projection of the elements that form the superego is easily understood. The superego (as an internalized agency) can only get in the way of megalomanic regression. The evaluation of the ego via commentary on one's actions seems to me to represent in itself less a mechanism of defence by projection than a symptom linked to the checking of delusions of grandeur and, hence, to the vestiges of homosexual object relations. Indeed, it seems to me that there too one can detect the effects of the homosexual instinct claiming its 'due' in some sort. 'The observer', experienced as external to the ego, seeks in this way to dismantle the megalomanic defence. In 'The Uncanny' (1919), Freud again takes up the question of the delusion of being watched, relating it to the 'double' (and also, after Otto Rank, to mirrors and to shadows):

> A special agency is slowly formed there, which is able to stand over against the rest of the *ego*, which has the function of observing and criticizing the self and of exercising a censorship within the mind, and which we become aware of as our 'conscience'. In the pathological case of delusions of being watched, this mental agency becomes isolated, dissociated from the *ego*, and discernible to the physician's eye. The fact that an agency of this kind exists, which is able to treat the rest of the *ego* like an object — the fact, that is, that man is capable of self-observation — renders it possible to invest the old idea of a "double" with a new meaning and to ascribe a number of things to it — above all, those things which seem to self-criticism to belong to the old surmounted narcissism of earliest times.

Originally — Freud takes up here an idea of Rank's — the double furnished an assurance of survival, a need that arose from primary narcissism, and thus the first 'double' was probably the immortal soul. The idea of a development of the double, from primary narcissism through to moral conscience, allows us perhaps to connect our observer to two phases of development, the first one of which does not imply an internalization of the post-oedipal superego. In another connection, Freud, in his 1914 paper, seems to allude to a similar eventuality when he writes about 'the activity of this critically observing agency — which becomes *heightened* into conscience and philosophic introspection'. In addition, the 'functional phenomenon' of Silberer that he quotes in support of his thesis, can with difficulty be accounted for by the activity of the moral conscience. If self-observation forms a necessary part of it, it is not reducible to it. Similarly, if the function of the ego depended solely on the superego, it would have to be admitted that in a disturbance such as depersonalization, for example, the part of the subject that observes the process that is taking place would be the superego. Numerous authors who have studied depersonalization have stressed the importance of self-observation in this phenomenon. However, it is all but certain that what is involved here is an ego function charged with reality-testing for the whole ego which, in certain cases, and for reasons that I have attempted to define, is delegated to external objects: the peer group. The subject does not then aspire to having his ego realize a moral ideal (which would be dependent on the superego), but to it being in conformity with what the group expects (or is deemed to expect) of it. This reflects back to him a satisfactory image, and thus brings him closer to his ideal. This distinction is of some importance in so far as the relationship between analytic and psychotherapeutic technique is concerned. It is known that the analyst must not reassure his patient when, for example, he shows a sense of guilt about his masturbatory practices, by saying to him: 'But everybody does that.' At that moment, not only has he failed to analyze the transference and abandoned his neutrality, but he has also favoured a regressive ego ideal, that which impels the ego to conformity with the wishes of the group in order to avoid shame, and to a consequent resexualization of homosexual impulses. Thus the analyst may conjure away the integration of the patient's homosexuality, which should lead him to greater autonomy in respect of his peers, to a reinforcing of his ego's narcissism, and hence to a real diminution of the margin between the ego and the ideal. The analyst may also thereby conjure away the analysis of the conflicts between the patient's instincts, his wishes and his superego.

CHAPTER SEVEN

The Superego
and the Ego Ideal

Following a law of nature, men may *generally* be divided into two
categories: the inferior category (ordinary men) as one might say,
the masses who serve only to reproduce other beings identical to
themselves, and the other category, that, in short, of real men, that
is to say those who have the gift or talent of being able to say
something new in their circle . . .

In the second category all fall outside the law, they are
destroyers . . . The crimes of such men are, evidently, relative and
diverse; most often they demand, under very varied forms, the
destruction of the present order of things in the name of
something better. But if such a man finds it necessary to go over
someone's dead body, then in my view he may do so in all
conscience . . .

The first perpetuate the world and increase its number; the
second cause it to move towards a goal. Both have an absolutely
equal right to existence. In a word, for me each have the same
rights and *vive la guerre éternelle* until the New Jerusalem, as it
should be.

Dostoyevsky, *Crime and Punishment*

Before putting forward a personal point of view, I should like
briefly to set out the views of some authors who have attempted to
define the relationship between the superego and the ego ideal.
This they have done, sometimes with the conclusion that the two
concepts do need to be differentiated, sometimes reducing the ego
ideal simply to a function of the superego. In doing this they adopt,
more or less, Freud's later formulations in which, when he does
not totally identify the two concepts, he makes the ego ideal a
function of the superego in so far as the latter proposes models to

the ego to which it obliges it to conform. As Joseph Sandler et al. (1963) remark, to my mind quite rightly,

> because Freud's early concept of ego ideal includes something other than his later concept of superego, a very wide spectrum of functions has to be subsumed under the term "superego", with the consequences that such statements as "conflict with the superego" or "tension between ego and superego" may be theoretically and clinically imprecise unless carefully qualified.

Amongst those authors who have been led to separate the ego ideal from the superego it is striking to find Nunberg and Jones, who did so even in Freud's lifetime.

1927. **Jones**

Jones assimilates the unconscious part of internalized prohibitions to the superego, whereas the conscious and more loving part would form the ego ideal.

1932. **Nunberg**

Nunberg considers that the ego ideal results because

> instinct gratification is renounced out of fear of losing the love object . . . this object is absorbed by the ego and cathected with libido; it becomes a part of the ego. In contrast to the ideal ego, it is called *ego ideal*. Out of love for this ideal, man clings to it and submits to its demands. Whereas the ego submits to the superego out of fear of punishment, it submits to the ego ideal out of love . . . the ego ideal is an image of the loved objects in the ego and the superego is an image of the hated and feared objects . . . The ego ideal seems to contain more maternal libido, the superego, more of the paternal.

1946–1954. **Edith Jacobson**

I have made some mention of Edith Jacobson's views (see Chapter 5). In 1954 she postulates the maternal origin of the ego ideal. Phantasies of a (total) incorporation of the gratifying object appear as an expression of the wish to re-establish the lost union.

> This desire probably never ceases to play a part in our emotional life. Even normally the experience of physical merging and of an "identity" of pleasure in the sexual act may harbor elements of happiness derived from the feeling of return to the lost, original union with the mother.
>
> Thus the earliest wishful fantasies of merging and being one with the mother (breast) are the foundations on which all future types of identification are built.

The primitive ego ideal is linked to the wish to be one with the love object. 'Even our never-ending struggle for oneness between ego and ego ideal reflects the eternal persistence of this desire.' However, the author does not separate the superego from the ego ideal.

> Forever close to the id and yet indispensable for the ego, the ego ideal is . . . part of the superego system, as a pilot and guide for the ego.
>
> The vicissitudes of the ego ideal reverberate, of course, the development of the infantile value measures. Its core harbors derivatives of early notions of value, such as the idea of eternal happiness, of glamor and wealth, of physical or mental power and strength, ideals which may play a paramount role in patients whose superego has never matured.

In the little girl there is a maternal ego ideal, 'the ideal of an unaggressive, clean, neat and physically attractive little girl who is determined to renounce sexual activities.'

In her 1954 article, Edith Jacobson studied the ego ideal of the depressive, which she sees as overly personified, having failed to reach a level of abstraction. Manic-depressives are proud of their ego ideal, 'as if their own idealism *per se* were capable of transforming them into human beings of worth'.

In 1946, however, this author had considered that the ego ideal appeared at the same time as the superego and given a definition of the little girl's ego ideal very similar to that which she would propose in 1954. The structure of the superego was considered essentially to be linked to the incorporation of the idealized parents, and its creation to be an attempt at restoring the ego, to mitigate the traumatizing effects of the object's deceit and depreciation. 'The superego is a life-saving response to a narcissistic injury.' The normal superego would only embody a single idealized parent, the one identified with. The superego of the depressive would be the result of an introjection of both idealized parents.

1953–1954–1960. **Annie Reich**

Annie Reich, in those works I have had occasion to refer to (chapter 5), distinguishes the superego, based on an acceptance of reality, from the ego ideal, 'based upon the desire to cling in some form or another to a denial of the ego's, as well as of the parents', limitations and to regain infantile omnipotence by identifying with the idealized parent'. A megalomanic ego ideal is linked to a weak ego and an insufficiently developed superego. It is a result of a disturbance in early relationships. Libido is insufficiently invested in objects and cathects the ego ideal. Originally the ego ideal is an identification with the primal mother, but it may subsequently be projected on to the father's penis with the aim of negating the fear of castration. The aim then becomes that of fusion with this idealized penis (1953). In her 1954 article, Annie Reich suggests: 'The ego ideal represents what one wishes to be, the superego what one ought to be.' The superego is the result of later identifications intended to restrain incestuous sexuality, but there are earlier identifications. Normally these primitive identifications would subsequently fuse with the later ones. These early identifications with the envied and admired qualities of the parents aim to repair a narcissistic injury. They represent a wish to be like the idealized parent (not necessarily to become like them). These aspirations must be described as ego ideals. The ego measures itself against them, and self-esteem is dependent on the distance between them and the ego, just as later it is dependent on the distance between the ego and the superego. The realization of these aspirations will depend upon the level of development of the ego. At a primitive level one is dealing with narcissistic phantasies of a magical, hallucinated fulfilment. These early identifications are but imitations of that which, at any given moment, the subject sees as offering a suitable means of wiping out the narcissistic injury. They are consequently subject to change. 'From many points of view the child cannot be entirely like the adults. Normally a capacity for self-evaluation develops which pushes in the direction of the gradual achievement of identification. The parent is himself then evaluated more realistically. This is the normal ego ideal.' Habitually, following puberty, the ego ideal and the superego merge, but 'it would seem that any attempt to understand non-psychotic narcissistic states requires the concept of the ego ideal'.

The pathology of the ego ideal becomes more apparent in those cases where the disturbance in the development of the ego is greater. Not only are the megalomanic aspects of the ego ideal pronounced, but frequently the ideals reveal crude, unsublimated sexual traits. The author was to take up this idea again in her 1960 article: at times the narcissistic phantasies and the demands of the superego find themselves in opposition, as the former contain numerous elements of an unsublimated instinctual character.

1953. **Piers**

I would just remind the reader of Piers' views, as outlined in the previous chapter and the distinction proposed by this author between shame (relating to the ego ideal) and guilt (which is of a superego order).

1955. **Novey**

Novey suggests (in 'The Role of the Superego . . .') that the ego ideal should be considered as 'a distinct psychic institution related to the ego and superego'. According to him, the ego ideal defines 'that particular segment of introjected objects whose functional operation has to do with proposed standards of thoughts, feeling, and conduct acquired later than the oedipal superego, but having its roots in the early pregenital narcissistic operations against anxiety'.

1958. P. Kramer

Kramer suggests that the superego consists of three parts: the ego ideal, the prohibiting superego and the benevolent superego. The ego ideal represents what a person wishes to be, the goals to which he aspires. Tension between the ego ideal and the ego produces shame, a sense of inadequacy, a lowering of self esteem. Harmony between the ego ideal and the ego leads to a sense of satisfaction with oneself, to a feeling of pride.

The prohibiting superego has entirely different qualities. It is demanding, severe, punitive. Its prototype is the prohibiting — and consequently hated — parent. It is cathected with aggressive forces. The benevolent superego is derived from the image of the loved parents (particularly the mother). Whereas one fears punishment from the prohibiting superego, one fears being abandoned by the benevolent superego. Normally the three elements merge with the resolution of the Oedipus complex. However, clinically, one can detect tensions between these elements. In fact the sense of guilt implies the presence of love, and the functioning of the prohibiting superego in isolation would lead to fear. The absence of the benevolent element prevents the real internalization of the superego and may lead the subject to anti-social behaviour.

1961. Jeanne Lampl de Groot

J. Lampl de Groot suggests examining separately the formation of the ideal and that of the punitive and self-criticizing agency. Hallucination (hallucinatory wish fulfilment) provides the basis for the ego ideal. 'The ego ideal is an agency of wish fulfilment.'

The superego is essentially restrictive and prohibiting. Ego ideal and superego have a fundamentally different origin, but their confusion is due to the fact that at the time of the Oedipus complex, being like the parents and doing what they demand are both equally based upon an identification with the parents. But in fact their functions have opposing goals. The ego ideal is a gratifying agency, the superego is restrictive. When development proceeds smoothly these two agencies coalesce and can no longer be distinguished, save at times of crisis (adolescence, menopause).

1964. John M. Murray

For J.M. Murray, the superego is a product of oedipal conflicts and its executive agent is the anxiety derived from fears of castration that are so powerfully operative at this time. The ego ideal is the heir of the original narcissism, in other words, 'it is born as an effort to restore the lost *Shangri-la* of the relations with the all-giving primary mother'. The transition from the primitive ego ideal to a more mature ego ideal represents a highly important problem of development.

1964. Hélène Deutsch

Hélène Deutsch has shown that in some cases the ego ideal can attain fulfilment via asceticism and in others via direct sexual satisfaction (one may be proud of one's sexual abilities); sublimations are not necessary.

1964. Grete Bibring

Grete Bibring seeks to define the ego ideal by contrasting it with the superego. It has predominantly narcissistic features. Whilst the superego operates through pressures and threats of punishment, the ego ideal exerts its pull by holding forth a promise. Genetically, the ego ideal derives its strength mainly from positive libidinal strivings; in the superego aggressive forces prevail. Despite these contrasts, however, she sees a close relationship between ego ideal and superego. Following Murray, the author believes that it is necessary to restore the ego ideal of certain patients and sees the analyst proposing his ego ideal (which she defines as being composed of the classical virtues of ancient Greece: wisdom, temperance, justice and courage) (*sic*) in lieu of the patient's primitive narcissism.

1964. **Hendrick**

Hendrick likewise separates ego ideal and superego. He thinks it important to take account of the fragility of the ego ideal in psychotic processes. The ego ideal has to develop in the direction of abstraction, and not become fixed to a living person. It is this latter eventuality that is present in depression. There have been insufficient displacements of the love object during the latency period. The ego ideal has remained pre-pubertal.

1964. **M. Laufer**

The ego ideal is defined by the author as 'an aspect of the superego'. For him, the ego ideal can only be defined as such when it becomes a function of the superego. He does, however, refer to 'pre-oedipal precursors' of the ego ideal, and even to 'oedipal precursors', in relation to the ego ideal of adolescents. He quotes Ritvo and Solnit (1960): 'The ego ideal can be considered to arise from three main sources: the idealization of the parents; the idealization of the child by the parents; and the idealization of the self by the child.' He defines the ego ideal as 'that part of the superego which contains images and attributes the ego strives to acquire in order to re-establish narcissistic equilibrium'. It sets goals for the ego. According to the author, the content of the ego ideal, as a part of the superego, remains unchanged after internalization. Adolescent idols are reflections of the perfect self (and not of the idealized parents). Where a struggle against the identification would be involved (a feminine identification for a boy, for example), there is a pseudo-ego ideal. Relationships with other contemporaries are possible because they represent a part of the self rather than the oedipal father. The ego fights to preserve the image of itself that it is struggling to acquire and attempts to deny any dependence on the original objects.

1962. **Evelyne Kestemberg.** — 1964. **R. Mises**

This last point of view may be compared to that of Evelyne Kestemberg, who writes about the adolescent's need to reject both his parents and their ideals in brutal fashion, and to that of R. Mises who remarked that the ego ideal may result from a tendency to refuse to submit to the superego, thereby proving to oneself one's freedom through giving oneself goals that are as far removed as possible from parental ideals.

1967. **B. Grunberger**

In a lecture given in February 1967, 'The Child's Treasure Hoard and the Avoidance of the Oedipus Complex', B. Grunberger saw the crisis of adolescence as being linked essentially to a rejection of the parents, the result, not of the Oedipus complex, but of the refusal of identification with the world of adults, and hence of an avoidance of the Oedipus complex. He adds that it seems to be very much a mark of contemporary civilization that this crisis is more and more frequently prolonged.

One might then summarize the views of the above authors as follows:

1. All, even when they assert that the ego ideal is a part of the superego, distinguish certain functions that belong to the ego ideal and which take account of its narcissistic, primitive and pre-oedipal character in relation to the superego;

2. Certain authors link the ego ideal with the wish for fusion with the mother;

3. The ego ideal is often considered to be linked to the libido, the superego to aggression;

4. Those authors who do make a clear distinction between ego ideal and superego do not indicate whether, for them, the ego ideal has the same status as an agency as does the superego;

5. Certain authors do not seem to differentiate the projection

of narcissism on to the object (which then constitutes the ego ideal) from the introjection of the idealized parents, or even from that of restrictive models imposed on the subject from without. Thus the ego ideal is sometimes seen as being the result of secondary identifications. Most of these authors see developments in the ego ideal taking place following the Oedipus complex, and particularly during adolescence. This would equally seem to be a characteristic that distinguishes it from the superego.

6. Normally, the ego ideal and the superego will ultimately coalesce.

1961. **Pierre Luquet**

Amongst French psychoanalytic views one finds positions that are more or less close to those quoted above. In his paper on 'Early Identifications', Pierre Luquet makes a distinction between early imagos and late imagos. In his view, the ego ideal is an early imago, that is to say, it is the result of the introjection of an object unassimilated by the ego, in the event a primitive, prohibiting object, whereas the superego is linked to the introjection of a late imago, that of the oedipal father.

1964. **B. Grunberger**

At the Colloquium of the Paris Psychoanalytic Society on *Narcissism*, Béla Grunberger maintained that in normal development superego and ego ideal cannot be distinguished. However, the superego has an instinctual origin (the Oedipus complex), and is in part imposed from outside, whereas the ego ideal, being of narcissistic origin, is essentially 'individualistic' and the expression of independence from the outside. When development does not go smoothly, the ego has to satisfy the sometimes opposing demands of the superego and the ego ideal. It is the existence of this conflict that leads him to see the ego ideal as an agency.

1964. **E. Kestemberg**. — 1965. **E. and J. Kestemberg**

Evelyne Kestemberg sees the ego ideal as being the result of early identifications with the parents and their values. She does not seem to have entirely retained this position as, in the paper she wrote in conjunction with Jean Kestemberg, the emphasis is on the necessity of distinguishing between the ego ideal and the introjection of idealized parental imagos.

1964. F. Pasche

F. Pasche, for his part, stresses the fact that the ego ideal is not an agency but a model, one or more images that condition certain demands of the superego (which here seems to be assimilated to the critical agency of 1914, charged with watching the ego to see that satisfaction in relation to the ego ideal is ensured).

1970. J. Bergeret

According to J. Bergeret one can observe, in borderline cases, a hypertrophy of the ego ideal and an atrophy of the superego.

1962. Hartmann and Loewenstein

In contrast, more or less, to the views of both French and foreign authors given above (though quite close, it seems to me, to F. Pasche's ideas), Hartmann and Loewenstein seek to re-place the ego ideal within the framework of the superego system, aligning themselves with Freud's formulation of 1932 according to which the superego is the vehicle of the ego ideal (see Appendix below). The authors state that the superego should not be attributed too early a role. One risks neglecting in this way the ego's own defensive capacities, as also the role played by reality in their development. They recall the views of Anna Freud, according to whom there is a primary hostility of the ego towards the instincts. (I would recall that this is in line with Freud's own views as expressed in 'Instincts and their Vicissitudes', 1915 and 'Repression', 1915.) The title of superego should be reserved for the product of the oedipal conflict.

We would not, as has occasionally been suggested, consider

the ego ideal as a separate system — separate from another system — that would comprise other superego functions such as, for example, conscience. As will be discussed later, the connections between the ego ideal and the prohibitive aspects of the superego are so close that both should be considered as aspects of one and the same system . . .

The ego ideal is 'an aspect of the superego'.

Studying the relationship between the ego ideal and the superego, the authors note that idealization of self and objects appears before the (oedipal) superego but, for them, the important thing is to distinguish between genetic continuity and functional characterization. And indeed, early idealizations and the early determinants of the superego must be viewed in parallel, and considered as precursors of the ego ideal. The ego ideal is just one function of the superego amongst others, just as there are numerous functions of the ego (perception, thought, defences, etc.). The ego ideal–superego unity forms a person's 'moral system'.

Melanie Klein

A separate place must be given here to Melanie Klein's views on the ego ideal and idealization. These have been very perceptively summarized in an unpublished work by Jean Bégoin in 1971. It must be noted that the concept of idealization appears very early on in Melanie Klein's work (1925), but is only fully developed in the course of her work on the depressive position and her description of paranoid-schizoid anxieties (especially Klein 1940, 1946). Idealization is linked to a denial of the subject's own aggression. It aims at combating persecution by the bad object by means of objects endowed with absolute perfection. Idealization is thus linked to the manic defence. At the same time it represents an essential mechanism of mourning since (manic) triumph over the object diminishes belief in the goodness of internal objects. Idealization allows fears of retaliation by the dead object (according to the talion principle) to be borne.

In 1947, Melanie Klein defined projective identification in

which the mechanisms of splitting, denial, omnipotence and idealization are operative. Idealization is linked to splitting: the idealized breast helps provide protection from the persecuting breast. Idealization is the result of persecutory fears. Equally, it is linked to the intensity of the instincts which seek unlimited gratification from the inexhaustible ideal breast.

Hallucinatory wish fulfilment is only possible through splitting of the object, accompanied by a denial of persecution and of the existence of the subject's bad objects and hence of his aggression. In other words, it occurs through the denial of a whole area of the object-relationship, of the ego and, therefore, of psychic reality. The infant must project good parts of himself into the object (the mother, the breast) in order to be able to establish a satisfactory object relationship. But if he does so to an excessive degree, this leads to an impoverishment of the ego due to the loss of good parts of the self projected into the object, which thus becomes the ego ideal. The introjected idealized object remains unassimilated, and the ego that is seeking to escape its persecutors thus becomes entirely dependent on its idealized internal object. The object relationship described here is schizoid and narcissistic. When the ego ideal is projected on to the object, the latter is loved because it is the repository of the 'good' parts of the subject.

Jean Bégoin, in his account of Melanie Klein's work on the concept of idealization, recalls that she postulates the existence of an ego from birth. It is evident, therefore, that the absence of a primary narcissistic phase fundamentally alters her whole conception of the ego ideal compared to that of Freud. I would differ somewhat from Jean Bégoin when he says in his work that 'the (Kleinian) concept of idealization is in direct line with the descriptions of Freud'. I think that we are in a different dimension here. For Freud, in 1914, the ego ideal can only be understood as a displacement of primary narcissism, by virtue of the non-renunciation of a satisfaction that has once been enjoyed. The defensive use of this search becomes possible secondarily, once object relations have been established. For Melanie Klein — and here Jean Bégoin underlines this point — idealization is a defence mechanism that she situates 'at the origin of narcissistic phenomena rather than being a consequence of them'. I feel myself to be in agreement with Bégoin's conclusions when he stresses the links between the Kleinian concept of idealization and the death instinct:

> Following Freud, she thinks that, in part, the ego, in the service of the death instinct, projects outside the threat represented by the internal death instincts. Whence the instant appearance of violent persecutory anxiety which leads to an immediate need for idealization and the phantasy of the existence, somewhere, of something that could satisfy *all* needs. The need for *idealization* is the need to deny the existence of the death instinct.

I would be very willing to believe that the 'object-relatedness' of the Ideal in Freud's writings from 1923, that I have indicated following Sandler et al. (1963), is directly linked, for Freud himself, to the introduction of the death instinct. It is nonetheless the case that Kleinian descriptions of idealization, which in a great number of instances are clinically strikingly accurate, seem to me to fail to recognize — by reason of the absence of primary narcissism from Melanie Klein's theory — the origin of the formation of the ego ideal, born of the primary de-fusion, and its function of preserving the perfectness of the subject, that the development of the ego has snatched from him.

1961. **H. Rosenfeld**

Melanie Klein makes no explicit mention of the link between superego and ego ideal. However, H. Rosenfeld (1961) defines the ego ideal as 'the aspect of the superego which arises from the identification with idealized objects'.

If we can now pick up again some of the propositions that have been put forward in the present work, we may perhaps be able to formulate some hypotheses concerning the relationship between the ego ideal and the superego that they imply.

First of all, I began by considering the ego ideal in its 1914 perspective, doubtless taking this as far as one could go, as a 'rescue operation' carried out by narcissism on the subject's own behalf and prompted by nostalgia for a time when he was his own ideal. This ideal is 'projected before him' as a hope, a promise, a guide. It is therefore, above all, a spontaneous creation. It is linked to the course of the subject's development, the child's wish being to 'grow up' (Freud, 1907–1908), that is to say to reconquer the lost perfection experienced in the world of primary fusion, by integrating the instinctual stages and the ego's levels of development which will allow him to achieve genitality, the identification with the father, possessor of the mother, in the accomplishment of incest. The incestuous phantasy contains within it that of a rediscovery of the primary object by another route. Seen in this way the ego ideal is maturative, that is to say, it encourages the subject to acquire an ego that has integrated all the phases of its development. The ideal education would therefore be that which corresponded to the optimum degree of integration allowing the ego to realize its project. It includes, essentially, a succession of identifications with different models, themselves renewed at each stage. These identifications with objects carrying the subject's narcissism (the idealized part or whole objects) do not seem to me to constitute the ego ideal but to be an effect of it, the ego aiming to reduce the margin separating it from the ideal by incorporating its idealized objects. These identifications are of prime importance for the development of the ego ideal (and the ego), since they permit the ego to come closer to its ideal:

1. Through the acquisition of real capacities;

2. Through the integration of its instincts and object relations;

3. Through the narcissistic satisfaction resulting from their partial realization, experienced unconsciously as taking the ego gradually towards the reattainment of its sense fulfilment. In this sense, it is no doubt inaccurate to say that the ego ideal becomes less demanding. The goal pursued is still equally grandiose (that is to say incest), but the subject is no longer bound by the law of all or

nothing, by the necessity for immediate and total gratification. These identifications must be distinguished — even if only from a heuristic point of view — from those which take as their object models imposed by the parents such as that of the little girl (literally a 'model') described by Edith Jacobson. The word model is a doublet of 'mould', and the neat, clean, attractive little girl devoid of sexuality, is the perfect anal product, cast in a mould, of an all-too-successful maternal toilet training. The maturative ego ideal does not necessarily coincide with that which, in the event, risks culminating in a poor integration of the anal phase, the mother having led the child to cathect narcissistically (to idealize) reaction formations, generally through the threat of loss of love or of punishment. I have shown in another connection that this maturative ego ideal may be eclipsed, given a prompt to the hope of eliminating the margin between the ego and the ego ideal by other routes than those of development. The mother is able to play a fundamental role here by 'misleading' the subject, that is to say, leading him away from the 'normal' path of development. Later the (ideological) leader is capable of taking on an identical function. In this sense, 'normal path of development' is to be understood in the same way as for physical development. A plant needs to be exposed to the light in a certain way. If the light-source (the ego ideal) is placed in an unsuitable position, phototropism will cause the plant to develop in a twisted fashion in the course of its growth.

I have suggested in chapter 4, 'The Ego Ideal and the Group', that there appeared to be a fundamental difference between the ego ideal, heir to primary narcissism, and the superego, heir to the Oedipus complex. The former is the product of an attempt to regain omnipotence, the latter of the castration complex, the former impelling the subject towards incestuous fusion, the latter separating the child from the mother by the incest barrier. Equally, I have stated that the ego ideal is the first rung of the ladder in the ego's development, whilst the superego is the final step.

Consider the person who has reached the stage of development at which the wish for the realization of incest through genital coitus, following the negotiation of the pregenital phases, is at its height. I have advanced the hypothesis that this moment occurs at the time of the classical oedipal phase and not only at puberty. One can understand that the setting up of the superego as incest barrier may play the role given it by Béla Grunberger: that of protecting the child's narcissism by attributing to an interdict (by the father) that which is above all a function of his own impotence. It may be noted, however, that the narcissism that is saved in this way changes face. For in principle the project, proposed by the ego ideal, that the reunification of the ego and the primary object take place through incest, must be abandoned. A real internalization of the superego should 'ideally', as Freud says, not only explode the Oedipus complex, but also bring about a real dissolution of the ego ideal if, as I have endeavoured to maintain, the ego ideal and the incest phantasy are closely linked. The superego should become the largest, if not the unique, source of food for the ego's narcissism. The ego should derive its sense of worth and its pride from conformity with the demands of the superego. It may be observed in passing that the nature of the narcissistic gratification is thereby greatly modified. To speak of the superego is to speak of limits as the word itself suggests. The third agency tops the ego, indeed, weighs down upon it: one *submits* to one's superego. As Annie Reich states, the superego is a powerful agent of reality. It should, however, be borne in mind that just as the exploding of the Oedipus complex is only relative, so the absorption of the ideal by the superego is incomplete. Doubtless it would be total if the setting up of the superego had taken place following a real recognition of the inferiority of the child's organs and of the role of the father in the primal scene, followed by the abandoning, at all levels, of the infantile theory of the ubiquity of the penis. But the superego is the product — in part at least — of the need to deny that reality. In short, the 'some things are his prerogative' (1923), to be truly integrated, must include an acceptance that one of the 'things' that is restricted to the father is genital coitus, not only because this is a prerogative of the father, but because he is capable of performing it, not only because coitus is forbidden the child, but because he does not have the necessary capability.

Given the hypothesis I have adopted, according to which incest includes fusion with the primary object and the fusion of the ego with the ideal, one can understand better the reasons for the perennial nature of oedipal wishes, which go far beyond the search for instinctual satisfaction. Besides, there is not an oedipal instinct, there is only a sexual instinct. Our oedipal wishes are carried along by the search for our lost omnipotence. I do not wish to minimize here the role of sexuality in oedipal wishes, I simply want to underline that, if 'love is much more than love', the wish to penetrate one's mother also includes that of rediscovering the boundless and the absolute, the perfection of an ego whose wound, left gaping by the tearing out of its narcissism, finds itself healed at last.

Indeed, if the hypothesis of a superego based upon a compromise with reality, and hence also, correspondingly, with narcissism, contains some truth, one can understand that the absorption of the ego ideal by this new formation will be neither total nor always definitive. This is because the ego, 'His Majesty the ego', does not seem to be disposed to give up his ancient splendour. This persistence — at least in latent form — of the ego ideal side by side with the superego, which gives rise to those promptings of the Illusion that I have referred to, should not be confused with the ego ideal 'imposed from without' such as F. Pasche has described in the case of depressives:

> In depression the ego feels itself to be abandoned because of a short-circuit of cathexis between the personified superego and a certain ego ideal. The characteristics of the latter must be specified. This ideal is indeed carried to an extreme, it goes beyond the subject's means, moreover it does not correspond to the ego, it does not belong to it, it is but a narcissistic production of the personified superego, hence it is imposed on the subject from without.

As I see it, this extreme ideal that one can, in fact, see at work in the depressive, along with a cruel and sadistic superego, is linked to that which I called to mind previously in relation to Edith Jacobson's model little girl. Although it seems as if these aspirations toward being perfect (imposed on the subject), can be likened in all respects to those grandiose models that some set themselves, I wonder whether one should consider them as belonging truly to the order of the ego ideal, at least as I understand it following the 1914 paper. Should we not rather consider them as being a function of the superego, regressed to the anal-sadistic phase, the subject's narcissism having in some sense been diverted to its profit? These models, 'imposed from without', restrict rather than enhance the subject, in just the same way as does the character armour of Reich, in relation to which I have suggested that it is, precisely, a phantasy representation of the parental rectum at the time of toilet training.

Come the adolescent crisis, one can see just how little the ego ideal has really been absorbed by the superego when, as numerous authors have observed, it finds itself in conflict with the latter. I believe one adolescent ego ideal that is in most striking contrast to the superego, is that of the *superman*. Note that two heroes of literature who are followers of Nietzsche, Lafcadio and Raskolnikov, are in fact adolescents. (See Lebovici, 1971, on Raskolnikov and the sense of guilt.) In the latter instance the struggle between the ego ideal and the superego is particularly evident. Now, the superman, in the generally accepted sense of the term — he who, all-powerful, is above the law — seems to me to be contrasted, point for point, with the superego as defined by Freud in the *New Introductory Lectures*:

> Thus a child's super-ego is in fact constructed on the model not of its parents but of its parents' super-ego; the contents which fill it are the same and it becomes the vehicle of tradition and of all the time-resisting judgements of value which have propagated themselves in this manner from generation to generation.

He again took up this notion of the superego as the vehicle of tradition in the *Outline*. I think that it is as an echo of this view that F. Pasche's description of the father of the depressive should be understood:

> As regards him, he would have needed to accept being placed *beneath his superego* rather than appropriating it to himself, pocketing it. Naturally, this subordination to the superego implies a form of passivity and corresponds to a castration; I believe this castration needs to be accepted by the father and that this is the most important consequence, at the same time as proof, of a dissolution of his own Oedipus complex. Furthermore the son must take note of the father's castration, which he cannot do without recognizing his guilt towards him (the original sin in the Freudian sense) and his irreducible inferiority, not in relation to the father, but in relation to the superego (Pasche, 1961).

Jean Gillibert (1967) equally presents a view that seems to derive from this final Freudian version of the superego when he writes:

> . . . in the superego. there is an ideality, not in the sense of a Platonic ideal that hovers in the air awaiting some form of incarnation before it descends, but in the sense that *my* father is not *the* father, that I cannot think of my father save within a context of a heritage of paternity. But *the* father is not God. In order to become it, he would need to represent a narcissistic ideality, product of all the perfections. The father is castration, its executor. The ego ideal, man's avatar in the image of God, infinitely, etc., is a transgressive and not a defensive means of denying castration . . . *my* father is that particular and privileged moment of human experience in which I have accepted finiteness (his, as mine).

In other words, it is as if the instinctual upheaval of adolescence again put in question, if not the entire superego, at least certain aspects of it, in particular that defined by Freud (1932–1938) and perceptively explicated by my two French colleagues. To accept the superego is to place oneself within a tradition, to become a link in a chain, to resign oneself also to being but a man. To be a superman is to refuse all that en bloc, that is, to refuse the human condition. One can appreciate that large upheavals of forces may make the ancient dream seem more realizable. 'No, I will not submit, I will not be like my father. I reject the world of *my* fathers.' This move of revolt, at a time when one is full of new vitality, is almost biological. I have, however, indicated that it can occur at other times if only the Illusion can be made to shimmer before eyes ready to be dazzled.

As for coming down on the side of whether the ego ideal is an agency in the same sense that the superego is, this strikes me as difficult. I think one would have to take into account the role it plays in each case. However, I do not in fact think that it can be reduced to the role of an image or model. From the moment that it leads the (whole) ego in a certain direction, that it comes into conflict with other agencies, as for example when it allies itself with the id against the superego, it seems to me to have sufficient autonomy to be classified as an agency. When, on the contrary, it lives in such harmony with the superego that it all but disappears as an autonomous entity, it no longer merits the title of agency. (This latter point must be distinguished from an absorption of the ego ideal by the superego, as occurs in the depressive.) Note that Laplanche and Pontalis, in *The Language of Psychoanalysis* (1967), call the ego ideal an agency.

In general it would seem that even a well-established superego is not sufficient to provide man with the food he requires for his narcissism. Where development has gone relatively smoothly, the subject is able to reconcile the demands of his superego with his old (dormant) wishes for fulfilment. He does this through love (as I have attempted to show) and through sublimation, by loving the object despite its finiteness and because of it, and by very reason of the trials the creative act imposes. Man needs both bread and roses. The ego ideal can live in friendship with the superego when it has itself acquired that maturative quality that I have spoken about and effected a certain number of instinctual integrations. It can then cathect, to some extent, qualities or behaviours linked to the successive disillusions that the ego has had to face: lucidity, intellectual courage, love of truth. These qualities can be integrated into the ego ideal when the superego is in place. They protect man from *hubris*. They are a necessity for whoever undertakes the work of *savant*. Whether all trace of infantile megalomania is absent therefrom, I remain unsure. Is that in any case required? I think not. On the contrary I am very ready to believe that any scientific work combines an approach to reality (be it psychical or material) with the narcissistic cathexis of the undertaking itself. 'Give me a lever and a fulcrum and I will move the world.' This celebrated cry seems to me to make clear the fact that at the heart of all our activities, even those made most 'secondary', lies — transformed no doubt but irreducible — our dream of omnipotence that 'presses ever forward unsubdued'.

By Way of Conclusion

Before taking leave of the reader who has been good enough to follow me so far, I should like to remind him or her of certain of the hypotheses I have put forward in this essay.

In order to study the 'malady of the ideal', that universal affliction of mankind, I have been led to focus my attention initially on the relationship between the ego ideal and perversion and to delineate a nucleus common to certain psychic disturbances, today increasingly widespread. The aim of all of this seems to be the obliteration of the painful limit imposed by *reality* on man's boundless wish to extend himself.

It is common, particularly since the article by Bertram Lewin (1948), to assimilate the apprehension of reality to that of the difference between the sexes. It is also now accepted, and this would in any event be my opinion, that such a view needs to be coupled with the recognition of the difference between the generations. These two points form the bedrock of reality. I nonetheless felt it necessary to demonstrate the links uniting these two points and causing them to correspond to each other as do the two faces of a single coin. The denial of the mother's lack of a penis masks the denial of the presence of a vagina, that is to say, of an organ that the little boy, at his oedipal age, is incapable of penetrating and satisfying. When, in speaking of the superego (1923), Freud says of the father that: 'many things are his prerogative', it seems to me indispensable to include in this genital coitus with the mother, not only because the accomplishment of this coitus is forbidden the little boy by the presence of his father, but also because he has not the capacity for it. It seems to me impossible here to endorse Freud's view, according to which the little boy has no wish to penetrate the mother, nor any awareness, even at an unconscious level, of her possessing a complementary organ to his own, both wish and knowledge only appearing with puberty.

It should be recalled that according to the theory of the male Oedipus complex as bequeathed to us by Freud, the little boy's penis is only involved in a vague way in his incestuous phantasies. Contrary evidence comes from clinical experience, with children in particular, and from Freud's own clinical material. How is one to interpret Little Hans' phantasy of seeing the plumber give him a big *wiwimacher*, as big as his father's, otherwise than as being linked to the wish to satisfy his mother genitally? The contrary evidence, as I say, that clinical experience supplies every day, and the existence of other theories of infantile sexuality that have been added to that of Freud, have not, however, eclipsed the latter. My hypothesis is that its success is largely linked to the fact that it robs the Oedipus complex of a large measure of its dramatic import. Moreover, it supplies a confirmation of masculine defences against the narcissistic injury inflicted by the anachronism of the oedipal wish in relation to the capacities for satisfying it, defences which culminate and triumph in the instigation of perversion. I have thus found myself to be 'more royalist than the king', as Jones had said (already!) of his own theory about the Oedipus complex. Certain factors favour perversion, generally the attitude of the mother herself, who encourages the little boy to go along with the deception that he, with his pre-pubertal penis, his pregenital sexuality, is capable of satisfying his mother, an adult object, and that he has no grounds for envying his — equally adult — father, since the latter does nothing with the mother that the little boy is not capable of doing. Thus the attrition of the difference between the sexes and the generations leads to the abolition of the very idea of evolution, of development, of maturation, in short of process. The future pervert has no reason to project his narcissism before him and to hope that he will one day be, like his father, a partner to his mother, through taking him as his ideal, since he lives under the illusion that he is, as of now, a suitable erotic object.

In order that nothing should shake his conviction, he must project his narcissism onto his pregenital erogenous zones and his part objects by subjecting them to a process of idealization. His ego ideal will thus remain attached to a pregenital model. Pregenitality has to be idealized by the pervert, in order that he may feed himself, and others, the illusion that it equals, and is even superior to, genitality. The blows that his illusion suffers, the fact that his peers manifest genital interests, makes this idealization an absolute necessity, for the pervert always lives under the threat, at some level, that the infantile nature of his sexual attributes, of his objects and of his ego will be discovered. To his oft-noted sexual compulsion I would suggest adding a compulsion to idealize which, to my mind, takes into account his paradoxical affinities with Art and Beauty. They are paradoxical in that he seeks a direct discharge of his component instincts, the raw material of the process of sublimation. The latter point led me, in the course of this study, to take up again, within the perspective of the ego ideal, problems which I had tackled previously (1968) concerning creativity. This pointed, in particular, to study of the mechanisms which give rise to the production of inauthentic aesthetic works, that of the creator's identifications allowing one to distinguish between works that have undergone a process of idealization, and those governed by sublimation.

I accord pre-eminent importance to man's immaturity and to the consequences that stem from this: the *Hilflösigkeit* that can be seen to occupy such a central place in Freud's work if one but reads it carefully. The primary loss of fusion, as I have maintained, leads both to a recognition of the object, of the not-me, and to the creation of the ideal from which the me, the ego, is then cut off. The gaping wound thus created in the ego can only be closed by a return to the fusion with the primary object. This hope will be transferred to the incestuous wish which implies a return to the inside of the mother's body by way of genital coitus. The genital insufficiency of the little man prevents him from realizing his wish immediately. He can attain incest only by projecting into the future his phantasy of union with the mother. He is thereby led to discover that which makes his father his mother's object and to set up the genital father as his ideal.

That which presses us ever forward would therefore be the wish to rediscover the hallowed time when we were our own ideal. We are ever in search of this era — lost, in fact, at the very moment the primary fusion was disrupted. Between this moment and that, projected before, when the incest is supposedly to be achieved, the whole of man's psycho-sexual development is situated. The pervert's solution, and that of those subjects with related structures, thus 'magics away' this developmental process. The latter is experienced as satisfying, that is, as engendering the minimum of tension between the ego and the ideal, when all its stages have been integrated; the incestuous project implies the acquisition of full genital capacity through the integration (and not the repression) of the pregenital phases. Whatever the apparent adult character of the ego, any evasion of one or other of the stages of development cannot be concealed from the ego ideal which is as punctilious in regard to any sham as the superego is in regard to any transgression.

The further study of examination dreams which I have made here allowed me to develop the hypothesis of an ego ideal having a maturative quality, when external events have not upset the normal course of development. I was thus led to suppose the existence of an innate programme of psychosexual development that follows laws comparable to those that govern biological phenomena, a thought that seemed to me to be not entirely alien to Freud's work. This programme is in some sense underpinned at each stage by the phantasy of the reunification of ego and ideal, which is merged with that of fusion with the primary object through realization of the incestuous wish.

If the state of being-in-love is examined in this light, Freud's assertion that it represents a limitation of narcissism may then be subjected to a new criticism. To my mind, the state of being-in-love — and this not only in the case of reciprocated love — exalts the ego. It creates an affect that is linked to an extension of narcissism. In this state subject and object represent the personification of the reunification (experienced in advance by a sort of hallucinatory wish fulfilment) of the ego (the subject) and the ego ideal (the object). Rather than saying, along with Freud, that 'the object absorbs the ego', it would seem more appropriate to say 'the ego ideal absorbs the ego'. One could then envisage the state of being-in-love as representing a celebration of the marriage of ego and ideal, as a return to the original bond that united them before the disruption of the primary state of fusion.

Being-in-love might be compared to the narcissistic regression that characterizes the initial stages of certain analyses. as described by Béla Grunberger, or to Freud's analytic 'honeymoon', the sense of elation characterizing this state being the result of the analysand finding himself in close proximity to his incarnate ego ideal: that is the analyst, the mainstay of his projection. Thus this experience of elation is linked to a reactivation of the Illusion, in other words, to the promise of a reunification of ego and ideal.

However, if analysis allows this unification to be achieved — in, it must be said, only very relative measure — the margin between the ego and the ideal will never be entirely eliminated. Groups often offer a much shorter route to the long-standing wish for the union of ego and ideal. Such groups are based upon an ideology which may be defined, psychoanalytically, as a system that appears to have a more or less rational basis, corresponding to the outward appearance of dreams and to secondary elaboration. An ideology always contains within it a phantasy of narcissistic assumption linked to a return to a state of primary fusion, which equally excludes conflict and castration and thus operates within the order of Illusion. The leader in these ideological groups does not appear to me to be a representation of the father. These groups aim at an eradication of the Oedipus complex and the world of the father. The leader is an analogue of the mother of the pervert. Just as the latter gives her little impubescent boy to believe that he has no need to grow or to mature in order to take his father's place, and thereby spares him having to face up to conflict and castration, the leader lulls the group with the possibility of being able to achieve total happiness, in a rediscovered land of plenty. It is a land of 'the total man' (Marx), where all needs will be satisfied, where 'the world of harmony' (Fourier) will reign, where contented humanity will dream no more. 'When men will be full and free, they will dream no more at night', says Paul Nizan in *Aden Arabie*.

Within the particular perspective I have adopted, it seems to me that the infantile prototype of these adult ideologies is the monistic theory of phallic sexuality which allows the little male to maintain the deception that it is possible, by the attrition of the difference between the sexes and, correspondingly, the difference between the generations, to by-pass the process of development. Freud initially ascribed the role of reality testing to the ego ideal (1921). Subsequently (1923) he made it the prerogative of the ego. It would seem that in groups dominated by ideology, and hence by Illusion, it is indeed to the group ego ideal that this function has been delegated.

The solitary individual who does not share in the Illusion is not only persecuted or killed, but declared to be mad. Indeed, any situation in which the Illusion is activated leads to reality testing being abandoned, to a greater or lesser degree, to the representative of the ego ideal: the group as a whole or its leader. It is thus not only in the state of being-in-love or in hypnosis, but also in the analytic situation itself. It seems to me that the abuse of power in this realm should not so much be ascribed to the 'historical' transference, in the strict sense of the term, as to the projection of the ego ideal on to the analyst. His counter-transference leads him to become the life-long repository of the analysand's narcissism, at the same time as continuing to dazzle him with the possible attainment of the Illusion. But at that point surely the analytic situation has swung over entirely to the side of magic, ideology and faith? 'I am the gate, and all who enter by me will be saved' (Gospel according to St John).

There is one area in which reality testing, which essentially consists in rediscovering in the external world the representation of a perception, is particularly uneasy. We have, indeed, no way of subjecting our psychic ego to reality testing in order to be able to confront it with our ego ideal. There is no object in the external world that corresponds to its internal presentation. We are therefore obliged to find some mirror for it, analogous to those we have for viewing our body ego, that is, some expedient that allows us to be both in the street and to see ourselves passing. There seem to me to be essentially three such expedients:

— We may create works which will represent a double of our ego.

— We may project our psychic ego into our body ego (the mechanism I have described does not seem to me to be quite the same as that delineated by Federn in relation to hysterical conversion). Our body ego may itself then be projected — giving rise, in the most extreme case, to the creation of the influencing machine.

— Finally, the way in which we are perceived by others, our peers, our *alter egos*, our homosexual doubles, may serve as a mirror to our psychic ego. We are all, therefore, dependent on opinion, though, it is true, to very differing degrees.

If the body ego is a mirror, a double, of the psychic ego, and the body itself an eventual persecutor; if, equally, the homosexual object plays a role in the evaluation of our ego, one can understand that Tausk's theory of delusions and that of Freud may be seen as complementary rather than contradictory. The difficulty of establishing ourselves, once and for all, as observers of our ego, enabling us to evaluate it in relation to our ideal, is at times very great and creates a constant and painful tension between the ego and the ideal.

If art and literature may in themselves constitute a bridge over the gulf that divides ego and ideal, the content of that literature is also replete with descriptions of the tension between these two parts of the complete ego, of the affects it arouses and its consequences, be it in relation to Lancelot or Percival in search of the Holy Grail, to the Knight of the Sad Face pursuing the impossible star or any other of the hundreds and thousands of examples.

The pathetic tale of the ever tireless and often tiresome Marie Bashkirtseff seems to me to illustrate well the effects of the painful rent that afflicted her ego by its distance from her ideal. When one reads her *Cahiers Intimes* (not the *Journal* which is an abridged and edulcorated version by André Theuriet), one discovers that her brief and breathless life (she died at twenty four of a tuberculosis that seems to have spread to the larynx, the eyes, the middle ear and the lungs) was entirely dominated by one absolute, suffocating compulsion, that of obtaining the food for the narcissism that was essential to her survival. This compulsion led her to exhaust herself in the pursuit of accomplishments that might furnish her with admiration and approbation. Although intended to keep her alive, the compulsion would finally be responsible for her death.

A few days before her death she consigned to her *Journal*, that first mirror in which she viewed herself and offered herself to the gaze of the reader who, she said, would read her in fifty years time, the following: 'I have not been understood, I have always been misjudged, even by my own family, and it is a little "of that that I am dying".' Each of her *Cahiers Intimes* carries as epigraph the motto *Gloriae Cupiditas*. To her mirror she confides: 'It is you I love.' But this apparent self-love, as in every instance where it appears to be excessive, is but a misleading effect of her insatiable narcissistic quest that masks a profound and piercing doubt as to her personal worth. She will equally write elsewhere: 'I am worthless', and also: 'I have a high opinion of myself and when I am becoming I am overcome with surprise and satisfaction.' Her *Cahiers* are full of descriptions of her appearance and her deportment: 'General Bihovitz, Collignon, my aunt and mother. I sat by the fireplace leaning on a small table, feet majestically posed and wearing a Mary Stewart bonnet, not the feet, me. The feet are in red mules made by Rubini after the style of the Egyptian slippers I was so struck by in *Aida*.' Or again:

> ... the real sensation awaited us at the Promenade des Anglais. White horses, white carriage, women in white, fair hair, lanterns catching the last rays of the sun, we look like something from a fairy story. Preoccupied with driving and

looking natural, but then, everyone noticed me and my name
went round the crowd in an astonishing manner . . .

There are a thousand descriptions of this type which, taken
together, would probably furnish a specialist with an incomparable
documentation of the fashions of the late seventies and early
eighties. 'Physical luxury is a requirement for moral luxury', she
writes of her dresses, a phrase that would seem to corroborate
what I have suggested about the evaluation of the psychic ego
through the intermediary of the body ego.

Marie is an avid reader of all that the papers carry in their
society columns about her appearances at balls, at the Opera, at
concerts, out skating and in the Chamber — for she takes an
interest in politics and is fascinated by famous politicians, be they
a Bonapartist like Paul de Cassagnac, with whom she was to fall in
love, or Gambetta. She races from Nice to Florence, Naples,
Rome, Madrid, Burgos, Seville, Cordova, Grenada, Paris,
Biarritz, San Remo: 'I should like to stay here until the races, then
go to Sorrento, and also to Trouville, Aix-les-Bains, and to the
bathing resorts in England; there is not enough time, life is so
short.' She was not yet aware of her illness when she wrote these
lines, and yet the first signs of tubercular laryngitis were
imminent. They were to prevent her from exercising her voice,
which she tells us was divine; she plays the mandolin, rides, hunts,
speaks French, Italian, German, Spanish, and, of course, Russian,
and is perfecting her Greek and Latin; she writes poetry, is
interested in the arts and paints. Whilst her taste is not very sound
— she prefers Carolus-Duran and Bastien-Lepage to Manet —
she has a very sincere talent that the years might have matured and
freed from its early influences. She wants to become famous:
'Reading Stendhal's account of Michelangelo I seriously feel like
killing myself out of despair for having no genius; why live
without genius?'

She paints relentlessly from morning till night, barely allowing
herself two hours rest in the afternoon when the illness starts to
progress; she is a pupil of Julian and watches closely for the slightest

sign of approbation from her masters, or from the public and the critics when she exhibits, for: 'No, don't you see, what I need if I am to live is to have lots of talent.' But also: 'Ah! I had a pleasant time with that old devil Carolus-Duran. But at the end of it all, what? Something rather forced . . . because after all I do not understand . . . Oh, I will never have any talent . . . Everything is scratched out and I have even given away the canvas so as never to see it again . . . it is killing. O painting, I cannot succeed at it. But as soon as one has destroyed what one's done, one feels relieved, free and ready to begin again . . .' And also:

> I no longer know where to go or what to do, I haven't the energy to do even a simple study, I always have to undertake too much and as that does not work out well I sink into despair and, at present, into a state of nerves . . . In any case, I shall never paint, I have never been able to paint a good piece. I have been painting now for three and a half years . . . I have lost half of that, I admit it, but it's all the same . . .
>
> I am finally out of breath . . . But then the terrible conviction arises that I could not, that I will not paint . . . Sculpture then . . . In any event you will return to painting, only even weaker . . . What then? Then one would be better dead.

The regulation of Marie's self-esteem proves, then, to be extremely difficult. The gulf that she is ever attempting to bridge between her ego and her ideal causes her to become hyperactive, ever on the look-out for new feats to accomplish to provoke the admiration of those around her. One does indeed feel her to be 'out of breath', short of wind, in the thousand and one undertakings that exhaust her, literally consuming her, committed as she is to this hopeless task: the obliteration of the fatal tear that wrested her ideal from her ego.

Without aiming to put forward here a theory of tubercular illness that claims any general validity, I have had occasion to note both in my analytic practice, and through direct observation, that a number of tubercular patients were in like pursuit of an ego ideal and pushed into a hyperactivity that drained them of their libidinal energy. It is a kind of haemorrhage that may either precede or accompany pitting of the lungs and haemoptysis, and which leaves them bloodless and gasping, like Kafka's fasting character accomplishing his vain and tragic feat. Previously, the fever and greatly increased powers of observation characteristic of the tubercular patient, which culminate, in fact, in a *consumption* that is as much libidinal as properly somatic, were ascribed to tubercular toxin and to the raising of the patient's temperature.

It must be noted that, in so far as her *Cahiers* are sufficiently revealing in this respect, Marie appears to have suffered a fundamental, though perhaps not primary, narcissistic injury, both she and her mother having been abandoned by her father. He went to live with another woman by whom he had several children. One might think of Marie as seeking, through her mirror, her journal, her creative works, her peers — so many doubles — a means of repairing the consequences of this paternal rejection. Now, it is probably this rejection itself that led her to refuse all the men who wished to marry her and to attach herself to one of them who, irony of fate, would ask her to accept the child he had had by another woman. She cannot resign herself to do this, and is unable to manage the crises she is also going through in her own family. Finally, she experiences a love that is without hope, for a man who is not interested in her and who will choose another. She writes at that point: 'I must, I absolutely must be married so he shall see that I don't care at all about him, and above all I must marry in great style . . . I must have either a brilliant revenge or die.' The following day, in her *Cahier*, she notes in relation to her father: 'I told him, my father, in order to annoy him, that I have had enough of all of them, that I want to have nothing in common with him, that he is useless to me.'

In other words, love, which is one of the essential human modalities whereby the two sides of the wound that divides ego and ideal may be brought closer together, escapes her, for it is precisely from this wound itself that the conflict arises which makes all love impossible. At the same time, in a manner close to

Jean Kestemberg's definition of the erotomanic relationship, she is attached to, or believes she appeals to, various notable figures. She seems, however, not to have had any actual sexual experience. When she considers it, it is with a mixture of shame and guilt in which, despite Epictetus, the ideal seems to predominate over the superego and the breach dividing ego and ideal appears to be consciously perceived:

> As for taking a lover, with a character like mine it is something that does not even bear thinking about. I would be so humiliated, so tormented, I would suffer so much. The first me would perhaps say nothing, but the second, that which wants all manner of things for the first, that which recalls Epictetus and wants nothing for itself, but has placed all its happiness in the former, that one would not permit it, and it is before her that the first would be ashamed of behaving badly.

Henceforth, the world of the instincts and the world of narcissism will remain separate for her; her body is no longer able to furnish her with object-related erotic satisfactions. With her characteristically ironic tone she recounts an episode when she was led to undress before some women:

> You should have seen those three old ladies, the looks they exchanged and their whispers; it doesn't flatter me, I have known for a long time that there is nothing in the world more beautiful than my body and that it is a real sin, a positive disgrace not to have myself sculpted or painted. Such beauties can belong to no one person. It is like a museum which is open for all to see.

One can, of course, see in this primarily narcissistic cathexis of the body, a defence against Oedipal feelings, faithfulness to the father, repression of homosexuality . . . Nonetheless, it still represents an impossible synthesis of narcissism and instincts. In part, probably, this split is itself an effect of the narcissistic injury inflicted by the father's rejection. Her oedipal wishes are indeed accompanied by a terrible hatred which becomes apparent in dreams involving wounded men, lying in pools of blood, whilst her aggression towards her mother, held responsible for the desertion to which they fall victim, remains deeply repressed. It becomes apparent, however, when Marie weeps and refuses to go out with a mother who, she claims, neglects herself, or in the complacent, extremely cruel account she gives of a bull fight, in which the bull's horns stir around the horse's innards. She also reports, in another context, several dreams of the primal scene.

Pregenitality, and particularly anality, is repressed or curbed. Writing about an operation on a scrofula or furuncle undergone by one of her entourage, she says:

> I admire Zola, but there are some things which everyone in the world says and which I cannot bring myself to say, or even to write. However, so that you should not think this is something terrible, I will let you know that the worst of these is the word *purged*; I am annoyed at putting such a word down here; I do not hesitate to say either blackguard, or other things of the sort, but as for these petty, innocent dirty little expressions, they revolt me.

And again: 'I dreamt that someone was explaining to me what is the matter with my right lung; certain parts of it the air cannot reach . . . this gives rise to . . . but it is too disgusting to relate, it is enough that I am afflicted.'

It will be appreciated that under these conditions one of the other routes that might lead to her being able to repair to some extent the fissure between her ego and her ideal, that of artistic creativity, should often find itself blocked. The process of sublimation is impeded by the repression of pregenital instincts. The defeat of her attempts at 'narcissistic recovery' (Grunberger, 1956) is perfectly expressed in the account she gives of a performance of *Faust* that she attended. Writing about the singer who was interpreting the role of Marguerite and who had no voice at all, she says: 'At first I thought that she was nervous, frightened and when she began the aria *Roi de Thulé*, I trembled on her behalf and I became so ashamed, so terrified, that I hid myself away at the back of the box as if I were myself the singer.' In this episode one again finds shame as the affect characteristic of a defeat, in this case through identification, at the level of the ego ideal. It is a defeat in front of witnesses (the audience) that leads to a wish to hide or to disappear. I have spoken in the course of this work of the link between shame and anality, the exhibition that aims at gaining narcissistic confirmation from peers (seen as homo-sexualized objects, *alter egos*) being the equivalent, when it fails to reach its goal, of a de-idealization of the ego, of a loss of face, or in other words of an uncovering of the anus with a resexualization of the concomitant homosexual instincts.

I have been able to note the following sequence in a patient, which seems to me to relate to this same problematic, albeit situated within the context of a different structure. This related to a young woman who had been left, in the course of her analysis, by the man she was in love with, who then married another woman. My patient reacted to this desertion with a violent hatred which was frequently acted out (letters, phone calls, etc.). In the transference I would sometimes represent the man who had abandoned her, at other times the rival, on occasion the two simultaneously. However, the maternal and homosexual aspect of the conflict, whose infantile roots will not detain us here, was obvious. In relation to one of my comments she accused me of being destructive because, she said, I appeared to suppose that she was not loved by this man (I would remind the reader that he had just married another woman and that, from her own accounts, he seemed to show clearly that he was tired of her acting out). Some time later she reported having met him and felt that he had been *captivated*; she gave out a *glow*, a *brilliance*, that had completely seduced him. Given the erotomanic tone of what she was saying, I said that it seemed as if it were unbearable to her that I might see her as having been rejected, as if that placed her in a humiliating position in relation to me. In saying this, I was hoping to indicate the significance of the dazzling (and hence idealizing) *aura* that she attempted to bestow on herself in front of me, by telling me of the way in which she had captivated her former friend.

In certain of her descriptions of herself, Marie Bashkirtseff takes on an almost identical 'glow'. It may be noted that this 'aura' is the pendant to that which the object takes on in the state of being-in-love, or in its manifestations in mystical states (see the chapter on 'Being-in-love'). She was indeed, as we have seen, rejected by her father. To be rejected, abandoned, as was Marie, and as was my patient may, in a general way, lead the subject to experience him or herself as a reject, a piece of rubbish, or in other words as excrement. Now, at the level of primary process contained and container are not distinguished. To show oneself as having been made into something fecal or to display one's anus are one and the same thing. This identity of contained–container is confirmed in language by such expressions as 'having a jar', for example.

As I understood at the time, my patient's narcissistic injury had to be concealed from me, the rejection she had suffered being experienced as the equivalent of the passive display of her anus to me. This interpretation had the effect of calming her immediately. To the following session she brought a dream in which she was to take two contraceptive pills; one had to do with her lover (this related to a passing, current liaison) and the other involved a blond person. She interpreted the dream for herself as expressing her wish to receive from me, as mother, a child. Not only did the indications of a positive, homosexual transference become clearer, but the somewhat disturbing aspect of her material gave way to increased insight.

At times shame, linked to narcissistic defeat, may lead not to delusion but, as we know, to suicide. This would then represent a realization of the phantasy that accompanies this affect: that of disappearing, of no longer having to meet the eyes of one's peers. The person who is ashamed is said to be unable to look others in the face, to be unable to face up to them, the hidden anus being now written on his face. One 'dies of shame'; and to claim that ridicule cannot kill is but a denial.

Likewise, the wish to have the witnesses to an affront, to a disgrace, disappear, thereby eradicating all trace and memory of it, is a fairly common motive for murder. I am not only speaking here of the wish to kill those who were the direct cause of the shame, as in the case of a vendetta, but of the murder of those before whom the subject was humiliated. The phantasy of having the witnesses to the shame disappear is very frequent. Thus one singer, who has a very beautiful voice, and is moreover one of the nicest people you could hope to meet, tells me that at the beginning of his career, being ill-advised, he included in his repertory a piece which, on the occasion of a certain gala, earned him various gibes. As it happened, he knew most of those present: it took place in a provincial town. Ever since, whenever he hears of the death of one of the audience he feels a sense of relief, and his confessed ambition is to thus work his way through the whole list! Only then will the burning shame be effaced. This phantasy may be likened to the order given by the ageing Castiglione, Napoleon III's beautiful mistress, to shroud all her mirrors, witnesses to her narcissistic injury. One might also recall the passage quoted above in which Marie Bashkirtseff scratches out one of her paintings — which both kills her, she says (for it involves a double of herself), but also relieves her.

For women, one modality for regulating self-esteem lies in the phantasy of possessing a penis. I have had occasion to note, in another context, that the first object on to which lost omnipotence is projected, the breast, then the mother, is at the same time experienced as the cause of the narcissism being wrenched away. In the course of the vicissitudes of pre-oedipal conflicts the possession of a penis, an organ in which the mother is lacking, may be phantasied as representing a triumph over the mother and hence as a regaining of lost omnipotence. Many women believe that all their problems, ultimately even that of the bringing together of their ego and their ideal, would be resolved by possession of the male organ.

Marie Bashkirtseff's penis envy is apparent. Not only does she shoot, hunt and ride horseback, but she also belongs to the movement 'The Right of Women'. She writes:

I have a shoemaker called D . . . who makes my foot, tiny as it already is, into an object of general curiosity. No one can understand how it is possible to walk with such a foot. It is narrow, pointed, unnatural but pretty and astonishing. The women of the Palace were stupefied and M. de M . . . cannot conceal his astonishment; he gazes on the foot. I don't believe in fact that it is found to be pretty, but it is extraordinary.

If penis envy is the result of coveting the organ that the mother lacks, nevertheless, in those cases where there is a high degree of tension between ego and ideal, penis envy may be seen as an attempt at providing a focus, analogous to that which occurs in phobia, for a pain rendered all the more torturing by its vagueness, permanence and extent. It is a pain of *being* and not of *possessing*, although the symbol necessarily brings us into the realm of possessions, since being cannot be symbolized. In a general sense, I think that women's penis envy and its relationship to the tension between the ego ideal and the ego, furnishes a further illustration of the interpretation that Green has made of the suicide of Ajax:

Ajax kills himself because Achilles' arms go to another. In this case it does indeed concern a possession, of which he has been deprived. But let us not be taken in. What Ajax suffers from is an injury to his being . . . From the loss of a phallic attribute, but only in so far as this would vouchsafe him the admiration of friend and foe. This is why his reaction is one of shame, as if their being accorded to another set the seal on his downfall and his worthlessness (Green, 1969).

Freud's description (1937) of the severe depression arising in certain analyses when he seeks to encourage his female patients to renounce their penis envy can, to my mind, only be understood if the penis is seen as the focus of hopes for the unification of ego and ideal. It is then a renunciation of the hope of rediscovering a fulfilment of *being* that the patient is being asked to make.

In this work I have emphasized certain Freudian formulations concerning the ego ideal: the wish to 'be grown up', the projection of the ideal 'before' the subject, which have led me to give it the sense of a *promise*, situated therefore in the *future*, and to adopt the terminology of Michel Fain and Pierre Marty who bring together ego ideal and *hope*. The affect that characterizes depression is the lack of hope, or despair, an indication that the project of uniting ego and ideal has been more or less completely abandoned.

Although of necessity considering only a part of the spectre of the malady of the ideal and having chosen not to make a full study of depression, I have nevertheless made some allusion to this. I have aligned myself with Francis Pasche, who sees in the ego ideal of the depressive 'a narcissistic production of the personified superego . . . imposed on the subject from without'. It even appeared to me that what was involved was a superego that had regressed to the anal–sadistic phase and been narcissistically cathected, a 'mould' offered by the educator, analogous to Reich's character armour, which I interpreted as representing the parental rectum at the time of toilet training. Often the ego ideal that is offered to the depressive is represented by a parent who has died prematurely and who, decked with every perfection by the surviving parent in consequence of their own conflicts in relation to their late partner, is presented to the child as an unattainable model.

A comparison between the schema of mania and that of depression leads, I think, to corroboration of the need for a distinction between ego ideal and superego. I have attempted to establish this distinction and give some nuance to it, in another connection, in the final chapter of this work. In depression the lost, ambivalently regarded object is included in the ego, and the superego, in alliance with this ego ideal 'imposed from without', dominates the ego. There is then, it seems to me, no place for a personal ego ideal.

In mania, as Freud again stated in 1921, the ego is fused with the ego ideal, and not with the superego as Rado and Lewin maintain, whatever the multiplicity of meanings given to the ego ideal in *Group Psychology and the Analysis of the Ego*. Lewin does, however, stress the unity of infant and breast in the course of states of manic elation. It seems to me that at an oral level this unity represents a state of fusion with the primary object, in other words a return to the state of undifferentiation of me (ego) and not-me that characterizes the time when narcissism has not yet been wrested from the ego. That this state should be accompanied by the breakdown of the segregation of the psychic agencies, and hence by the disappearance of the superego, seems self-evident. When it comes to the anal level, omnipotence is exercised in relation to objects, which, as the work of Karl Abraham has shown, are subject to a rapid and incessant process of incorporation and expulsion, like some kind of intra-psychic 'cotton reel'. This omnipotence may encourage in the subject the well-known megalomanic phantasy of being able to revive (incorporate) and to kill off (expel) the object *ad libitum*. Thus, one woman patient of mine dreamt, when I was away, that she left a plant to die off and then gave it some water, doing this several times in succession. Similarly, she fed a little hamster and then allowed it to starve till it became limp and could barely open an eye, when a fresh mouthful would bring it back to life.

The object is thus reduced to the status of a part object, belonging to the subject, over which he then has absolute mastery, thus insuring himself against any loss of which he is not the author. In this instance it is the ego ideal that has united with the ego, in so far as an absolute union of this order is possible outside of the earliest stages of life or of death. It is precisely this coincidence that has swept away the superego, though this is to some extent a secondary effect. There is moreover an additional reason for the disappearance of the superego in mania, namely the control that the subject then exercises over his introjects and hence over his superego.

Proof that the coincidence between ego and ideal is not, however, absolute is furnished by the evidence that the categories of outside and inside are maintained. This means that the manic ego is similar to the pure pleasure-ego, with objects taken in (swallowed) or expelled (spat out) according to whether they are pleasant or unpleasant (cf. 'Negation'). The body of the manic subject (and that of the drug addict) is like that described by Evelyne and Jean Kestemberg and Simone Decobert in their study on anorexics (1973): a tube, open at both ends, that objects can pour into and flow out of endlessly. Not that I mean to reduce anorexia to a form of mania or drug-addiction, but I have been struck by the similarity between this process and that which can be observed in these two nosological entities. The manic subject and the drug-addict, who exercise this omnipotent control over their objects, seek thereby to make themselves as independent as possible of any external source. They do this in an attempt to create a self-sufficient system that would protect them from being abandoned, and hence from depression, and which tends to maintain the ego in close proximity to its ideal. Thus, an alcoholic patient of mine dreamt that he was in an institution where the urine was collected and processed in such a way that the alcohol it was thought to contain could be extracted and recycled.

Two women patients of mine, although not anorexic, would make themselves vomit after eating. One of them was for a short while addicted to drugs. Both had had multiple abortions, thus reproducing at another level this same cycle of filling up and emptying out that was apparent in their bouts of vomiting following the taking in of food. They experienced their bodies as being like the barrel of the Danaids. I will come back in a moment to the case of one of these patients. But before doing so, I should like to emphasize that, given the proviso that manic subjects have not got to the point of being totally confused with their object, it is nonetheless the case that what is involved here is the bringing nearer together of their ego and their ideal. Otherwise, how is one to explain the complete reversal of affects that one can observe in hypomanic subjects as against depressives. The former have an incurable optimism, hope having been maintained far beyond the bounds of anything that seems credible. This is the world of the 'happy ending' (through the denial of whole aspects of reality).

Depressives give up all hope, or, in other words, no longer even entertain the phantasy of a reunification of ego and ideal. I have referred here to hypomanic and not manic subjects because if one wishes to contrast hope and hopelessness one cannot really compare manic subjects with depressives, the former being 'beyond' hope, for hope still locates happiness somewhere in the future. It is here and now that the manic subject fulfills himself in the 'feast'.

One of the two patients I have just spoken of who made themselves vomit seemed to me to bring some material that throws light on a point that I have, perhaps, not brought into sufficient prominence. I think it is present as a strand running through the greater part of this work; that is the role of the anal instincts in the process of idealization.

Mélanie Blanche was a young woman of twenty eight when she came to consult me. She complained of not being able satisfactorily to complete her studies in literature and of being anxious. This, as far as I remember, was the main reason for her seeking treatment. She had had an analysis in her adolescence, the latter part of which had taken place with her sitting up. She is a pretty, intelligent and cultured young woman, excessively affected, who in her sessions would often hold a lock of her (long) hair in a dreamy way, play with her antique jewellery in a rather precious manner and spend literally hours stopping herself from uttering certain words such as vagina, buttocks, pubis, hairs, etc. For ever on the point of giving, she left me forever frustrated. I interpreted this behaviour successively as a means of 'arousing' me without allowing me any satisfaction, then as a means of refusing me her stools. The first interpretation is linked to the fact that she told me right at the beginning of the analysis that she was pregnant and pleased to be so, since she then appeared before me 'equipped', that she was not going to keep the baby, that it was her third pregnancy and that this last one would, like the preceding one, be cut short by her father. The analysis of her relationship to her father showed how much she was constantly trying to seduce him. She felt awkward in front of him, could not stay in the same room with him, etc. She was also to tell me that her parents had no sexual relationship, that they slept in separate beds. The attitude of her father seemed to confirm her phantasies of being his sole sexual object. When she was going off on holiday with a boyfriend, her father gave her a vaginal douche and instructions on how to use it and, when she was pregnant, used a catheter on her. To arouse me and then leave me thirsting, was to make me experience what her father made her experience, by sustaining her in the illusion that she was his partner, without however really satisfying her, unless through a sadistic and mutilating form of penetration.

During this same period she told me about how, as a young girl, she was in the habit of gluttonously stuffing herself with chocolates until she felt sick, then making herself vomit. We were then able to elaborate her difficulties in being able to retain what she had taken in, and then her difficulty in expelling it if she thought that someone (her mother or I) could take from her whatever she had in her belly (her words, her child, her stools . . .). Thus she attempted to cut me out of this: by arriving 'full'; she showed me that she had no need to take anything from me. She was, in her own words, already 'equipped'. If, nonetheless, she got rid of what she had in her belly, it was not to give it to me, but to reinternalize it. Naturally all of this suggested to me a problem of un-worked-through mourning, but nothing in the material at that time enabled me to support my hypothesis. Corresponding to this self-sufficient circulatory system of the object, the patient confessed to a poor actual sex life in relation to her considerable masturbatory activity, which was equally the case with my other vomiting and multi-aborted patient. Her phantasies were principally centred around the initiation of a young girl by a severe woman, the headmistress of a school, for example. There then appeared the figure of an old nanny, Mme Hortense, now some eighty years old, who had remained in the family till my patient was twenty. But the only memories to emerge were of this woman's severity and devotion. At the same time the patient, who by now had a bit more courage about calling a spade a spade, nevertheless clung on to this same mannerism and often had dreams of snow and whiteness. She also dreamt about Greta Garbo, who seemed to her to be a feminine ideal of beauty and purity. But she dreamt that 'the Divine' died. I then suggested that perhaps she had had enough of her 'purity' and that in fact her ideal was a cover for other wishes. It was at this time that we elaborated the problem that lay behind her rejection of her Jewishness. She had in fact become a Catholic in her adolescence, but was no longer practising. That whish is Jewish was identified by her with anality. She began to dream about Anouk Aimée, née Dreyfus. At the same time, she consciously praised me to the skies; having read one of my papers, it was positively idolized. One particular dream was to come and deliver a blow to this beautiful edifice. An artist called Altamira was having an exhibition in a gallery. There was a wind blowing in the neighbourhood. Altamira, she said, was the analyst, and this expressed her 'high admiration' for my work. I then added, 'but it's only wind'. (One might note, moreover, that Altamira is also the name of some caves and that one can thus see the place where, secretly, she situates my work: in her windy cave.) Her idealization of myself and of her instincts as well as her general aestheticism are a cover for her anal–sadistic instincts.

These interpretations were to lead to the emergence of material that was to leave me perplexed for many a long month. An uncle's cancer and the artificial anus he acquired were the day's residues of a series of dreams that were to occupy the field of the analysis. Thus she dreamt successively and repetitively of the death of all the members of her family: father, mother, uncles, aunts, etc. I, too, died. At other times it was a very aged and cancerous Freud who made an appearance. In one dream her father had a large stain of blood on his pyjamas, in the area of his anus. In another dream she found herself in his company in a circular library of leather-bound volumes; it was windy. That same night she was also with the uncle with the artificial anus. There was a rubber sack that collected the excrement. She was excited. Then there were cemeteries that reappeared every night with coffins and the smell of rotting flesh. I could make little of these hecatombs, this stench that got up my nostrils, invading me and almost making me regret the time when these decomposing bodies were covered by the pure white of idealization. I took consolation in absolving myself for the counter-transference irritation that had accompanied the affectation and aestheticism of my patient during the long preceding phase, an affectation and aestheticism that had concealed a charnel house in the same way that it is the most delicate flowers that flourish over graves.

I also took consolation in telling myself that it isn't everybody who has a necrophilic patient on their couch. At that point Mme Hortense fell ill with hemiplegia following on a stroke. Mélanie Blanche immediately went to her in the country where she lay bed-ridden and incontinent, in her old house, a toilet-bucket stinking next to her bed, the photographs of her dead on the wall. Mélanie Blanche, lying down in the next room, the door ajar, masturbated herself. I could see the perverse elements, but could not understand why those particular ones. Why death, the cemeteries? Certainly, it would have been much easier if some occasion of infantile mourning had allowed me to see Mélanie Blanche as having made herself the receptacle, the tomb for the lost object, identified with faeces according to the classic description of Karl Abraham. But there was no such occasion, and in any event this would not have sufficed to explain the perverse, anal–sadistic and necrophilic elements.

Mélanie Blanche's cemetery dreams continued. Thus, standing in front of a tomb covered with flowers, she had the thought that these flowers were feeding off the corpse that lay rotting in the ground. It made her vomit. I said that she was no longer able to repress the rot, the blackness, the anal instincts with these flowers which were themselves contaminated by that which they now sought in vain to mask. She is, herself, the flower that feeds off the corpse. Faced with this awareness of her necrophagia (this was not, of course, the term I used), she is forced to expel that which she has swallowed. The interpretation seemed to me to be correct, but incomplete. What corpse was this? She said some more about

Mme Hortense. Suddenly, from the flow of my associations, I stepped outside the analytic situation and asked her a question:

> Did Mme Hortense have a husband? — Yes, but no one ever saw him, — And what did he do? — He was a *grave-digger*. Ah, yes, I'd never thought of that. It's funny. Mme Hortense had had a previous husband who had died. For some reason I never knew he had had to be exhumed. Mme Hortense often used to talk about that exhumation ... One day Mme Hortense opened a cupboard. I hadn't told you this, but although I used to be sick in the toilet, sometimes I would be sick into bags which I lined up inside a cupboard. Mme Hortense discovered them. I must have been about eighteen. She caught me but said nothing. When I was younger I used to hide blood-stained underclothing in a doll's pram. It was my father who discovered them.

'Exhumed them?' I suggested. It was obviously not without significance that it was I who, after six years of analysis, should be the one to dig up Mme Hortense's husbands, husbands who had never been mentioned until then.

This session marked a turning point in the treatment. Mélanie Blanche has almost completely given up her precious way of speaking and her mannered aestheticism. Her intellectual inhibitions have in part diminished. This has left room for a more authentic kind of sublimation. She has more insight. She is trying to understand what she herself has called her necrophilia and her perversion. For my part, I would imagine that the nanny's own phantasies must have played a major role in the elaboration of the sexual themes in those of Mélanie Blanche. Indeed, before being the father's sexual object, she must have been that of the nanny, and the absence of the latter's husband, his occupation, the oft-recounted exhumation of the first husband must all have contributed to entrenching Mélanie Blanche's phantasies of the primal scene. The corpse is surely the husband, swallowed up in the entrails of Mme Hortense, and reduced to a part-object, a fetish. There were still some elements missing before I could communicate this reconstruction to Mélanie Blanche, which a greater lifting of the infantile amnesia would supply.

She later told me about her grandmother who died when Mélanie Blanche was eight and away in the mountains in winter. (Again the snow of her first dreams.) The death was kept hidden from her. She slept with her grandmother's muff until she was eighteen. She had another cemetery dream: the cemetery was covered with a layer of ice on which people were skating very gracefully. She said to a man with whom she associates me: 'They are elves, not worms.'

This is precisely how one might define idealization, as I have attempted to illustrate, in the case of the pervert in particular, contrasting it with sublimation. A layer of ice, of beauty, of purity, that covers over the faeces; only a link between the two levels makes sublimation possible. 'They are elves, not worms', is also what is proclaimed, in the area of the instincts, by those who make a display of their moral ideals. It is well known that such an exhibition is often suspect. Ferenczi, in an interview that I only came across very recently and which appears in the French edition of his works, says that one should not be surprised to find that the private lives and personal relationships of the great idealists are so often marked by gross brutality, their idealism serving as a mask for unsublimated sadistic instincts.

One cannot possibly write about the ego ideal without also writing about that which is, according to Freud, the prototype of Illusion, namely religion. The path I shall adopt to do this will, I hope, allow me to put forward certain hypotheses concerning the development of the pathology that I have attempted to delineate in taking perversion as a model. When Freud came to consider the origin of religions in *Totem and Taboo*, the book which, he told Abraham, was to deal a mortal blow to religion, he took as his basis, it will be recalled, the Darwinian 'scientific myth' of the primal horde, as taken up by Atkinson. 'A violent and jealous father who keeps all the females for himself and drives away his sons as they grow up', is one day killed by the brothers who have been driven out and have come together against him. His body is then devoured by these primitive cannibals who thus seek to appropriate to themselves his envied qualities. But soon a profound sense of guilt, fostered no doubt by the futility of the murder — none of the sons could anymore take the place of the dead father — leads the members of the brotherhood to choose a totem, generally an animal, common to the tribe. It is forbidden to kill the totem, save on one occasion each year when the animal is ritually sacrificed and devoured by the whole tribe. At the same time, by a sort of 'deferred obedience' to their dead father, they renounced the fruits of their deed by forbidding themselves sexual relations with the women they had now set free. They thus created out of their filial sense of guilt 'the two fundamental taboos of totemism' which correspond to the two repressed wishes of the Oedipus complex.

Religion expresses reverence towards the dead father, henceforth worshipped in the form of the totem, and at the same time serves as a remembrance of the triumph over the dead father by the reproduction of the rite of the totem meal. Affection and remorse in relation to the father are thus the unique source of morality and religion. One can see in this description of totemism that the dead father is idealized in the form of the totem. The ego ideal thus erected is ultimately projected on to numerous divinities and then on to the unique God of monotheistic religions in the form of the omnipotence attributed to him. This ego ideal seems to me to be linked to complex factors which mean that it is not the direct heir of primary narcissism. Indeed the idealization of the dead father is here based on the necessity of repressing the aggressive instincts of which he was the object. This leaves room for the positive half of the ambivalent love–hate couple, which makes this idealization akin to the mechanism described by Melanie Klein. Furthermore, and this seems to me to be fundamental to religions, the father is at least as much the representative of the superego as of the ego ideal. Once again, as Freud emphasizes, moral code and religion are inseparable. It should be noted in passing — but since the superego is not our topic we will not dwell on it — that the moral agency, as it is phylogenetically constituted in the Freudian schema, appears in a more evolved form than when it makes its appearance in the course of individual development. In the former case it is a product of the sense of guilt (and hence of concern for the object), in the latter of the fear of castration and hence of fears for the self. However that may be, the Oedipus complex and the superego hold a pre-eminent place in religion.

Freud supposed, in optimistic fashion for once, that Illusion, of which religion was for him the prime example, had but a limited future and that one day science would take over in its place. For him, not only was *Totem and Taboo* to demolish religion, whose unconscious and historical roots he had brought to light, but humanity, he let it be understood, must one day enter into the scientific era for good. 'May intellect and reason one day hold sway over the human mind, such is our most ardent wish', he proclaimed (1932). Contrasting science and religion, he felt that psychoanalysis, as a branch of the former, would hasten this joyous event. In fact, if, since he wrote *Totem and Taboo*, *The Future of an Illusion* or the *New Introductory Lectures*, science has indeed made giant progress, the human mind, for its part, is far from having entered the scientific era. Religion has certainly suffered a serious blow, but it has merely given way to ideologies and superstition or been degraded into mysticism. Thus, more than ever, 'real life happens somewhere else'. Freud's optimism was not, paradoxically, that of Saint-Simon who, on his death-bed, is supposed to have uttered the prophetic statement: 'Religion cannot disappear, it can only be transformed' (1825).

Max Weber, whose work in the field of sociology may in some respects be likened to that of Freud, has said that science produces a disenchantment with the world. It is as if science, by its rational explanations of phenomena, had destroyed religions in so far as they, too, represent systems for explaining the universe. Yet the need for Illusion has remained, at which point this unsatisfied need has swept reason aside in much more violent fashion than religion ever did. For there are degrees of Illusion, and a system in which the oedipal dimension of the psyche is preserved does not merit the title to the same extent as one which abolishes that dimension. Mysticism, unlike religion, has nothing to do with the Oedipus complex or the superego, any more than do ideologies as I have attempted to define them. It corresponds, rather, to the need for the uniting of ego and ideal via the shortest possible route. It represents fusion with the primary object, and even when the latter is represented consciously by God, it is nonetheless, at depth, an equivalent of the mother-prior-to-the-loss-of-fusion. Numerous descriptions of mystical ecstasy bear witness to this. Thus Saint François de Sales says that in this state the soul is like a small child still at the breast whose mother, to coddle him whilst he is still in her arms, feeds the milk into his mouth so that he has no need even to move his lips. Freud admitted the existence of an oceanic feeling, the primary feeling of the ego, but claimed never to have experienced it. He maintained that the father was the first object to be identified with, and thus seems to have left aside a whole aspect of the human psyche which today is tending to occupy an ever larger place. The attempt to recapture this oceanic feeling through drugs, mysticism and ideologies, has replaced the much longer route offered by religions in which paradise had to be earned through expensive sacrifices, if it was promised at all, as it is not in the Jewish religion. It is never, in any event, Paradise Now. Religion itself, in so far as it continues to exist, is undergoing a change in the direction of a weakening of the oedipal dimension. In *Moses and Monotheism* (1939) Freud, taking up once again the history of the origin of religions, shows that in Christianity the son's wish to take the father's place is all but realized, God the Father being relegated to the background. The religious compromise at the basis of morality, which reconciles remorse and triumph in relation to the father, comes down here clearly on the side of triumph.

However, I would want to add that the fact that the Father does continue to exist alongside the Son, even if only as a brilliant second, does represent the vestiges of repentance and hence the maintenance of the superego. Karl Barth, giving expression to a powerful current in today's Christian world, advocates a Christ-centred orientation which does away with the figure of the father and thus crosses the boundary which, to my mind, separates religion and mysticism, the absolute reign of the Son implying, in latent form, union with the mother. A slogan of the American Jesus Freaks recommends: 'After religion, try Jesus.'

What is more, if science itself stands dishonoured for destroying the spiritual food, the Illusion, for which man is so avid, it is, in other respects and at a much more profound level, experienced as encouraging this self-same Illusion. Scientific progress may need to employ secondary process, demanding as it does a whole sequence of actions, trials and tests, being the product of work that is forever having to be recommenced, the fruit of vast patience, and operating within a psychic context that acknowledges differences and hence development. It is none-theless experienced at the level of the primary process, in relation to its results, as magic itself. When man sees the moon-landing on his television, not only does he see some grey dust taking the place of the 'silver-aspected star', the 'Queen of the Night', the 'funereal torch', 'Diana', 'Phoebe' or 'Selena', thus annihilating 'this realm of dreams, province of illusions, capital of the Soap Bubble', to cite but a few of the celebrated poetic metaphors our satellite has evoked. He also soon experiences as entirely natural, banal and boring, the extraordinary feat of prowess which he has been invited to witness. And the result of this, at the level of the primary process, seems to me to be an increasing level of impatience, as if man can no longer adjust himself to life's natural rhythms but has begun to function on the model of the machines he has himself created. Thus science itself, paradoxically, appears to function as a powerful activator of Illusion.

It is always in the interest of psychoanalysis to concern itself above all with internal factors in attempting to explain the phenomena with which it has to deal. Psychoanalysis should never consider society as somehow divorced from unconscious roots within the individual, like a kind of Golem that has escaped its creator, or, at its most extreme, like an 'influencing machine'. In so far as the ego ideal — this link concept between the individual and the collectivity — is concerned, it seems to me legitimate to take into account the external activating factors (which nonetheless have their roots in the individual psyche of every human being) of this ancient wish for the reunification of ego and ideal, by the shortest possible route, namely Illusion. The development of the pathology I have attempted to outline is to be set to the account of those factors which take the progress made by science as confirmation of the possibility of an immediate reunification of ego and ideal, replacing religion by mysticism and ideology. The man who functions on the model of a machine cannot even anymore be a 'machine with wishes' (a phrase from Deleuze and Guattari). To wish implies process, development and differences. He is not, therefore, a 'machine with wishes' but only a machine that simply ticks over and finally destroys itself like some of Tinguely's creations. Thus 'anti-Oedipus' cannot but culminate in death.

Appendix

THE EGO IDEAL IN FREUD'S WORK

As is well known, Freud first used the term 'ego ideal' in 'On Narcissism: an Introduction' in 1914. However, it would seem appropriate from a methodological point of view also to examine texts prior to 1914 in which the concept appears, more or less clearly, without actually being named as such. This chronological orientation will no doubt make it easier to follow the developments which encouraged Freud formally to introduce the concept of the ego ideal into psychoanalysis.

1895. **Project for a Scientific Psychology.**

The first reference to note is from the first part of the *Project*, 'General Scheme':

> At first, the human organism is incapable of bringing about the specific action [i.e. an alteration in the external world capable of bringing about a lowering of internal stimuli, for example the supply of nourishment bringing an experience of satisfaction that is then linked to the disappearance of tensions]. It takes place by extraneous help, when the attention of an experienced person is drawn to the child's state by discharge along the path of internal change (e.g. by the child's screaming). In this way this path of discharge acquires a secondary function of the highest importance, that of *communication*, and the initial helplessness of human beings is the *primal source of all moral motives*.

It seemed to me preferable to adopt this fragmented approach initially, quoting from Freud's texts one after the other, even if it entails subsequently having to reconstruct the puzzle which thus cannot fail to emerge.

1897. **Letters to Fliess.**

On three occasions in these letters Freud refers to the *family romance* which was the subject of one of his 1908 papers, to which I shall return later. In letter 57, dated January 24th, he contrasts the humble attitude of the hysteric towards his magnified father, which forms the basis of his aspirations to inaccessible ideals (which also makes marriage impossible for him) with the 'combination in paranoics of megalomania with fictions of an alienation of parentage'. In a note to letter 63 of the same year he again takes up his idea of the family romance of the paranoic. In the famous letter 71 of October 15th, in which he announces to Fliess his discovery of the Oedipus complex through his self-analysis, he again writes about the family romance of paranoics — heroes or founders of religions — (the model being the family romance of Christ). In these texts the family romance is linked to the megalomania of the paranoic.

1905. **The Three Essays.**

Here we find idealization mentioned once, in relation to perversion, and more precisely to the mental factor in perversions:

> It is perhaps in connection precisely with the most repulsive perversions that the mental factor must be regarded as playing its largest part in the transformation of the sexual instinct. It is impossible to deny that in their case a piece of mental work has been performed which, in spite of its horrifying result, is the equivalent of an *idealization* of the instinct.

Here we glimpse what is to my mind a very important aspect of the problem of the perversions in general, namely: the pervert's ego ideal, which seems to me to play a fundamental role in the understanding of the perversions in general on the one hand, and of normal development on the other (a point I have attempted to grapple with in the chapter 'The Ego Ideal and Perversion'). Similarly, it can contribute to our understanding of the relationship between the ego ideal and sublimation, to which I have also devoted a chapter in the present work: 'The Ego Ideal, Sublimation, and the Creative Process'. The 'discharge' of the pervert is indeed, as we know, that of the non-repressed, non-sublimated component instincts which have nonetheless undergone a process of idealization, as stated by Freud in the text.

1907-1908. 'Creative Writers and Day-Dreaming'.

Two years later he developed some more contributions to this area of interest. First of all, studying the play of children, he wrote that: 'A child's play is determined by wishes: in point of fact by a single wish — one that helps in his upbringing — *the wish to be big and grown up. He is always playing at being 'grown up', and in his games he imitates what he knows about the lives of his elders*' (my italics). I have suggested that the wish to be 'grown up', to be adult and like the adults, constitutes one of the essential ingredients of the ego ideal of a child in the normal course of development (in the chapter 'The Development of the Ego Ideal'). Parallel to the child's play at 'being grown up', Freud studied the phantasies of adults. And the first thing he describes is the adult's attitude towards his phantasies: 'The adult', he says, 'is ashamed of his phantasies and hides them from other people. He cherishes his phantasies as his most intimate possessions, and as a rule he would rather confess his misdeeds than tell anyone his phantasies.' And a little further on he attempts to explain this shame of the adult in relation to his phantasies: the grown man 'knows that he is expected not to go on playing or phantasying any longer, but to act in the real world; on the other hand, some of the wishes which give rise to his phantasies are of a kind which it is essential to conceal. Thus he is ashamed of his phantasies as being childish and as being unpermissible.'

Here again, in my view, Freud makes reference to the concept of the ego ideal, albeit prior to its formulation, in considering the problem of the adult's relation to his phantasies. Indeed one must anticipate the 1914 paper and recall that for Freud the ego ideal is 'projected before' even if its roots are in the lost and hallowed time when the ego was its own ideal, that is to say in primary narcissism. The ego ideal is thus a *project* in the full sense of the term, and if, in this sense, being grown up is, for a child, entirely syntonic with his ideal, the phantasies of the adult, seen in this light, represent a backward step to infantile modes, that are non-adult. Is it necessary to add that phantasizing appears in this instance as an anal type of auto-erotic activity? ('He cherishes his phantasies as his most intimate possessions', writes Freud . . .) And that auto-erotic activity, in addition to always being linked to a strong sense of guilt, is linked even more to the narcissistic injury inflicted by the primal scene and the child's profound sense of being a sexually inadequate object, rejected and humiliated by the very objects of his wishes (cf. 'The Ego Ideal and Perversion')?

Phantasy activity, independently even of its content, therefore represents a dip into a world in which the child has attempted to overcome his frustration and his powerlessness through the omnipotence of his thought. It would seem to have its own particular status, since in comparison to the adult ego ideal, which gives an impetus towards reality, it is regressive, ridiculous and, representing as it does a reminder of a fundamental narcissistic injury, is a prompter of shame. At the same time, by its contents, it is able to compensate for the shortcomings that brought it into being. 'The motive forces of phantasies are unsatisfied wishes . . . They are either ambitious wishes, which serve to elevate the subject's personality; or they are erotic ones', writes Freud in the same text. He adds that the two types of wish co-exist for the most part, 'the lady for whom the creator of the phantasy performs all his heroic deeds' being often easily discovered behind the ambitious phantasies.

One might well consider the co-existence, which is so common, of phantasies that we would now call narcissistic, with erotic phantasies, to be linked to the attempt to repair the early and profound shock suffered by infantile megalomania by virtue of the primal scene. As for the feelings of shame, which would in this instance be stronger than that of guilt, this would refer, according to certain authors to whom I have had occasion to refer, to the relation between the ego and the ego ideal and not the superego (which would prompt guilt). It should also be recalled that for Freud any return to an activity or to cathexes that have been superseded is accompanied by shame and that the person who has progressed along the road of his development has, so to speak, raised up new Gods (new ideals) whilst the Gods that have been abandoned (that regression rediscovers) have become dangerous and repugnant (*Totem and Taboo*, 1912–1913; 'The "Uncanny" ', 1919).

1908–1909. 'Family Romances'.

The following year Freud was to define more precisely the child's wish to be 'grown up'. Here we are coming very close to the concept of the ego ideal, at least on a descriptive level: 'The child's most intense and most momentous wish during these early years is to be like his parents (that is, the parent of his own sex) and to be big like his father and mother.' In this text Freud again takes up his idea of the two types of phantasy: erotic and ambitious. From the child's frustrated love and from his ambition there will spring the family romance in which the parents that he will invent for himself will always be of high social rank. Often it will only be the father who is a man of position, the child being the product of maternal infidelity; but according to Freud the child should not be attributed purely hostile feelings towards his father. The latter is indeed exalted, overvalued. We might say he is 'idealized', as if the child wished to rediscover in this substitute father the magnified father of his early childhood. An addition of 1909 to *The Interpretation of Dreams*, chapter VI, the section dealing with symbols, mentions that 'The Emperor and Empress (or the King and Queen) as a rule really represent the dreamer's parents; and a Prince or a Princess represents the dreamer himself or herself.'

Approaching Freud's seminal 1914 text we find that from 1910 there also starts to appear in a number of his works the concept that Freud will actually introduce at the same time as that of the ego ideal, and from which it is, at that point, inseparable, namely: narcissism.

1910. **Notes to the Three Essays.**

The first written reference that we have to this concept is in a note of 1910 to the *Three Essays*, although narcissism was referred to by Freud at a meeting of the Vienna Psychoanalytic Society on 10th November, 1909. Unfortunately the minutes of that meeting have disappeared. The note to the *Three Essays* concerns homosexuality. Freud writes about a short-lived and very intense fixation to the mother, followed by identification subsequent to which the future homosexual takes himself as a love object. That is to say, he proceeds from a narcissistic basis, looking for a young man who is like himself and that he can love as his mother loved him.

1910. **Leonardo.** — 1911. **Schreber.**

That same year, in *Leonardo*, he again takes up exactly this idea. But is it to my mind in 'The Case of Schreber' and, in some ways, in *Totem and Taboo* that Freud touches most closely on the problems of the ego ideal and of narcissism before he has yet given a name to the first of these two concepts. To recall some of the essential points made in the Schreber case: Freud's exposition emphasizes particularly the development of the illness — passing from a persecution paranoia to a religious paranoia — and the reconciliation of the phantasy of passive homosexuality that this development made possible.

Originally the transformation into a woman (being emasculated) was felt to be, says Freud 'a serious injury and persecution . . .'

> It only became related to his playing the part of Redeemer in a secondary way. There can be no doubt, moreover, that originally he believed that the transformation was to be effected for the purpose of sexual abuse and not so as to serve higher designs. The position may be formulated by saying that a sexual delusion of persecution was later on converted in the patient's mind into a religious delusion of grandeur. The part of the persecutor was at first assigned to Professor

Flechsig, the physician in whose charge he was; later, his place was taken by God himself.

As will be recalled, Schreber himself, in a passage of his *Memoirs* quoted by Freud who accords it decisive importance, demonstrates the salutary nature of the transformation in his delusion of emasculation: 'I shall show later on [it is Schreber speaking] that emasculation for quite another purpose — a purpose *in consonance with the Order of Things* — is within the bounds of possibility, and indeed, that it may quite probably afford the solution of the conflict.' The transformation into a woman is originally experienced, and Freud emphasizes this point, as a matter of 'sexual shame'. Freud came back to this question of shame on another occasion: 'He considered the transformation into a woman as a shame, a disgrace that must have been inflicted on him with a hostile intention.' When the object of the President's passive homosexual wish itself undergoes a transformation, and from being a doctor becomes God, this shame disappears:

It was impossible for Schreber to become reconciled to playing the part of a female wanton towards his doctor; but the task of providing God himself with the voluptuous sensations that He required called up no such resistance on the part of his ego. Emasculation was now no longer a disgrace; it became "consonant with the Order of Things".

On rereading 'The Case of Schreber' once again, I have been struck by the tremendous importance given to that which, three years later, he would call the ego ideal. Feminization is indeed, for a man, incompatible with his ego ideal. It will have been noted that, as on each occasion when it is narcissism that is put into question, the dominant sensation is that of shame. I do not mean to suggest that it might not be possible to detect, behind all that, a sense of guilt, particularly since Schreber did go through depressive episodes. But in the persecutory phase of his illness it is shame that predominates. What is more, the phantasy of castration — so terribly dangerous to the ego — becomes acceptable from the moment the ego ideal takes up its side. This seems to demonstrate that there is — at least in psychosis — a fear that is more fundamental than that of a strictly sexual castration, namely a loss of the person's narcissistic worth, a profound blow to his ego in relation to his ideal. From the moment that this castration is for the benefit of God, it is felt to be narcissistically acceptable. He loses his penis but gains a narcissistic phallus by serving God's designs.

But who is God? If the relationship to the father is too erotized or too aggressive this makes the projection of the ego ideal on to the father and his penis impossible. The penis remains a penis, a sexual object, without becoming a phallus. The person has no other recourse than to set up his own ego as his ego ideal, the seedbed for his future megalomania. Now we know that in reality Schreber's father was the kind of father who makes the desexualization of the relationship to his penis extremely difficult and in any event precarious (cf. Racamier and Chasseguet-Smirgel, 1966). One might therefore suppose that in this instance narcissistic fixation will be very important. It is precisely à propos of President Schreber and paranoia that Freud will write about 'a stage in the development of the libido which it passes through on the way from auto-erotism to object-love', which he calls narcissism. In this text auto-erotism corresponds to a stage in which me and non-me (ego and non-ego) are intermingled and in which libidinal cathexis remains indistinct and without boundaries. Narcissism represents a stage when 'the individual . . . unifies his sexual instincts (which have hitherto been engaged in auto-erotic activities) in order to obtain a love-object; and he begins by taking himself, his own body, as his love object, and only subsequently proceeds from this to the choice of some person other than himself as his object.' In other words, narcissism is here seen as the cathexis of an ego that is already clearly delimited and separate from the object. The necessity to rediscover in the other the characteristics of the ego and, particularly, the sexual characteristics, leads to the following stage — that of homosexual object choice — and only then to heterosexuality. At that point the homosexual instincts do not disappear but are diverted from their goal, sublimated, and go to form the social instincts.

If, as Freud says in his 1914 paper, the projection of the ego ideal on to the object does not *ipso facto* bring with it the sublimation of the instincts in question, it seems to me to go without saying that if the erotic and aggressive link with the object is maintained, preventing it from becoming an adequate prop to the ego ideal, this must lead to the sublimation of the homosexual instincts being precarious.

> People who have not freed themselves completely from the stage of narcissism — who, that is to say, have at that point a fixation which may operate as a disposition to a later illness — are exposed to the danger that some unusually intense wave of libido, finding no other outlet, may lead to a sexualization of their social instincts and so undo the sublimations which they had achieved in the course of their development.

'Paranoics', Freud was to say, 'have brought along with them a *fixation* at the stage of *narcissism*, and we can assert that the length of the step back from *sublimated homosexuality to narcissism* is a measure of the amount of *regression* characteristic of paranoia.'

It is the flowing back of libido to the ego that is the basis of megalomania (or rather of a return to infantile megalomania). The point of departure for this process may be found most commonly in those humiliations, those social rebuffs in which one detects — says Freud — 'the participation of the homosexual component of affective life'.

All of these propositions of Freud anticipate the 1914 text in which he will establish the link between the ego ideal and homosexual libido. Furthermore, if we return to the question, 'Who is God?', we could say that he is the end result, and indeed the salvation of (Freud sees the development towards mystical paranoia as 'a sort of healing'), an attempt to project narcissism on to the object. That is to say, God is the result of an attempt to create an ego ideal, the same attempt having failed when it took

Flechsig as its prop, although many traces of this can still be detected (Flechsig is supposed to have belonged to 'the highest celestial nobility' for example). One can see that development in the direction of religious paranoia is only possible from the starting point of the existence of an a-conflictual nucleus in the relationship to the primary object, the ego ideal being fed from this source. It would seem that the more the relationship to the homosexual object, in this event the father, has been conflicted and therefore has remained sexualized, the more the ego ideal will be projected on to an abstract and grandiose figure — in the extreme, on to God himself. One can therefore appreciate — and I shall come back to this in relation to *Totem and Taboo* — that part of the megalomania is relieved, to the extent that the phantasied homosexual object relationship is made possible, whereas in the persecutory form of paranoia there is an almost total withdrawal of libido into the ego, the person then only being able to take himself as his own ideal, thus arriving at a final stage of megalomania. Seen in this light paranoia is, *par excellence*, a malady of the ego ideal.

1912–1913. Totem and Taboo.

It seems to me that in this text Freud demonstrates fairly clearly the particular status that he accords the ego ideal, a year before having given it its name, placing it between infantile megalomania and object love, between the pleasure principle and the reality principle. He does so in relation to the magic of the primitive animist that depends upon the omnipotence of thought. As will be recalled, he distinguishes three phases in the evolution of man's view of the universe: animistic, religious and scientific and he traces the fate of the omnipotence of thoughts through these three phases:

> At the animistic stage men ascribe omnipotence to themselves. At the religious stage they transfer it to the gods but do not seriously abandon it themselves, for they reserve the power of influencing the gods in a variety of ways according to their

wishes. The scientific view of the universe no longer affords any room for human omnipotence; men have acknowledged their smallness and submitted resignedly to death.

He compares the animistic phase to narcissism, the religious phase to the point at which, having developed object relations, narcissism is projected on to the parents, and the scientific phase to the stage of maturity in which ' the individual accepts the exigencies of reality (although he is sceptical that this phase is ever completely attained, detecting traces of animism in 'modern life').

It is the religious phase, says Freud, that 'would correspond to the stage of object choice of which the characteristic is a child's attachment to his parents'. The projection of infantile narcissism on to the parents is indeed constitutive of the ego ideal, which thus represents a step forward in the achievement of a sense of reality, a progressive compromise between the pleasure principle and the reality principle, the child having accepted that he must give up his primary megalomania in favour of his object.

If we now quickly attempt to put together the several elements that we can gather from these pre-1914 texts, we see that the ego ideal:

1. is a project of the child's to become adult ('Creative Writers and Day-Dreaming') and more precisely to become like the parents and especially the parent of the same sex ('Family Romances'). The libido in question is therefore essentially homosexual ('The Case of Schreber');

2. is of narcissistic origin at the same time as representing a development towards object relatedness. It tends to maintain the original narcissism at the same time as projecting it on to the object ('The Case of Schreber', *Totem and Taboo*), but it is the product of a shock to this primitive narcissism and of man's original helplessness which obliged him to seek satisfaction and the discharge of tension through an external object, an adult ('The Project').

1915. **'Instincts and their Vicissitudes'.**

Anticipating somewhat, we might put together this last text with a note to 'Instincts and their Vicissitudes'. 'Indeed, the primal narcissistic state would not be able to follow the development (that is to be described) if it were not for the fact that every individual passes through a period during which *he is helpless* and has to be looked after and during which his pressing needs are satisfied by an external agency.' It is at this point, it would seem, that the first formation of the ego ideal is to be located, a projection (on to the object that enables the helpless ego to survive) of the battered megalomania. The birth of the ego ideal would then be contemporaneous with the first frustrations and the birth of the object;

3. That it maintains links with sublimation ('The Case of Schreber') but is not to be confused with this. It concerns the object whereas sublimation concerns the instinct. However, Freud does write about the idealization of the instinct by the pervert (*Three Essays . . .*);

4. If it is possible to draw together from these pre-1914 texts certain aspects of what was to become the ego ideal, it is on the contrary very difficult to divine the links that Freud was to establish in 'On Narcissism: an Introduction' between these aspects of the ego ideal — which appear essentially as a phantasy, the child's project of identification with an adult, with the parent of the same sex — and the moral agency (except in the 'Project'). A glance at Chapter VII of *The Interpretation of Dreams* allows us indeed to assure ourselves that the censorship that Freud places, in the first topography, between the unconscious and the pre-conscious on the one hand, and the pre-conscious and the conscious on the other, has no explicit links with the 'latent' ego ideal as we have tried to define it. This is true, even if it does have links with what Freud would describe in 1914 as constituting a critical agency, this function having become that which we would now be in the habit of assigning to the superego.

1914. 'On Narcissism: an Introduction'.

As we have seen, Freud had already written about narcissism before introducing the concept into the body of psychoanalytic theory. Without rehearsing the whole of the concept of narcissism as expressed in this text, I would just remind the reader that, to the extent that this notion is indispensable for an understanding of the ego ideal, here Freud sees narcissism as not only one, or even several, stages of development, but as a permanent cathexis. It transforms the ego; as a result, objects can be cathected to different degrees, without the ego ever being able to give up entirely its libido in favour of its objects.

It is in the third part of this work that Freud introduces the concept of the ego ideal. S. Shentoub has rightly pointed out to me that Freud must have spoken about the ego ideal to the Viennese psychoanalysts from 1912, as one can confirm from the correspondence between Freud and Lou Andréas Salomé (1970). 'Man has shown himself incapable of giving up a satisfaction he has once enjoyed', says Freud. This satisfaction is that which resulted for him from the narcissistic perfection of his childhood. 'He seeks to recover this early perfection that has been taken from him in the new form of an ego ideal. What he projects before him as his ideal is the substitute for the lost narcissism of his childhood in which he was his own ideal.' It should be noted that here, referring to the loss of the child's initial perfection, Freud has in mind the 'admonitions of others' and the awakening of the critical judgement, and not a spontaneous development of the ego, which links the ego ideal to moral conscience and in particular to the repression that will come from the ego's 'self-respect'.

It is a mistake to interpret the ego ideal in this text, as is sometimes done, as the equivalent of a psychical agency. As we have said before it is much better conceived of as a phantasy 'projected before', a phantasy which can seemingly remain in part unconscious, and which is the product of the narcissistic perfection that has been lost under the influence of parental criticism. On the other hand there does exist, side by side with the ego ideal, an agency 'which performs the task of seeing that narcissistic satisfaction from the ego ideal is ensured' and which, with this end in view, constantly watches the actual ego and measures it by that ideal. The delusion of being watched of paranoics demonstrates the genesis of this agency, the incorporation of parental criticism being dissolved, and reprojected in the form of voices.

It is essentially homosexual libido that has been utilized in the formation of the ego ideal. Self-esteem is linked to evaluation by the critical agency of the ego (moral conscience and censor) in relation to the ego ideal.

'The development of the ego', says Freud, 'consists in a departure from primary narcissism and gives rise to a vigorous attempt to recover that state. This departure is brought about by means of the displacement of libido on to an ego ideal imposed from without; and satisfaction is brought about from fulfilling this ideal.'

The idea of an ideal imposed from without seems to me to be an important point for discussion to the extent that one might well question whether there may not be a much more spontaneous formation of the ego ideal linked on the one hand to identifications with parental models, independently — in part at least — of the formulation by them of interdicts and admonitions, and on the other hand to the existence of an innate programme of psycho-sexual development, that is to say of the wish to be 'grown up', a point I have emphasized in the chapter on 'The Development of the Ego Ideal'.

Freud concludes his article by assigning the ego ideal a very important role in the understanding of group psychology. It represents, indeed, a linking concept between the individual and the group, a theme that he will develop in 1921 in *Group Psychology and the Analysis of the Ego*. 'It binds', he writes, 'not only a person's narcissistic libido, but also a considerable amount of his homosexual libido . . . The want of satisfaction which arises from the non-fulfilment of this ideal liberates homosexual libido, and this is transformed into a sense of guilt (social anxiety).' The term 'social anxiety' was taken up again by Freud in *Civilization and its*

Discontents (1929), at a time when he no longer used the term ego ideal but only that of superego. At that time, this social anxiety is related to a lack of internalization of the superego. The profoundly narcissistic tone of this anxiety, which is linked to the image of ourselves that we wish to convey to others, the reflection that we get back from them representing an appreciation of the degree of conformity that exists between our ego and our ideal, the shame that accompanies it. All that disappears in this second formulation, which at the same time sets aside the links between this affect and homosexuality. I have addressed this problem in the chapter on 'The Development of the Ego Ideal'.

Finally, Freud concludes his paper by writing again about the paranoic in relation to this, and about the precipitating factor in paranoia:

> The frequent causation of paranoia by an injury to the ego, by a frustration of satisfaction within the sphere of the ego ideal, is thus made more intelligible, as is the convergence of ideal-formation and sublimation in the ego-ideal, as well as the involution of sublimations and the possible transformation of ideals in paraphrenic disorders.

1916. **Introductory Lectures on Psycho-Analysis.**

In the *Introductory Lectures on Psycho-Analysis* (chapter XXVI, 'The Libido Theory and Narcissism'), Freud in essence repeats the propositions contained in his 1914 paper concerning the ego ideal and the existence of a critical agency charged with gauging the conformity of the ego to the ideal.

1921. **Group Psychology and the Analysis of the Ego.**

As will be recalled, *Group Psychology and the Analysis of the Ego* takes as its starting point the existence of an identity between the nature of group psychology and that of individual psychology. The project of the book is in line with that of *Totem and Taboo*, at the same time as constituting, in some ways, a continuation and a

development of 'On Narcissism: an Introduction', most particularly of the last paragraph. I shall only address the elements
relating to the subject that concerns us here.

In the chapter on 'Identification', Freud seeks to study the
affective relations between the individuals making up a group.
Two points deserve our attention. Firstly, the chapter begins with
an affirmation of the importance of identification in relation to
the Oedipus complex: the boy wishes to be like his father who he
takes as his ideal. 'He exhibits', says Freud, 'an identification with
his father which takes him as his model.' Three sorts of
identification are possible:

1. Identification constitutes the most primitive form of link
with the object;

2. Through regression it can take the place of a libidinal
attachment to the object;

3. Identification can take place each time a person discovers
that he has a trait in common with another person. It is this that
explains the attachment of the individuals who make up a group to
one another by reason of the shared affect that results from the
link that connects each individual to the leader.

But identification is also present in other instances. Having
taken up again the example of the *Three Essays* and of *Leonardo*
concerning identification in the homosexual, Freud retraces the
process of introjection of the object by the melancholic, as he had
described it earlier in 'Mourning and Melancholia' (1916–1917).
The ego, explains Freud, is divided into two pieces, one of which
rages against the second, which has been altered by introjection
and which contains the lost object. The aggressive part of the ego
comprises 'the voice of conscience', the critical agency within the
ego. 'We have called it', says Freud, 'the "ego ideal", and by way
of functions we have ascribed to it self-observation, the moral
conscience, the censorship of dreams, and the chief influence in
repression. We have said that it is the heir to the original
narcissism in which the childish ego enjoyed self-sufficiency.'

It may be noted here that, although he makes reference to his
1914 work, Freud tends to confuse the ego ideal with the critical

agency (which he did not do in 1914), and even to have this agency absorb the ego ideal. It must be added that it is his work on 'Mourning and Melancholia' — in which the critical agency occupied the whole stage (there is no question of the ideal) — that lies at the source of Freud's elaboration of the concept of the superego, bringing with it a disappearance of the ego ideal, if not in name at least as regards its particular characteristics and its primarily narcissistic origin.

However, in *Group Psychology and the Analysis of the Ego*, the ego ideal still retains some of its autonomous status and its specific characteristics. Pursuing his aim of studying the libidinal organization of the group, Freud is led to examine the state of being-in-love and hypnosis. In the state of being-in-love the loved object is subjected to idealization.

> the object is being treated in the same way as our own ego, so that when we are in love a considerable amount of narcissistic libido overflows on to the object. It is even obvious, in many forms of love-choice, that the object serves as a substitute for some unattained ego ideal of our own. We love it on account of the perfections which we have striven to reach for our own *ego*, and which we should now like to procure in this roundabout way as a means of satisfying our narcissism.

Freud says that in every case of being in love one finds traits of humility, of the limitation of narcissism, and that the object has, so to speak, absorbed, consumed the ego, which sacrifices itself before the loved object. Contemporaneously with this 'devotion' of the ego to the object 'the functions allotted to the ego ideal entirely cease to operate. The criticism exercised by that agency is silent; everything that the object does and asks for is right and blameless.' Love is blind and 'the whole situation can be completely summarized in a formula', says Freud, '*The object has been put in the place of the ego ideal.*' I have had occasion to make some remarks on this problem in the chapter 'The Ego Ideal, Being in Love and Genitality'.

For Freud, the hypnotist is, in relation to his subject, in

the same position as the loved object. The hypnotist has been put in the place of the ego ideal (with the exclusion of the sexual element). It may be noted in passing that in this text Freud attributes the function of reality testing to the ego ideal, a function that will later revert to the ego. Now, says Freud, the hypnotic relation is similar to that which links the individual in a group to the leader. '*A primary group of this kind is a number of individuals who have put one and the same object in the place of their ego ideal and have consequently identified themselves with one another in their ego.*' Note that in this text the ego ideal does indeed retain its specific, and in particular its narcissistic characteristics, and that it would prove very difficult to substitute 'superego' for 'ego ideal' throughout.

The group has this in common with the primal horde, that the leader 'is still the dreaded primal father; the group still wishes to be governed by unrestricted force . . . it has a thirst for obedience. The primal father is the group ideal, which governs the ego in the place of the ego ideal.' Indeed the individual ego ideal is given up in favour of the group ego ideal personified in the leader. Individual peculiarities disappear in the group, the members composing it identifying themselves with each other. Thus, at the level of the ego there is identification of the members of the group between themselves, whilst a common external object is put in place of the ego ideal. Such is the libidinal structure of the group. The character of the leader as father has been discussed in the chapter on the relationship between the ego ideal and the group.

The ego ideal constitutes 'A Differentiating Grade in the Ego' (title of chapter XI). Now, the separation of the ego from the ego ideal cannot be borne for long. Certain institutions permit a regression to a state of non-differentiation between the ego and its ideal, for example, the festival. '*But the ego ideal comprises the sum of all the limitations in which the ego has to acquiesce, and for that reason the abrogation of the ideal would necessarily be a magnificent festival for the ego, which might then once again feel satisfied with itself*' [my italics]. This is what would take place in mania: the ego and the ego ideal would become as one. At the other extreme the misery of the melancholic is the expression of an extreme tension between the two agencies.

1923. **The Ego and the Id.**

Freud introduced the term superego as an equivalent of the ego ideal and, in so doing, rather surprisingly referred to his 1914 text: 'The considerations that led us to assume the existence of a grade in the ego, a differentiation within the ego, which may be called the "ego ideal" or "super-ego", have been stated elsewhere' (whereas he had never referred to the superego prior to the 1923 text). In a note he adds that he was mistaken in ascribing the function of reality testing, which belongs to the ego, to this superego. Freud then gives consideration to the process of identification and the building up of 'character' resulting from identification with lost objects (an introjection into the ego of the object which offers itself to the id's love, the libido that the ego receives subsequent to its identifications is the source of secondary narcissism). The effects of the first identifications are general and lasting.

> This leads us back to the origin of the ego ideal; for behind it there lies hidden an individual's first and most important identification, his identification with the father in his own personal prehistory. This is apparently not in the first instance the consequence or outcome of an object-cathexis; it is a direct and immediate identification and takes place earlier than any object-cathexis. But the object-choices belonging to the first sexual period and relating to the father and mother seem normally to find their outcome in an identification of this kind, and would thus reinforce the primary one.

The intricacy of the problem is due to the triangular character of the Oedipus situation and to the individual's constitutional bisexuality.

Originally the boy's object is the mother's breast. The boy deals with his father by identifying himself with him. For a time these two relationships proceed side by side.

The father then becomes a rival and the identification takes on a hostile colouring owing to the wish to get rid of him; this is the Oedipus complex in its proper sense.

The demolition of the Oedipus complex may lead either to an identification with the mother or in normal cases to an intensification of the identification with the father.

The normal dissolution of the Oedipus complex would consolidate the masculinity in a boy's character.

This does not constitute an identification with the abandoned object, although at times this may take place. In fact the existence of the *full Oedipus situation comprises four trends and two identifications*:

> *The broad general outcome of the sexual phase dominated by the Oedipus complex may, therefore, be taken to be the forming of a precipitate in the ego, consisting of these two identifications in some way united with each other. This modification of the ego retains its special position; it confronts the other contents of the ego as an ego ideal or super-ego.*

The superego is not simply a residue of the earliest object-choices of the id; it also represents an energetic reaction-formation against those choices. The superego says to the ego: ' "You ought to be like this (like your father)". It also comprises the prohibition: "You may not be like this (like your father) — that is, you may not do all that he does; some things are his prerogative." '

Here we can see an old acquaintance looming up, which in fact Freud does not refer to in this text, namely 'the incest barrier' of the *Three Essays*. We can see that the superego-ego ideal confusion acquires precise object roots: the repression of the Oedipus complex. In fact it does not entirely lose its narcissistic foundations and Freud will give it a dual origin:

> If we consider once more the origin of the superego as we have described it, we shall recognize that it is the outcome of two highly important factors, one of a biological and the other of a historical nature: namely, the lengthy duration in

man of his childhood helplessness and dependence, and the fact of his Oedipus complex, the repression of which we have shown to be connected with the interruption of libidinal development by the latency period and so with the diphasic onset of man's sexual life.

The superego therefore represents the natural culmination of development. The ideal ego, the superego, are the summation of our relationship to our parents: 'When we were little children we knew these higher natures, we admired them and feared them; and later we took them into ourselves.' Thus we have here a coalescence of narcissism (admiration) and the prohibition of the instincts (fear), but with the accent on the instincts.

The ego ideal is therefore the heir of the Oedipus complex . . . Owing to the way in which the ego ideal is formed, it has the most abundant links with the phylogenetic acquisition of each individual — his archaic heritage . . . [at the same time as it] answers to everything that is expected of the higher nature of man. As a substitute for a longing for the father, it contains the germ from which all religions have evolved. The self-judgement which declares that the ego falls short of its ideal produces the religious sense of humility to which the believer appeals in his longing . . . The tension between the demands of conscience and the actual performances of the ego is experienced as a sense of guilt. Social feelings rest on identifications with other people, on the basis of having the same ego ideal.

Religion, morality and a social sense form the chief elements in the higher side of man and have been acquired by virtue of the father complex. At the end of this chapter Freud calls the superego 'the heir to the id' and also 'a reaction formation to the Oedipus complex'. The relation of the ideal ego or superego to the id explains the fact that this creation is in large measure unconscious.

At the beginning of chapter V, called 'The Dependent

Relationships of the Ego', Freud once more gives a description of the formation of the superego:

> On the one hand it was the first identification and one which took place while the ego was still feeble, and on the other hand it is the heir to the Oedipus complex and has thus introduced the most momentous objects into the ego . . . It is a memorial of the former weakness and dependence of the ego, and the mature ego remains subject to its domination.

The negative therapeutic reaction can be seen as linked to the sense of guilt produced by the superego preventing the person from giving up his illness. The sense of guilt (and of inferiority) represents the state of tension between the ideal ego or superego and the ego.

The extremely powerful superego of melancholia has gained hold of all the individual's sadism and turned it against the id; the superego becomes 'a pure culture of the death instinct'. According to this view the superego represents the turning against the ego of the death instinct that has not been directed outwards (cf. *Civilization and its Discontents*). Whence the fact that the less a person is aggressive in the external world, the more severe will be his superego (this being due to the fate of the death instinct).

1923. 'Remarks on the Theory and Practice of Dream Interpretation'.

Freud will make scarcely any further reference to the ego ideal from the time of *The Ego and the Id*. In the 'Remarks' of the same year he writes: 'It is enough that we should keep firmly to the fact that the separation of the ego from an observing, critical, punishing agency (an ego ideal) must be taken into account in the interpretation of dreams as well.' It can be seen that this version of the ego ideal no longer has anything in common with its narcissistic predecessor of 1914 and that it is, in fact, restricted to the critical agency.

1924. 'The Economic Problem of Masochism'.

The following year, in 'The Economic Problem of Masochism', Freud considered the superego itself to be a model and an ideal resulting from the introjection of the idealized parents. It is, however, essentially their aggressive characteristics that are retained because of the defusion of instinct which occurs along with the process of identification.

> We have attributed the function of conscience to the superego and we have recognized the consciousness of guilt as an expression of a tension between the ego and the superego. The ego reacts with feelings of anxiety (conscience anxiety) to the perception that it has not come up to the demands made by its ideal, the superego. What we want to know is how the superego has come to play this demanding role and why the ego, in the case of a difference with its ideal, should have to be afraid.
>
> We have said that the function of the ego is to unite and to reconcile the claims of the three agencies which it serves; and we may add that in doing so it also possesses in the superego a model which it can strive to follow. For this superego is as much a representative of the id as of the external world. It came into being through the introjection into the ego of the first objects of the id's impulses — namely, the two parents. In this process the relation to those objects was desexualized; it was diverted from its direct sexual aims. Only in this way was it possible for the Oedipus complex to be surmounted. The superego retained essential features of the introjected persons — their strength, their severity, their inclination to supervise and to punish. As I have said elsewhere [The Ego and the Id], it is easily conceivable that, thanks to the defusion of instinct which occurs along with this introduction into the ego, the severity was increased. The super-ego — the conscience at work in the ego — may then become harsh, cruel and inexorable against the ego which is in its charge. Kant's Categorical Imperative is thus the direct heir of the Oedipus complex.

But the same figures who continue to operate in the super-ego as the agency we know as conscience after they have ceased to be objects of the libidinal impulses of the id — these same figures also belong to the real external world. It is from there that they were drawn; their power, behind which lie hidden all the influences of the past and of tradition, was one of the most strongly-felt manifestations of reality. In virtue of this concurrence, the super-ego, the substitute for the Oedipus complex, becomes a representative of the real external world as well and thus also becomes a model for the endeavours of the ego.

The view of the superego as representative of tradition (the parents' parents) will be taken up again in the *New Introductory Lectures* (Freud, 1932).

1932. **New Introductory Lectures on Psycho-Analysis.**

Finally, in the third of the *New Introductory Lectures*: 'The Dissection of the Psychical Personality' (1932), Freud, who here brings in some new elements to the definition of the superego, introduces 'ideal models' even more clearly: 'In the course of development the super-ego also takes on the influence of those who have stepped into the place of parents — educators, teachers, people chosen as ideal models . . .'

> [The super-ego] is also the vehicle of the ego ideal by which the ego measures itself, which it emulates, and whose demand for ever greater perfection it strives to fulfil. There is no doubt that this ego ideal is the precipitate of the old picture of the parents, the expression of admiration for the perfection which the child then attributed to them.

If we attempt to summarize briefly these views, we can note:

1. That even before the introduction of the superego, the sense given to the ego ideal differs noticeably from one text to another. Thus in 'On Narcissism: an Introduction' and in the

Introductory Lectures on Psycho-Analysis it is distinct from the critical agency; in *Group Psychology and the Analysis of the Ego* the critical agency is incorporated into the ideal.

2. It is in this latter text that it seems to include the greatest number of narcissistic significations at the same time as it starts to embrace characteristics that will subsequently be recognized as belonging to the superego and explicitly attributed to the critical agency (the conscience) in 'Mourning and Melancholia'. It is of interest, in this respect, to situate the 1921 text as 'heir' of the 1914 paper, but equally as having been written a year after *Beyond the Pleasure Principle*, that is to say after the introduction of the death instinct.

3. As one gets further and further away from the 1914 paper, the rare allusions to the ego ideal imply less the *projection* of narcissism on to the parents than the *incorporation* of idealized parents. Here I find myself in agreement with a very important observation made by Joseph Sandler and his colleagues (1963). These authors emphasize that in the development of this concept Freud moved from that of an ego ideal that the subject creates for himself (in order to recapture his lost perfection) to that of an ideal that is related to parental models.

Although these two movements may be correlative, the accent that is put on instinctual conflicts after 1923, on the prohibiting and restrictive character of the superego (for, whatever may be said, it is only very exceptionally that any of Freud's texts present this agency in a benign light [perhaps only in 'Humour', 1927]), confers on the ideals a character that is equally object related and restrictive. Although it must be noted (cf. above) that as of 1914 an ambiguity is introduced by the term 'ego ideal imposed from without'.

4. No single text of Freud's brings together all of the characteristics ascribed separately to the ego ideal in these different works.

To conclude this review, I should like to say a word about the 'ideal ego'. It will of course be understood that this is not a Freudian concept. Even the most attentive reading of Freud's texts does not allow one to detect the slightest difference between *Ideal-Ich* and *Ichideal* (that is, between ideal ego and ego ideal). Only the most passionate exegetists (in France) have been able to try and find some significance in what is simply a linguistic device to try and avoid repetition. However Nunberg, and in his wake a number of other authors (most notably, in France, Lagache), have sought to distinguish two concepts within that of the ego ideal, basing themselves not upon an erroneous interpretation of Freudian texts, but on what seemed to them to be a clinical reality.

For Nunberg (1932), the ideal ego corresponds to the unorganized ego that still feels itself to be fused with the id. This is the ego of the little child and also that which reappears in certain catatonic or manic states, in dementia 'and even to a degree also in the neuroses . . . In the phantasy of "returning to the mother's womb", the individual seeks to realize this ideal state of his ego . . .' For Daniel Lagache (1966), it is of interest to try and distinguish the ideal ego from the ego ideal–superego system. 'The ideal ego viewed as a narcissistic ideal of omnipotence cannot be reduced to the fusion of ego and id, but includes a primary identification with another being, cathected with omnipotence, that is to say the mother.'

For my part I have not judged it necessary to distinguish between ego ideal and ideal ego, in as much as any study of the ego ideal implies a study of the different forms that the attempt to recapture lost narcissism may take. That some of these forms are regressive, that others coincide with the gains made from development, is indeed just one of the things that I hope to have been able to demonstrate. This does not seem to me to justify the introduction of a separate concept to designate the more archaic modalities of re-uniting ego and ideal. Unless this is simply to be a linguistic convenience, it must not be forgotten that we are still concerned here with a wish whose origin is analogous, even if it takes a different road to its realization: We are, in any event, in the presence of narcissism and its vicissitudes.

BIBLIOGRAPHY

Abbreviations

I.J.P. = *The International Journal of Psycho-Analysis*
R.F.P. = *Revue Française de Psychanalyse*
S.E. = *The Standard Edition of the Complete Psychological Works of Sigmund Freud*, London, The Hogarth Press.

THE EGO IDEAL IN FREUD'S WORK

Freud (S.) (1895) Project for a Scientific Psychology. *S.E.*, I, pp. 281–397.
——(1887–1902) Letters to Wilhelm Fliess (1887–1902). *S.E.*, I, pp. 177–282.
——(1905) Three Essays on the Theory of Sexuality. *S.E.*, VII, pp. 123–243.
——(1907–1908) Creative Writers and Day-Dreaming. *S.E.*, IX, pp. 141–154.
——(1908–1909) Family Romances. *S.E.*, IX, pp. 235–244.
——(1910) Leonardo da Vinci and a Memory of his Childhood. *S.E.*, XI, pp. 63–138.
——(1911) Psycho-Analytic Notes on an Autobiographical Account of a Case of Paranoia (Dementia Paranoides). *S.E.*, XII, pp. 9–84.
——(1912–1913) Totem and Taboo. *S.E.*, XIII, pp. 1–161.
——(1914) On Narcissism: An Introduction. *S.E.*, XIV, pp. 76–104.
——(1916) Introductory Lectures on Psycho-Analysis. *S.E.*, XV–XVI, pp. 15–463.
——(1921) Group Psychology and the Analysis of the Ego. *S.E.*, XVIII, pp. 69–144.
——(1923) The Ego and the Id. *S.E.*, XIX, pp. 13–68.
——(1923) Remarks on the Theory and Practice of Dream Interpretation. *S.E.*, XIX, pp. 109–124.
——(1924) The Economic Problem of Masochism. *S.E.*, XIX, pp. 159–172.
——(1932) The Dissection of the Psychical Personality. in: New Introductory Lectures on Psycho-Analysis. *S.E.*, XXII, pp. 57–80.

SUBLIMATION IN FREUD'S WORK (Compiled by P. Letarte)

Freud (S.) (1905) Three Essays on the Theory of Sexuality. *S.E.*, VII, pp. 123–243.

—— (1908) 'Civilized' Sexual Morality and Modern Nervous Illness. *S.E.*, IX, pp. 177–204.

—— (1908) Character and Anal Erotism. *S.E.*, IX, pp. 167–176.

—— (1907–1908) Creative Writers and Day-Dreaming. *S.E.*, IX, pp. 141–154.

—— (1910) Leonardo da Vinci and a Memory of his Childhood. *S.E.*, XI, pp. 63–138.

—— (1910) Five Lectures on Psycho-Analysis. *S.E.*, XI, pp. 3–57.

—— (1910) Letter to Pfister on 2 May. in: *Correspondence de Sigmund Freud avec le pasteur Pfister (1909–1939)*, Paris, Gallimard, 1966, p. 72.

—— (1911) Psycho-Analytic Notes on an Autobiographical Account of a Case of Paranoia (Dementia Paranoides). (Schreber Case). *S.E.*, XII, pp. 9–84.

—— (1911) Formulations on the Two Principles of Mental Functioning. *S.E.*, XII, pp. 213–226.

—— (1912) Contributions to the Psychology of Love. *S.E.*, XI, pp. 163–208.

—— (1912) Recommendations to Physicians Practising Psycho-Analysis. *S.E.*, XII, pp. 109–120.

—— (1912) Types of Onset of Neurosis. *S.E.*, XII, pp. 227–238.

—— (1913) The Disposition to Obsessional Neurosis. *S.E.*, XII, pp. 311–326.

—— (1913) The Claims of Psycho-Analysis to Scientific Interest. *S.E.*, XIII, pp. 165–190.

—— (1914) On Narcissism: An Introduction. *S.E.*, XIV, pp. 67–104.

—— (1915) The Unconscious. *S.E.*, XIV, pp. 159–216.

—— (1916) Introductory Lectures on Psycho-Analysis. *S.E.*, XV–XVI, pp. 15–463.

—— (1917) Mourning and Melancholia. *S.E.*, XIV, pp. 237–258.

—— (1917) On Transformations of Instinct as Exemplified in Anal Erotism. *S.E.*, XVII, pp. 127–133.

—— (1918) From the History of an Infantile Neurosis (The Wolf Man). *S.E.*, XVII, pp. 7–122.

—— (1919) 'A Child is Being Beaten': A Contribution to the Study of the Origin of Sexual Perversions. *S.E.*, XVII, pp. 175–204.

—— (1920) Beyond the Pleasure Principle. *S.E.*, XVIII, pp. 1–64.

—— (1921) Group Psychology and the Analysis of the Ego. *S.E.*, XVIII, pp. 69–143.

—— (1922) The Libido Theory (Encyclopaedia article). *S.E.*, XVIII, pp. 255–262.

—— (1922) Psycho-Analysis (Encyclopaedia article). *S.E.*, XVIII, pp. 235–254.

—— (1922) Some Neurotic Mechanisms in Jealousy, Paranoia and Homosexuality. *S.E.*, XVIII, pp. 223–232.

—— (1923) The Ego and the Id. *S.E.*, XIX, pp. 13–68.

—— (1924) The Dissolution of the Oedipus Complex. *S.E.*, XIX, pp. 173–182.

—— (1924) A Short Account of Psycho-Analysis. *S.E.*, XIX, pp. 191–212.

—— (1926) Inhibitions, Symptoms and Anxiety. *S.E.*, XX, pp. 87–179.

OTHER WORKS

Abraham (K.) (1910) 'Remarks on the Psychoanalysis of a Case of Foot and Corset Fetishism', in Abraham, K. (1949) *Selected Papers*, London, Hogarth Press, pp. 125–136.

—— (1924) 'A Short Study of the Development of the Libido, Viewed in the Light of Mental Disorders', in Abraham, K. (1949) *Selected Papers*, pp. 418–502.

—— (1925) 'The History of an Impostor in the Light of Psychoanalytical Knowledge', in Abraham, K. (1955) *Clinical Papers and Essays on Psycho-Analysis*, London, The Hogarth Press, pp. 291–305.

Alexander (F.) (1938) 'Remarks about the Relation of Inferiority Feelings to Guilt Feelings', *I.J.P.*, 19, pp. 41–49.

—— (1956) 'Two Forms of Regression and their Therapeutic Implications', *The Psychoanalytic Quarterly*, 25, pp. 178–196.

—— (1965) 'A Note to the Theory of Perversions', in Lorand, S. and Balint, M. (eds.), *Perversions – Psychodynamics and Therapy*, New York, Random House, pp. 3–15.

Alpert (A.) (1949) 'Sublimation and Sexualization', *The Psychoanalytic Study of the Child*, vol. III–IV, New York, International Universities Press, pp. 271–278.

Andreas Salomé (L.) (1965) *The Freud Journal of Lou Andreas-Salomé*, London, The Hogarth Press.

—— (1970) *Correspondance avec Sigmund Freud (1912–1936)*, trad. Lily Jumel, Paris, Gallimard.

Anzieu (D.) (1966) 'L'étude psychanalytique des groupes réels', *Les Temps Modernes*, 242, pp. 56–73.

—— (1971) 'L'illusion groupale', *Nouvelle Revue de Psychanalyse*, 4, pp. 73–93.

Anzieu (D.) and Martin (J.) (1968) *La Dynamique des groupes restreints*, Paris, Presses Universitaires de France.

Arlow (J.-A.) (1972) 'Les perversions caractérielles', trad. Green, A., *R.F.P.* (1972) 36, pp. 207–225.

Aulagnier-Spairani (P.) et al. (1967) *Le Désir et la perversion*, Paris, Seuil.

Bak (R.) (1952) 'Psychodynamics of Fetishism', *Bulletin of the American Psychoanalytic Association*, 8, p. 228.

—— (1968) 'The Phallic Woman. The Ubiquitous Fantasy in Perversions', *The Psychoanalytic Study of the Child*, vol. XXIII, New York, International Universities Press, pp. 15–36.

—— (1971) 'Object Relationships in Schizophrenia and Perversion', *I.J.P.*, 55, pp. 235–242.

Balint (A.) (1953) *The Psycho-Analysis of the Nursery*, London, Routledge & Kegan Paul.

Balint (M.) (1948) 'On Genital Love', *I.J.P.*, 29, pp. 34–40.

Barande (I.) (1964) 'Discussion of the paper by Braunschweig, D., "Le narcissisme: aspects cliniques" ' (Colloquium on Narcissism, Artigny), *R.F.P.* (1965) 29, pp. 601–606.

Baranger (W.) (1958) 'The Ego and the Function of Ideology', *I.J.P.*, 39, 191–195.

Bazaine, (R.) (1959) *Notes sur la peinture d'aujourd'hui*, Seuil.

Begoin, (J.) (1971) *L'Idéalisation dans l'oeuvre de M. Klein* (unpublished).

Benassy (M.) (1964) 'Théorie du narcissisme de Federn (Psychologie du Moi) (Colloquium on Narcissism, Artigny), *R.F.P.* (1965) 29, pp. 533–559.

Beres (D.) (1958) 'Vicissitudes of Superego Functions and Superego Precursors in Childhood', *The Psychoanalytic Study of the Child*, vol. XIII, New York, International Universities Press, pp. 407–429.

Berge (A.) (1966) 'Le Surmoi, son origine, sa nature et sa relation avec la conscience morale'. Discussion of the paper by Roch, M., 'Du Surmoi "heritier du complexe d'Oedipe" ' (27th Congress of Psychoanalysts of Romance Languages, Lausanne), R.F.P. (1967) 31, pp. 1079–1080.

Bergeret (J.) (1970) 'Les états limités', R.F.P., 34, pp. 601–634.

Bergler (E.) (1947) 'Differential Diagnosis between Spurious Homosexuality and Perversion of Homosexuality', in Bergler, E. (1969) Selected Papers, New York, Grune and Stratton, pp. 614–622.

——— (1955) 'A Few Examples of Superego's Cruelty', Samiska, 9, pp. 63–71.

Besançon (A.) (1967) Le Tsarévitch immolé, Paris, Plon.

——— (1971) 'La psychanalyse dans ou devant l'idéologie', Histoire et expérience du Moi, Paris, Flammarion.

Bibring (G.) (1964) 'Some Considerations Regarding the Ego Ideal in the Psychoanalytic Process', Journal of the American Psychoanalytic Association, 12, pp. 517–523.

Bion (W.R.) (1961) Experiences in Groups and Other Papers, London, Tavistock.

Boehm (F.) (1921) 'Sexual Perversions', I.J.P., 2, p. 435.

Bourdier (P.) (1966) 'Réflexions sur le bonheur et l'amour, le possible, l'impossible et l'interdit.' Discussion of the paper by Luquet-Parat, C.-J., 'L'organisation oedipienne du stade génital' (27th Congress of Psychoanalysts of Romance Languages, Lausanne), R.F.P. (1967) 31, pp. 883–889.

Bouvet (M.) (1956) 'La relation d'objet', in Bouvet, M. (1968) Oeuvres Psychanalytiques, Paris, Presses Universitaires de France, pp. 41–122.

Braunschweig (D.) (1964) 'Le narcissisme: aspects cliniques' (Colloquium on Narcissism, Artigny), R.F.P. (1965) 29, pp. 589–600.

——— (1966) Contribution to the 27th Congress of Psychoanalysts of Romance Languages, Lausanne, R.F.P. (1967) 31, pp. 853–857.

——— (1971) 'Psychanalyse et Réalité' (Paper given to the 31st Congress of Psychoanalysts of Romance Languages, Lyon), R.F.P., 35, pp. 655–800.

——— and Fain (M.) (1971) Eros et antéros. Réflexions psychanalytiques sur la sexualité, Paris, Payot, p. 282.

——— (1972) 'Comment on the paper by Flagey, D., "L'inhibition intellectuelle" ' (32nd Congress of Psychoanalysts of Romance Languages, Brussels), R.F.P., 36, nos. 5–6.

Brenner (Ch.) (1955) 'A Reformulation of Parapraxes', *Bulletin of the Philadelphia Association for Psycho-Analysis*, 3, pp. 110–113.

Bychowski (G.) (1969) 'Social Climate and Resistance in Psychoanalysis', *I.J.P.*, 50, pp. 453–459.

Cain (A.) (1961) 'The Presuperego "Turning-Inward" of Aggression', *The Psycho-Analytic Quarterly*, 30, pp. 171–209.

Castaigne (M.) (1970) 'Réflexions sur un patient obsédé présentant des conduites perverses'. Membership paper for the Paris Psychoanalytic Society (unpublished).

Chase (C.) (1961) 'Comment on "The Superego and the ego-ideal" ' (22nd International Psycho-Analytical Congress, Edinburgh), *R.F.P.* (1963) 27, pp. 565–570.

Chasseguet-Smirgel (J.) (1958) Discussion of the paper by Nacht, S. and Racamier, P.C., 'La théorie psychanalytique du délire' (20th Congress of Psychoanalysts of Romance Languages, Brussels), *R.F.P.*, 22, pp. 558–562.

—— (1962) 'L'Année dernière à Marienbad', in Chasseguet-Smirgel, J. (1971) *Pour une psychanalyse de l'art et de la créativité*, Paris, Payot, pp. 49–80.

—— (1963) 'Réflexions sur le concept de "réparation" et la hiérarchie des actes créateurs', in Chasseguet-Smirgel, J. (1971) *Pour une psychanalyse*, pp. 89–106.

—— (1965) 'A propos d'Auguste Strindberg: contribution à l'étude de la paranoia', in Chasseguet-Smirgel, J. (1971) *Pour une psychanalyse*, pp. 110–164.

—— (1965) 'L'Idéal du Moi et les indications de la cure psychanalytique' (Feurs Colloquium) (unpublished).

—— (1966) 'Oedipe et religion'. Discussion of the paper by Luquet-Parat, C.-J., 'L'organisation oedipienne du stade génital' (27th Congress of Psychoanalysts of Romance Languages, Lausanne), *R.F.P.* (1967) 31, pp. 875–882.

—— (1966) 'Notes de lecture en marge de la revision due cas Schreber', *R.F.P.*, 30, pp. 41–62.

—— (1967) 'A propos de la technique active de Ferenczi', in Chasseguet-Smirgel J. (1971) *Pour une psychanalyse*, pp. 165–176.

—— (1967) 'Note clinique sur les rêves d'examen', in Chasseguet-Smirgel, J. (1971) *Pour une psychanalyse*, pp. 177–182.

—— (1967) 'Les ambiguités sexuelles'. Talk given to the Saint-Vincent-de-Paul Hospital (unpublished).

—— (1968) 'Le rossignol de l'empereur de Chine' (Essai psychanalytique sur le faux) in Chasseguet-Smirgel, J. (1971) *Pour une psychanalyse*,
pp. 183–216.

Clancier-Gravelat (A.) (1964) Discussion of the paper by Braunschweig,
D., 'Le narcissisme: aspects cliniques' (Colloquium on Narcissism,
Artigny), *R.F.P.* (1965) 29, pp. 609–611.

—— (1966) 'Oedipe et création littéraire'. Discussion of the paper by
Luguet-Parat, C.-J., 'L'organisation oedipienne du stade génital'
(27th Congress of Psychoanalysts of Romance Languages, Lausanne),
R.F.P. (1967) 31, pp. 891–895.

Cosnier (J.) (1970) 'Investissements narcissiques et objectaux', *R.F.P.*,
34, pp. 575–600.

Dalibard (Y.) (1964) Discussion of the paper by Braunschweig, D., 'Le
narcissisme: aspects cliniques' (Colloquium on Narcissism, Artigny),
R.F.P. (1965) 29, pp. 608–609.

Dante (1969) 'Paradise, Canto I', *The Divine Comedy* trans. Sayers, D.L.
and Renolds, B., Harmondsworth, Penguin Books.

David (Ch.) (1966) 'De la valeur mutative des remaniements postoedi-
piens'. Discussion of the paper by Luquet-Parat, C.-J., 'L'organisation oedipienne du stade génital' (27th Congress of Psychoanalysts of
Romance Languages, Lausanne), *R.F.P.* (1967) 31, pp. 813–817.

—— (1971) *L'État amoureux. Essais psychanalytiques*, Paris, Payot, p.
308.

—— (1972) 'La perversion affective', in *La Sexualité perverse*, Paris,
Payot, pp. 195–230.

Deleuze (G.) and Guattari (F.) (1983) *Ant-Oedipus: Capitalism and
Schizophrenia*, trans. Hurley, R. et al., Minneapolis, University of
Minnesota Press.

Deutsch (H.) (1934) 'Some Forms of Emotional Disturbance and their
Relationship to Schizophrenia', *The Psychoanalytic Quarterly* (1942) 11,
pp. 301–321.

—— (1937) 'Don Quixote and Don Quixotism', *The Psychoanalytic
Quarterly*, 6, pp. 215–222.

—— (1955) 'The Impostor. Contribution to Ego Psychology of a Type
of Psychopath', *The Psychoanalytic Quarterly*, 24, pp. 483–505.

—— (1964) 'Some Clinical Considerations on the Ego Ideal', *Journal of
the American Psychoanalytic Association*, 12, pp. 512–516.

—— (1967) *Selected Problems of Adolescence*, London, The Hogarth
Press.

Diatkine (R.) (1964) Discussion of the paper by Benassy, M., 'Théorie du narcissisme de Federn' (Colloquium on Narcissism, Artigny), R.F.P. (1965) 29, p. 559.

—— (1964) Contribution to the Colloquium on Narcissism, Artigny, R.F.P. (1965) 29, p. 526.

—— and Simon (J.) (1972) La Psychanalyse précoce, Paris, Presses Universitaires de France, p. 423.

Drake (D.) (1955) 'A Psychoanalytic Interpretation of Social Ideology', American Imago, 12, pp. 193–196.

Fain (M.) (1961) Discussion of the paper by Luquet, P., 'Les identifications précoces dans la structuration et la restructuration du Moi' (22nd Congress of Psychoanalysts of Romance Languages, Paris), R.F.P. (1962) 26, numéro spécial, pp. 267–271.

—— (1964) Contribution to the Colloquium on Narcissism, Artigny, R.F.P. (1965) 29, pp. 586–588.

—— (1964) Discussion of the paper by Mendel, G., 'La sublimation artistique', R.F.P., 28, pp. 801–804.

—— (1966) Discussion of the paper by Luquet-Parat, C.-J., 'L'organisation oedipienne du stade génital' (27th Congress of Psychoanalysts of Romance Languages, Lausanne), R.F.P. (1967) 31, pp. 818–824.

—— (1966) Contribution to the Colloquium of the Paris Psycho-Analytic Society on 'Analysis Terminable and Interminable', R.F.P. (1968) 32, pp. 284–286.

—— and Marty (P.) (1959) 'The Synthetic Function of Homosexual Cathexis in the Treatment of Adults', I.J.P. (1960) XLI, parts 4–5, pp. 401–406.

—— (1964) 'A propos du narcissisme et de sa genèse' (Colloquium on Narcissism, Artigny), R.F.P. (1965) 29, pp. 561–572.

Favez (G.) (1966) 'Le complexe d'Oedipe et l'ironie'. Discussion of the paper by Roch, M., 'Du Surmoi "héritier du complexe d'Oedipe" ' (27th Congress of Psychoanalysts of Romance Languages, Lausanne), R.F.P. (1967) 31, pp. 1069–1075.

Favreau (J.) (1964) Contribution to the Colloquium on Narcissism, Artigny, R.F.P. (1965) 29, pp. 526–528, 587–588.

—— (1964) Discussion of the paper by Benassy, M., 'Théorie du narcissisme de Federn' (Colloquium on Narcissism, Artigny), R.F.P. (1965) 29, pp. 556–557.

Federn (P.) Ego Psychology and the Psychoses, New York, Basic Books.

Fenichel (O.) (1934) 'Rationalization and Idealization of Instinctual

Impulses', in Fenichel, O. (1945) *The Psycho-Analytic Theory of Neuroses*, New York, Norton, p. 485.

Ferenczi (S.) (1913) 'Stages in the Development of the Sense of Reality', in Ferenczi, S. (1952) *First Contributions to Psycho-Analysis*, London, The Hogarth Press, pp. 213–239.

—— (1913) 'The Ontogenesis of Symbols', in Ferenczi, S. (1952) *First Contribution*, pp. 276–281.

—— (1914) 'The Ontogenesis of the Interest in Money', in Ferenczi, S. (1952) *First Contributions*, pp. 319–332.

—— (1924) *Thalassa: A Theory of Genitality*, New York, Psychoanalytic Quarterly (1938). Also New York, Norton (1968).

Flagey (B.) (1972) 'L'inhibition intellectuelle' (Paper given to the 32nd Congress of Psychoanalysts of Romance Languages, Brussels), *R.F.P.*, 36, nos. 5–6.

Flournoy (O.) (1965) Discussion of the paper by Sandler, J. and Jaffe, W.G. (26th Congress of Psychoanalysts of Romance Languages, Paris), *R.F.P.* (1967) 31, pp. 19–21.

—— (1965) 'La sublimation' (presented to the Swiss Psychoanalytic Society, Lausanne), *R.F.P.* (1967) 31, pp. 59–93.

Fornari (F.) (1966) 'Sentiments de culpabilité et structuration du Surmoi'. Discussion of the paper by Roch, M., 'Du Surmoi "héritier du complexe d'Oedipe" ' (27th Congress of Psychoanalysts of Romance Languages, Lausanne), *R.F.P.* (1967) 31, pp. 1081–1087.

Freeman (Th.) (1964) 'Some Aspects of Pathological Narcissism', *Journal of the American Psychoanalytic Association*, 12, pp. 540–561.

Freud (A.) (1966) *Normality and Pathology in Childhood*, London, The Hogarth Press.

Freud (S.) (1895) 'Draft H: Paranoia (24.1.1895)', *S.E.*, I, pp. 206–212.

—— (1897) 'Letter 57 (24.1.1897). Extract of a letter to W. Fliess', *S.E.*, I, pp. 242–244.

—— (1900) *The Interpretation of Dreams*, *S.E.*, IV and V.

—— (1905) *Jokes and their Relation to the Unconscious*, *S.E.*, VIII.

—— (1908) 'On the Sexual Theories of Children', *S.E.*, IX, pp. 205–226.

—— (1910) 'A Special Type of Choice of Object Made by Men', *S.E.*, XI, pp. 165–175.

—— (1912) 'On the Universal Tendency to Debasement in the Sphere of Love', *S.E.*, XI, pp. 179–190.

—— (1914) 'Letter of 29.7.1914', *A Psycho-Analytic Dialogue: The Letters of S. Freud and K. Abraham*, ed. Abraham, H.C. and Freud, E.L. (1965) London, The Hogarth Press.

——— (1914) 'On the History of the Psycho-Analytic Movement', *S.E.*, XIV, pp. 7–66.

——— (1915) 'Instincts and their Vicissitudes', *S.E.*, XIV, pp. 111–140.

——— (1916) 'A Mythological Parallel to a Visual Obsession', *S.E.*, XIV, pp. 337–338.

——— (1919) 'The "Uncanny" ', *S.E.*, XVII, pp. 219–256.

——— (1920) 'Beyond the Pleasure Principle', *S.E.*, XVIII, pp. 1–64.

——— (1921) 'Being in Love and Hypnosis', in *Group Psychology and the Analysis of the Ego*, *S.E.*, XVIII, pp. 111–116.

——— (1921) 'Identification', in *Group Psychology and the Analysis of the Ego*, *S.E.*, XVIII, pp. 105–110.

——— (1923) 'The Ego and the Super-ego (ego ideal)', in *The Ego and the Id*, *S.E.*, XIX, pp. 28–62.

——— (1924) 'The Resistances to Psycho-Analysis', *S.E.*, XIX, pp. 213–222.

——— (1925) 'Negation', *S.E.*, XIX, pp. 235–239.

——— (1925) 'An Autobiographical Study', *S.E.*, XX, pp. 7–74.

——— (1927) 'Fetishism', *S.E.*, XXI, pp. 152–157.

——— (1927) 'Humour', *S.E.*, XXI, pp. 159–166.

——— (1929) 'Civilisation and its Discontents', *S.E.*, XXI, pp. 64–145.

——— (1931) 'Female Sexuality', *S.E.*, XXI, pp. 225–243.

——— (1937) 'Analysis Terminable and Interminable', *S.E.*, XXIII, pp. 216–253.

——— (1938) 'An Outline of Psycho-Analysis', *S.E.*, XXIII, pp. 144–207.

——— (1939) 'Moses and Monotheism', *S.E.*, XXIII, pp. 3–137.

——— and Breuer (J.) (1895) 'Anna O...', in *Studies on Hysteria*.

Gaddini (E.) (1969) 'On Imitation', *I.J.P.*, 50, pp. 475–482.

Garma (A.) (1957) 'The Meaning and Genesis of Fetishism', *I.J.P.*, 37, pp. 414–415.

Gillespie (W.) (1940) 'A Contribution to the Study of Fetishism', *I.J.P.*, 21, pp. 401–415.

——— (1952) 'Notes on the Analysis of Sexual Perversions', *I.J.P.*, 33, pp. 397–402.

——— (1956) 'The General Theory of Sexual Perversions', *I.J.P.*, 37, pp. 396–404.

Gillibert (J.) (1967) 'Deuil, mort, même', *R.F.P.*, 31, pp. 143–171.

Glover (E.) (1931) 'Sublimation, Substitution and Social Anxiety', *I.J.P.*, 12, pp. 263–297.

—— (1932) 'On the Etiology of Drug Addiction', *I.J.P.*, 13, pp. 298–328.

—— (1933) 'The Relation of Perversion Formation to the Development of Reality Sense', *I.J.P.*, 14, pp. 486–503.

—— (1933) 'A Note on Idealization', *I.J.P.* (1938) 19, pp. 91–96.

Green (A.) (1962) 'Une variante de la position phallique narcissique', *R.F.P.* (1963) 27, pp. 117–184.

—— (1964) Contribution to the Colloquium on Narcissism, Artigny, *R.F.P.* (1965) 29, pp. 525, 586–588.

—— (1964) Discussion of the paper by Benassy, M., 'Théorie du narcissisme de Federn' (Colloquium on Narcissism, Artigny), *R.F.P.* (1965) 29, pp. 558–559.

—— (1966) 'Les fondements différenciateurs des images parentales'. Discussion of the paper by Luquet-Parat, C.-J., 'L'organisation oedipienne du stade génital' (27th Congress of Psychoanalysts of Romance Languages, Lausanne), *R.F.P.* (1967) 31, pp. 896–906.

—— (1968) 'Sur la mère phallique', *R.F.P.*, 32, pp. 1–38.

—— (1969) 'Le narcissisme moral', *R.F.P.*, 33, pp. 341–371.

Greenacre (Ph.) (1955) 'Further Considerations Regarding Fetishism', *The Psychoanalytic Study of the Child*, vol. X, New York, International Universities Press, pp. 187–194.

—— (1958) 'The Family Romance of the Artist', *The Psychoanalytic Study of the Child*, vol. XIII, pp. 9–31.

—— (1958) 'The Relation of the Impostor to the Artist', *The Psychoanalytic Study of the Child*, vol. XIII, pp. 521–540.

—— (1958) 'The Impostor', *The Psychoanalytic Quarterly*, 27, pp. 359–381.

—— (1960) 'Further Notes on Fetishism', *The Psychoanalytic Study of the Child*, vol. XX, pp. 191–207.

—— (1964) 'The Fetish and the Transitional Object', *The Psychoanalytic Study of the Child*, vol. XXIV, pp. 144–164.

—— (1968) 'Perversions. General Considerations Regarding their Genetic and Dynamic Background', *The Psychoanalytic Study of the Child*, vol. XXIII, pp. 47–62.

Gressot (M.) (1961) Discussion of the paper by Luquet, P., 'Les identifications précoces dans la structuration et la restructuration du Moi' (22nd Congress of Psychoanalysts of Romance Languages, Paris), *R.F.P.* (1962) 26, numéro spécial, pp. 283–285.

—— (1966) Discussion of the paper by Roch, M., 'Du Surmoi "héritier du complexe d'Oedipe" ' (27th Congress of Psychoanalysts of Romance Languages, Lausanne), R.F.P. (1967) 31, pp. 1061–1068.

Grunberger (B.) (1956) 'The Analytic Situation and the Dynamics of the Healing Process', in Grunberger, B. (1979) Narcissism, Psychoanalytic Essays, New York, International Universities Press, pp. 35–89.

—— (1959) 'Study of Anal Object Relations', in Grunberger, B. (1979) Narcissism, pp. 143–164.

—— (1960) 'Observations on the Distinction between Narcissism and Instinctual Maturation', in Grunberger, B. (1979) Narcissism, pp. 165–190.

—— (1963) 'On the Phallic Image', in Grunberger, B. (1979) Narcissism, pp. 202–218.

—— (1964) 'Study on Narcissism' (Colloquium on Narcissism, Artigny), R.F.P. (1965) 29, pp. 573–588 and Contribution to the same Colloquium, pp. 525–526.

—— (1964) 'Outline for a Study of Narcissism in Female Sexuality', in Female Sexuality, ed. Chasseguet-Smirgel, J., and David, C. (1970), Ann Arbor, University of Michigan Press, pp. 68–85.

—— (1965) 'A Study of Depression', in Grunberger, B. (1979) Narcissism, pp. 219–240.

—— (1966) 'Suicide of Melancholics', in Grunberger, B. (1979) Narcissism, pp. 241–264.

—— (1967) 'The Child's Treasure Hoard and Avoidance of the Oedipus Complex', in Grunberger, B. (1979) Narcissism, pp. 281–302.

—— (1967) 'The Oedipus Complex and Narcissism', in Grunberger, B. (1979) Narcissism, pp. 265–280.

Guillaumin (J.) Personal communication.

Harries (M.) (1952) 'Sublimation in a Group of Four-Year-Old Boys', The Psychoanalytic Study of the Child, vol. VII, pp. 230–240.

Hartmann (H.) (1955) 'Notes on the Theory of Sublimation', The Psychoanalytic Study of the Child, vol. X, pp. 9–29.

—— Kris (E.) and Loewenstein (R.) (1947) 'Comments on the Formation of Psychic Structure', The Psychoanalytic Study of the Child, vol. II, pp. 11–38.

—— and Loewenstein (R.) (1964) 'Notes on the Super-ego', The Psychoanalytic Study of the Child, vol. 17, pp. 42–81.

Hendrick (I.) (1964) 'Narcissism and the Prepuberty Ego Ideal', Journal of the American Psychoanaytic Association, 12, pp. 522–528.

Hesselbach (C.) (1962) 'Superego Regression in Paranoia', *The Psychoanalytic Quarterly*, 31, pp. 341–350.

Jacobson (E.) (1946) 'The Effect of Disappointment on Ego and Superego Formation in Normal and Depressive Development', *The Psychoanalytic Review*, 33, pp. 129–147.

—— (1953) 'Contribution to the Metapsychology of Cyclothymic Depression', in *Affective Disorders*, ed. Greenacre, Ph., New York, International Universities Press, pp. 49–83.

—— (1954) 'The Self and the Object World', *The Psychoanalytic Study of the Child*, vol. 9, pp. 75–127.

Jones (E.) (1925) 'The Value of Sublimating Processes for Education and Re-Education', in Jones, E., *Papers on Psychoanalysis*, London, Bailliere, Tindall & Cox.

—— (1926) 'The Origin and Structure of the Superego', *I.J.P.*, 7, pp. 303–311.

—— (1927) 'The Development of the Concept of the Superego', *Journal of Abnormal and Social Psychology* (1928) 23, pp. 276–285.

—— (1929) 'Fear, Guilt and Hate', *I.J.P.*, 10, pp. 383–397.

—— (1935) 'Early Female Sexuality', *I.J.P.*, XVI, pp. 263–273.

—— (1947) 'The Genesis of the Superego', *Samiksa*, 1, pp. 3–12.

Joseph (B.) (1960) 'Some Characteristics of the Psychopathic Personality', *I.J.P.*, 41, pp. 526–531.

Kanzer (M.) (1957) 'Acting-out, Sublimation and Reality Testing', *Journal of the American Psychoanalytic Association*, 5, pp. 663–684.

—— (1964) 'Freud's Uses of the Terms "Autoerotism" and "Narcissism" ', *Journal of the American Psychoanalytic Association*, 12, pp. 529–539.

Katan (M.) (1964) 'Fetishism, Splitting of the Ego and Denial', *I.J.P.*, 45, pp. 237–245.

Kestemberg (E.) Personal Communication.

—— (1962) L'identité et l'identification chez les adolescents', *La Psychiatrie de l'Enfant*, vol. V, no. 2, Paris, Presses Universitaires de France, pp. 441–522.

—— (1964) Contribution to the Colloquium on Narcissism, Artigny, *R.F.P.* (1965) 29, p. 526.

—— (1964) Discussion of the paper by Benassy, M., 'Théorie du narcissisme de Federn' (Colloquium on Narcissism, Artigny), *R.F.P.* (1965) 29, p. 558.

Kestemberg (J.) and Kestemberg (E.) (1965) 'Contribution à la perspective genetique en psychanalyse' (Paper given to the 26th Congress of Psychoanalysts of Romance Languages, Paris), *R.F.P.* (1966) 30, pp. 569–580.

Kestemberg (E.), Kestemberg (J.) and Decobert (S.) (1973) *La Faim et le corps*, Presses Universitaires de France, Coll. Le Fil Rouge.

Khan (M.R.) (1969) 'Role of the "Collated Internal Object" in Perversion Formations', *I.J.P.*, 50, pp. 555–565.

Klein (M.) (1923) 'Early Analysis', in Klein, M. (1975) *The Writings of Melanie Klein*, vol. 1, London, The Hogarth Press, pp. 77–105.

—— (1925) 'A Contribution to the Psychogenesis of Tics', in Klein, M. (1975) *Writings*, vol. 1, pp. 106–127.

—— (1928) 'Early Stages of the Oedipus Conflict', in Klein, M. (1975) *Writings*, vol. 1, pp. 186–198.

—— (1930) 'The Importance of Symbol Formation in the Development of the Ego', in Klein, M. (1975) *Writings*, pp. 219–232.

—— (1932) *The Psychoanalysis of Children*, London, The Hogarth Press.

—— (1940) 'Mourning and its Relation to Manic-Depressive States', in Klein, M. (1968) *Contributions to Psychoanalysis*, London, The Hogarth Press, pp. 311–338; and in Klein, M. (1975) *Writings*, vol. 1, pp. 344–369.

—— (1945) 'The Oedipus Complex in the Light of Early Anxieties', in Klein, M. (1968) *Contributions*.

—— (1946) 'Notes on Some Schizoid Mechanisms', in Klein, M. (1975) *Writings*, vol. 3, pp. 1–24.

—— (1957) 'Envy and Gratitude', in Klein, M. (1975) *Writings*, vol. 3, pp. 176–235.

Kramer (P.) (1958) 'Note on One of the Preoedipal Roots of the Superego', *Journal of the American Psychoanalytic Association*, 6, pp. 38–46.

Kris (E.) (1955) 'Neutralization and Sublimation. Observations on Young Children', *The Psychoanalytic Study of the Child*, vol. X, pp. 30–46.

Lagache (D.) (1966) 'La psychanalyse et la structure de la personnalité', *La Psychanalyse*, vol. VI, Paris, Presses Universitaires de France, pp. 5–54.

Lampl De Groot (J.) (1961) 'Ego Ideal and Superego', *The Psychoanalytic Study of the Child*, vol. 17 (1962) pp. 94–106.

Laplanche (J.) and Pontalis (J.-B.) (1967) *The Language of Psycho-Analysis*, London, The Hogarth Press.

Laufer (M.) (1964) 'Ego Ideal and Pseudo Ego Ideal in Adolescence', *The Psychoanalytic Study of the Child*, XIX, pp. 196–221.

Lebovici (R.) (1956) 'Perversion sexuelle transitoire au cours d'un traitement psychanalytique', *Bulletin de l'Association des Psychanalystes de Belgique*, 25, pp. 1–15.

Lebovici (S.) (1964) 'A propos de la lecture des textes freudiens sur le narcissisme' (Colloquium on Narcissism, Artigny), *R.F.P.* (1965) 29, pp. 485–493.

—— (1970) Advanced Seminar. Verbal Communication.

—— (1971) *Les Sentiments de culpabilité chez l'enfant et chez l'adulte*, Paris, Hachette, p. 223.

Lechat (F.) (1951) 'Du Surmoi', *Bulletin de l'Association des Psychanalystes de Belgique*, 12, pp. 1–8.

Levin (S.) (1971) 'The Psychoanalysis of Shame', *I.J.P.*, 52, pp. 355–362.

Lewin (B.) (1948) 'The Nature of Reality', *Psychoanalytic Quarterly*, 17.

—— (1951) *The Psychoanalysis of Elation*, London, The Hogarth Press, p. 200.

Lichtenstein (H.) (1970) 'Changing Implication of the Concept of Psycho-Sexual Development. An Inquiry Concerning the Validity of Classical Psycho-Analytic Assumptions Concerning Sexuality', *Journal of the American Psychoanalytic Association*, 18, pp. 300–318.

Loewald (H.) (1961) 'Superego and Time', *I.J.P.* (1962) 43, pp. 264–268.

—— (1962) 'Internalization, Separation, Mourning and the Superego', *The Psychoanalytic Quarterly*, 31, pp. 483–504.

Lopez (D.) (1966) Discussion of the paper by Roch, M., 'Du Surmoi "héritier du complexe d'Oedipe" ' (27th Congress of Psychoanalysts of Romance Languages, Lausanne), *R.F.P.* (1967) 31, pp. 1089–1090.

Luquet (C.-J.) (1961) Discussion of the paper by Luquet, P., 'Les identifications précoces dans la structuration et la restructuration du Moi' (22nd Congress of Psychoanalysts of Romance Languages, Paris), *R.F.P.* (1962) 26, numéro spécial, pp. 289–292.

Luquet, P. (1961) 'Les identifications précoces dans la structuration et la restructuration du Moi' (Paper given to the 22nd Congress of Psychoanalysts of Romance Languages, Paris), *R.F.P.* (1962) 26, numéro spécial, pp. 117–303.

—— (1963) 'Ouvertures sur l'artiste et le psychanalyste. La fonction esthétique du Moi', *R.F.P.*, 27, pp. 585–606.

—— (1964) Introduction to the Discussion on Secondary Narcissism (Colloquium on Narcissism, Artigny), R.F.P. (1965) 29, pp. 519–524.

—— (1966) 'Le mouvement oedipien du Moi.' Discussion of the paper by Luquet-Parat, C.-J., 'L'organisation oedipienne du stade génital' (27th Congress of Psychoanalysts of Romance Languages, Lausanne), R.F.P. (1967) 31, pp. 841–852.

Luquet-Parat (C.-J.) (see also Parat) (1966) 'L'organisation oedipienne du stade génital' (Paper given to the 27th Congress of Psychoanalysts of Romance Languages, Lausanne),R.F.P. (1967) 31, pp. 743–812.

Luzes (P.) (1966) Discussion of the paper by Roch, M., 'Du Surmoi "héritier du complexe d'Oedipe" ' (27th Congress of Psychoanalysts of Romance Languages, Lausanne), R.F.P. (1967) 31, pp. 1076–1078.

Mack-Brunswick (R.) (1940) 'The Pre-oedipal Phase of the Libido Development', Psychoanalytic Quarterly, 9, p. 293.

Mallarmé, S. 'Igitur ou la Folie d'Elbehuon', Oeuvres complètes, Gallimard, coll. de la Pléiade.

Mallet (J.) (1964) 'De l'homosexualité psychotique', R.F.P., 28, pp. 721–728.

—— (1966) 'Une théorie de la paranoia', R.F.P., 30, pp. 63–68.

Marty (P.) (1961) 'Discussion of the paper by Luquet, P., 'Les identifications précoces dans la structuration et la restructuration du Moi' (22nd Congress of Psychoanalysts of Romance Languages, Paris), R.F.P. (1962) 26, numéro spécial, pp. 293–301.

—— (1965) Discussion of the paper by Sandler, J. and Joffe, W.G., 'A propos de la sublimation' (26th Congress of Psychoanalysts of Romance Languages, Paris), R.F.P. (1967) 31, pp. 22–25.

McDougall (J.) (1968) 'Le spectateur anonyme. Le complexe d'Oedipe et la structure perverse', Inconscient, 6, pp. 39–58.

—— (1972) 'Scène primitive et scénario pervers', in La Sexualité perverse, Paris, Payot, pp. 51–96.

—— (1971) 'Primal Scene and Sexual Perversion', I.J.P. (1972) 53, pp. 371–384.

Mendel (G.) (1964) 'La sublimation artistique', R.F.P., 28, pp. 729–808.

Mises (R.) (1964) Contribution to the Colloquium on Narcissism, Artigny, R.F.P. (1965) 29, p. 526.

Moliere (J.B.P.) (1969) The Misanthrope, trans. Wood, J., Harmondsworth, Penguin Classics.

Murray (J.) (1964) 'Narcissism and the Ego Ideal', *Journal of the American Psychoanalytic Association*, 12, pp. 477–511.

M'Uzan (M. de) (1964) Contribution to the Colloquium on Narcissism, Artigny, *R.F.P.* (1965) 29, pp. 586–588.

——— (1965) 'Aperçus sur le processus de la création littéraire', *R.F.P.*, 29, pp. 43–77.

——— (1972) 'Un cas de masochisme pervers', in *La Sexualité perverse*, Paris, Payot, pp. 13–50.

Mynard (J.) (1961) Discussion of the paper by Luquet, P., 'Les identifications précoces dans la structuration et la restructuration du Moi' (22nd Congress of Psychoanalysts of Romance Languages, Paris), *R.F.P.* (1962) 26, numéro spécial, pp. 287–288.

Nacht (S.) (1961) Discussion of the paper by Luquet, P., 'Les identifications précoces dans la structuration et la restructuration du Moi' (22nd Congress of Psychoanalysts of Romance Languages, Paris), *R.F.P.* (1962) 26, numéro spécial, pp. 249–255.

——— (1964) 'Le narcissisme, gardien de la vie' (Colloquium on Narcissism, Artigny), *R.F.P.* (1965) 29, pp. 529–532.

Nacht (S.), Diatkine (R.) and Favreau (J.) (1956) 'The Ego in Perverse Relationships', *I.J.P.* (1956) 37, pp. 404–413.

Novey (S.) (1955) 'The Role of the Superego and Ego Ideal in Character Formation', *I.J.P.*, 36, pp. 254–259.

——— (1955) 'Some Philosophical Speculations about the Concept of the Genital Character', *I.J.P.*, 36, pp. 88–94.

Nunberg (H.) (1932) *Principles of Psychoanalysis*, New York, International Universities Press.

Ottenheimer (C.) (1955) 'On the Nature and Early Development of the Ego Ideal', *American Journal of Psychotherapy*, 9, pp. 612–629.

Parat (C.-J.) (1966) 'L'organisation oedipienne du stade génital' (27th Congress of Psychoanalysts of Romance Languages, Lausanne), *R.F.P.* (1967) 31, nos. 5–6.

——— Personal communication.

Pasche (F.) (1955) 'Notes sur les perversions', *R.F.P.*, 19, pp. 381–384.

——— (1956) 'Regression, perversion, névrose', in Pasche, F. (1969) *A Partir de Freud*, Paris, Payot, pp. 95–114.

——— (1959) 'Freud et l'orthodoxie judéo-chrétienne', in Pasche, F. (1969) *A Partir de Freud*, pp. 129–156.

——— (1961) 'De la dépression', in Pasche, F. (1969) *A Partir de Freud*, pp. 181–200.

—— (1964) 'L'antinarcissisme' (Colloquium on Narcissism, Artigny), *R.F.P.* (1965) 29, pp. 503–518.

—— (1964) Contribution to the Colloquium on Narcissism, Artigny, *R.F.P.* (1965) 29, p. 525.

—— and Renard (M.) (1956) 'Psychanalyse et troubles de la sexualité. Des problèmes essentiels de la perversion', in *La Psychanalyse d'aujourd'hui*, ed. Nacht, S., vol. I, Paris, Presses Universitaires de France, pp. 344–345.

Payne (S.M.) (1950) 'The Fetishist and His Ego', in *The Psychoanalytic Reader*, ed. Fliess, R., London, The Hogarth Press, pp. 21–30.

Pfister (O.) (1910) *Die Frömmigkeit des Grafen von Zinzendorf*, Leipzig and Vienna, Deuticke, p. 132.

Piers (G.) and Singer (M.) (1953) *Shame and Guilt. A psychoanalytic and a cultural study*, Springfield, Ill., Charles C. Thomas.

Racamier (P.-C.) (1961) Discussion of the paper by Luquet, P., 'Les identifications précoces dans la structuration et la restructuration du Moi' (22nd Congress of Psychoanalysts of Romance Languages, Paris), *R.F.P.* (1962) 26, numéro spécial, pp. 279–281.

—— and Chasseguet-Smirgel, (J.) (1966) 'La révision du cas Schreber: revue', *R.F.P.*, 30, pp. 3–26.

Reich (A.) (1953) 'Narcissistic Object Choice in Women', *Journal of the American Psychoanalytic Association*, 1, pp. 22–44.

—— (1954) 'Early Identifications as Archaic Elements in the Superego', *Journal of the American Psychoanalytic Association*, 2, pp. 218–238.

—— (1960) 'Pathologic Forms of Self Esteem Regulation', *The Psychoanalytic Study of the Child*, vol. XV, New York, International Universities Press, pp. 215–232.

Reich (W.) (c.1950) *Character Analysis*, London, Vision Press.

—— (c.1950) 'From Psychoanalysis to Orgone Biophysics', in Reich, W. *Character Analysis*, London, Vision Press.

Renard (M.) (1964) 'Le narcissisme primaire dans la théorie des instincts' (Colloquium on Narcissism, Artigny), *R.F.P.* (1965) 29, pp. 495–501.

—— 'Le narcissisme', in *La Théorie psychanalytique*, t. II of *Traité de psychanalyse*, ed. Nacht S. (1969), Paris, Presses Universitaires de France, pp. 181–214.

Ritvo (S.) and Solnit (A.) (1960) 'The Relationship of Early Ego Identifications to Superego Formation', *I.J.P.*, 41, pp. 295–300.

Roch (M.) (1966) 'Du Surmoi "héritier du complexe d'Oedipe" ' (Paper given to the 27th Congress of Psychoanalysts of Romance Languages, Lausanne), *R.F.P.* (1967) 31, pp. 913–1060.

Rosenfeld (H.) (1961) 'The Superego and the Ego Ideal', *I.J.P.* (1962) 43, pp. 258–263.

Rosenman (S.) (1956) 'Black Magic and Superego Formation', *The Psychoanalytic Review*, 43, pp. 272–319.

Rosolato (G.) (1967) 'Le désir et la perversion', in Aulagnier-Spairani, P. et al., *Le Désir et la perversion*, Paris, Seuil, p. 207.

Ross (N.) (1970) 'The Primacy of Genitality in the Light of the Ego Psychology', *Journal of the American Psychoanalytic Association*, 18, pp. 267–284.

Rouart (J.) (1961) Discussion of the paper by Luquet, P., 'Les identifications précoces dans la structuration et la restructuration du Moi' (22nd Congress of Psychoanalysts of Romance Languages, Paris), *R.F.P.* (1962) 26, numero spécial, pp. 273–277.

―――― (1968) 'Acting out and the Psycho-analytic Process', *I.J.P.*, 49, pp. 185–187.

Rycroft (C.) (1955) 'Two Notes on Idealisation, Illusion and Disillusion', *I.J.P.*, 36, pp. 81–87.

―――― (1960) 'On the Concept of the Superego', *The Psychoanalytic Study of the Child*, vol. XV, New York, International Universities Press, pp. 128–162.

―――― Holder (A.) and Meers (D.) (1963) 'The Ego Ideal and the Ideal Self', *The Psychoanalytic Study of the Child*, vol. XVIII, New York, International Universities Press, pp. 139–158.

―――― and Joffe (W.G.) (1965) 'On Skill and Sublimation', *Journal of the American Psychoanalytic Association* (1966) 14, pp. 335–355.

Sarlin (Ch.N.) (1970) 'The Current Status of Genital Primacy', *Journal of the American Psychoanalytic Association*, 18, pp. 285–299.

Sauguet (H.) (1968) 'Le processus analytique' (Notes for an Introduction to the 29th Congress of Psychoanalysts of Romance Languages, Lisbon), *R.F.P.* (1969) 33, pp. 913–927.

Saussure (R.de) (1964) 'Les sources subjectives de la théorie du narcissisme chez Freud' (Colloquium on Narcissism, Artigny), *R.F.P.* (1965) 29, pp. 483–485.

Schmideberg (M.) (1956) 'Delinquent Acts as Perversions and Fetishes', *I.J.P.*, 37, pp. 422–424.

Sebaoun (W.) Verbal communication.

Sechehaye (M.) (1950) *Autobiography of a Schizophrenic Girl*, New York, Grune and Stratton.

Sedat (J.) (1972) 'Autour de l'amour courtois. La naissance du féminisme au XIIe siècle', *Topique*, nos. 7–8, pp. 183–213.

Shentoub (S.) Personal communication.

Socarides (Ch.) (1960) 'The Development of a Fetishistic Perversion', *Journal of the American Psychoanalytic Association*, 8, pp. 281–311.

Soule (M.) (1968) 'Contribution clinique à la compréhension de l'imaginaire des parents', *R.F.P.*, 32, pp. 419–464.

Sperling (M.) (1963) 'Fetishism in Children', *The Psychoanalytic Quarterly*, 33, pp. 374–392.

Spitz (R.A.) (1957) *No and Yes. On the Genesis of Human Communication*, New York, International Universities Press.

Stewart (S.) (1972) 'Quelques aspects théoriques du fétishisme', *La Sexualité perverse*, Paris, Payot, pp. 159–194.

Tausk (V.) (1919) 'On the Origin of the "Influencing Machine" in Schizophrenia', *Psychoanalytic Quarterly* (1933) 2, pp. 519–556.

Weigert (E.) (1961) 'The Superego and the Ego-Ideal', *I.J.P.* (1962) 43, pp. 269–271.

Index